MARY STUART

THE MAID OF ORLEANS

FRIEDRICH von SCHILLER

MARY STUART

THE MAID
OF ORLEANS

Two Historical Plays

Translated by
CHARLES E. PASSAGE
Associate Professor of World Literature
Brooklyn College

FREDERICK UNGAR PUBLISHING CO.
NEW YORK

MARY STUART

INTRODUCTION

It was from a province of obscurity and fear that Elizabeth Tudor found herself unexpectedly summoned forth in 1558, at age twenty-five, to become the Queen of England. As recently as the beginning of the decade of the 1550's her succession to the throne had been merely a remote possibility, and since that time she had passed close to the brink of death by either execution or assassination. In 1553 her half-brother, King Edward VI, had died childless after a reign of only six years. As the sole male heir of Henry VIII he had been his father's fond preference over two daughters, though he was the offspring of Henry's third marriage. Moreover, that third marriage had been solemnized under the new Protestantism, Edward was himself necessarily Protestant, and the powerful Protestant leaders of the country supported him as the mainstay of their cause. At his death without children to succeed him they were seized with consternation, because the throne had then unquestionably to revert to the elder of Henry's daughters, Mary Tudor, the intensely Catholic child of Henry's Catholic first marriage to the Spanish Princess Catherine of Aragon. In desperation, the Protestant leaders had precipitated civil war and attempted to place Henry's Protestant grandniece, Lady Jane Grey, upon the throne of England.

Amid cruelties of that civil disorder Mary Tudor ascended the throne in 1553. She suppressed the rebellion with harshness. Lady Jane Grey, after a nominal queenship of nine days, was apprehended, committed to prison, and eventually beheaded. As yet unmarried, Mary Tudor now selected for her spouse none other than King Philip II of Spain, the most

powerful monarch in Catholic Christendom and militant foe
of Protestantism everywhere. The English people, however,
who had loyally taken her as their rightful Queen and who
were acceding to her reconversion of the country to the old
Faith, would not brook rule from the alien King, and Philip,
to his discomfiture, was coldly accepted as the Queen's consort
but icily refused the title of King of England. In the process of
eradication of Protestantism from the realm Mary met strong
opposition. The severity of her persecutions won her the hateful name of "Bloody Mary" and a memory forever tainted in
the history of her country. Yet objective critics must judge her
as a woman understandably embittered and sincerely dedicated to a supremely difficult task.

Her young womanhood had endured atrocious humiliation.
As royal Princess of England she had been suddenly relegated
to an indeterminate position between legitimacy and illegiti-
macy by Henry VIII's belated divorce of her mother. The
divorce itself was a monstrous sin in her eyes, and the sin was
increased hundredfold when the divorce served as the pretext
for Henry's removal of all England from the Roman Catholic
religion and his institution of the new Protestant order. The
final humiliation came with her father's second marriage to
the upstart Anne Boleyn. It was understandable, therefore,
that she should bear small affection to the half-sister Elizabeth
that was born of that union. By the time of her accession in
1553 the human agents in the drama of religious conflict had,
by the working of Providence it seemed, been removed from
the scene of life. The erring King and father was in his grave;
the Protestant Edward VI had died without issue; Anne
Boleyn had long since perished on the scaffold publicly dis-
graced as an adulteress and condemned to death with her royal
husband's consent; four additional Protestant wives of Henry
were also dead. Her mission to turn England back to the old
religion seemed expressly indicated by the Deity in the dis-

position of human events. There remained to be dealt with only the unwanted half-sister Elizabeth. For a time Queen Mary Tudor had her committed to the Tower of London, from which prisoners often emerged only to the place of execution. Subsequently she caused her to be removed from there and installed in Woodstock House under surveillance, wresting from her an overt profession of Catholicism.

Nevertheless all things conspired to frustrate her great mission. The love of her subjects withered away in the searing sun of fanaticism, projects did not advance, her husband bore her almost a contemptuous aversion, and, worst of all, her womanhood was blighted with childlessness. In her final illness, after a mere five years of reign, she realized that she had failed on every count she deemed important and that Elizabeth, as her successor, would prove false to the Catholic cause. And so it proved. Childless and defeated Queen Mary Tudor died in 1558, and Elizabeth, summoned from obscurity and the shadow of death, lost no time in proclaiming herself and England Protestant.

The action was all but mandatory for the new Queen. Catholic law could not countenance Henry VIII's divorce, still less his remarriage to Anne Boleyn according to rites unhallowed by the Catholic religion. Before Catholic law, therefore, Elizabeth was a mere illegitimate offspring of her royal father and without any rightful claim to the throne of England. Before Protestant law the reverse was true, and the tide of national feeling was also running strong in the direction of Protestantism. Her personal convictions reinforced the choice.

What, then, must have been the young Queen's feelings when, in the very year of her accession, her right to rule was publicly and spectacularly challenged by her first cousin once removed, Mary Stuart, heiress to the throne of Scotland! As granddaughter of Margaret Tudor, a sister of Henry VIII, Mary Stuart considered herself the only legitimate heir to the

English throne. That she was next in line after Elizabeth, in case the latter had no issue, no one denied; it was her assertion of rightful queenship *now* that offered such galling offense. Mary's maternal relatives, the Dukes and Cardinals of Guise, had taught her to look upon Protestantism as a work of devils, upon Protestant law as no law at all, and upon Elizabeth as a bastard and usurper. The occasion for the public challenge was the resplendent marriage in Paris between Mary Stuart and Prince Francis, heir to the crown of France. In the solemn procession Mary displayed the royal emblems of Scotland, of France, and of England, as though she were already Queen of all three realms. With defiance thus proclaimed, the struggle was to continue between the two women for almost thirty years. It was to end with Elizabeth's sending Mary to her death in 1587.

Unglamorous duty proved to be Elizabeth's lot for many years, while glamorous adventure and misadventure befell Mary time and again. During the next quarter of a century Elizabeth worked as a dedicated servant of a nation that was lifting itself into greatness, herself hardly existing as a private individual apart from her Queenship, while Mary ranged freely through life as a personage of independent destiny. The story and the romance are hers, and even the most skeptical and antipathetic cannot help but be struck by her brilliant and tragic course of existence.

The deaths of kings formed the milestones of her career, the first of these being the death of her father, King James V of Scotland, which occurred only a few days after her birth. Already a Queen in her infancy, she was sent abroad to France at age three to be betrothed to the equally young heir to the throne of France. Her rearing was that of a French Princess amid the sophistication and elegance of the Parisian court, and there, as an uncommonly lovely girl in her teens she fell fondly in love with her husband-to-be. Their tender mutual devotion was a rare phenomenon in the life of courts. It could not but promise a happy future, was the common opinion. Their marriage in 1558 was the occasion for that provocative display of the English royal emblems whereby her English cousin was so gravely offended, but the action must be construed as sinister inspiration from other parties and accepted by Mary's naiveté. Within a year the princely couple was thrust into the position of reigning monarchs by a bizarre and tragic coincidence. In 1559 the French King, while participating in one of those mediaeval tournaments which he fondly perpetuated in the midst of the Renaissance, galloped in a joust against a visiting knight and received his opponent's lance-thrust through his visor and died instantaneously as the weapon pierced his eye and brain. As Queen of France, Mary reached all too early and all too briefly the apogee of her life's good fortunes. The health of King Francis II was precarious. A year later he died, and once again Mary's fate was radically altered. From Queen she was relegated over night to the ambiguous position of widow of the late monarch, the mere sister-in-law of the new King Charles IX, and subject to the unwelcome control of the ambitious Queen Mother, Catherine of Medici, who overshadowed her sons. The situation was intolerable. Moreover, Mary's own mother had recently died in Scotland, and thus all events joined to make it imperative that she return to her native land, which, as viewed from Paris, seemed remote and drab indeed. The return itself was fraught with perils. In that same year, 1560, representatives of England, Scotland and France had attempted to draft the Treaty of Edinburgh, wherein it was stipulated that Mary should renounce all claim to the English throne as long as Elizabeth lived, but Mary perversely refused to agree to that article. Now, as she prepared to sail from France to Scotland, English naval forces vowed they would intercept her ship if they encountered it and take her captive. Amid her own tears and amid tributes

from famous poets she did set sail, however, and by good luck
arrived safely in Scotland. She was not yet twenty years of age.

Her Scottish subjects received her very well at first, capti-
vated by her youthful beauty and charm, although the radical
adherents of the new Presbyterian faith recently imported
into the country by John Knox were less enthusiastic than
the Catholics. For a time Mary sought to rule effectively, yet
even from the beginning her political obtuseness made signifi-
cant mistakes. The feudal clans of Scotland could not be
managed by methods patterned on those of the French court.
It was also Mary's decided policy now to conciliate her English
cousin. Solicitously she consulted her "dear sister" Elizabeth,
—for Queens addressed each other as "sisters,"—asking her
advice in the matter of choosing a second husband. She herself
proposed Don Carlos, son of Philip II and Infante of Spain,
but Elizabeth frowned on the politically dangerous alliance of
Spain and Scotland. The counterproposal was Robert Dudley,
Earl of Leicester, Elizabeth's own lover. What devious plan
underlay such a proposal is hard to imagine. When the suggestion was declined, Elizabeth made a new suggestion, namely
their common cousin Henry Darnley, the only remaining
descendant of the Tudor family and therefore the only possible
heir, other than the two women themselves, to the throne of
England. Mary agreed to receive Lord Darnley as a suitor.
Accordingly, Darnley came to Edinburgh, a handsome, petu-
lant youth, his good looks temporarily masking his petulance,
and to the amazement of all inspired Mary with sudden and
vehement passion so that she presently married him. Directly
his disagreeable nature became manifest, his paramount concerns being the outward show of kingship and morbid jealousy
of his beautiful wife. Soon Mary's passion turned to cordial
dislike; the dislike turned to active hatred when Darnley burst
into her apartments one night with a band of assassins and
before her eyes slew her favorite court singer, David Rizzio.

Three months later, in June of 1566, she bore Darnley's child, the future James I of England.

At this point there came into Mary's life the man who was to decide her destiny. He was James Hepburn, Earl of Bothwell, a forceful and possessive man with great power in the complex political life of the kingdom. Their headlong passion could not long be kept secret, yet Darnley's folly seems to have been dark suspicion of Rizzio when suspicion was unwarranted and now a total underestimation of Bothwell. For Bothwell now planned nothing less than the assassination of Darnley and kingship of Scotland through marriage with Mary. Whether Mary herself actively or passively was engaged in the murder plan is one of history's unresolved mysteries. Proof of her guilt or non-guilt rests with the famous "Casket Letters," which, if genuinely hers, demonstrate her full involvement in the scheme to kill her detested husband. In any case, Darnley, returning from a trip to Glasgow, was prevailed upon by his wife to spend the night of February 9, 1567 in a lonely house outside of Edinburgh rather than cover the last short lap of his journey back to the capital. During the night the house was blown up by an explosion of gunpowder and Darnley's body was discovered next morning, strangled to death, in the garden. Bothwell was accused of murder and brought to trial. Mary insisted on standing aloof from the proceedings and Bothwell was acquitted. Almost immediately thereafter Bothwell seized Mary and carried her off a prisoner to his castle at Dunbar. He now announced his intention of divorcing his wife and keeping the Queen in his castle until she agreed to marry him. This was too much even for Mary's staunchest friends, while her enemies, political, religious, and personal, had long since vowed her ruin. Civil war broke out; the forces of Bothwell and Mary were defeated; Bothwell fled abroad; Mary was imprisoned in the castle of Loch Leven; her infant son was proclaimed King of Scotland, while Mary's illegitimate half-

brother, the Earl of Murray, was named regent until the child
should come of age. Not the least fantastic of Mary's adventures
was her romantic escape in disguise from her prison on Loch
Leven, but her brief effort to regain her crown met with fresh
defeat. Escaping anew, she fled to the west coast and took ship
with a small company of friends. Return to France now seemed
more of a humiliation than an escape; Spain was distant and
the voyage there hazardous around the English coasts. She
determined to stop at the nearest English port and announce
herself as a temporary visitor in Elizabeth's country. She
landed at Carlisle, proclaimed her presence there, and asked to
proceed to an interview with the English Queen. She was informed that she was being temporarily detained. It soon became apparent that the detention was outright captivity.

For nineteen years she remained Elizabeth's prisoner, now
at one castle, now at another. The situation was at a complete
impasse. Elizabeth was well aware that she had no legal right
whatsoever to hold Mary captive, much less to bring her before
a court for trial. Yet she dared not let her go. Neither did she
dare confront her, knowing herself to be legally in the wrong.
And the longer the state of affairs continued, the more difficult
it became to take any step at all. In 1570 the Pope excommuni-
cated Elizabeth, thereby absolving her Catholic subjects from
their allegiance to her. This action, together with an armed
Catholic uprising in the north of England, only served to
prompt Parliament to pass stricter laws against the Catholic
religion and to debar Mary permanently from succession to the
English throne. Conspiracies were repeatedly organized to
liberate the imprisoned Queen. All such attempts failed. In
1572 the Duke of Norfolk was executed for such a treasonable
attempt, while his confederate, the Bishop of Ross, was banished. The Spanish ambassador Mendoza was implicated in the
conspiracy of James Throckmorton in 1584. After the unsuccessful attempt by Dr. Parry in 1585 Parliament passed an Act

which would hold the prisoner herself responsible in the event of a further plot. Murder of Elizabeth was repeatedly discovered to be one of the plotters' objectives, and such was the avowed plan of Babington and Savage, who paid with their lives for the next attempt. To enforce the Parliamentary Act, a commission of forty-two judges was sent down to Castle Fotheringhay, the last of Mary's prisons, to bring her to trial for conspiracy against the life of the English monarch. At first, the captive refused to answer before the court; then, changing her mind, she pleaded her cause with admirable dignity. Nevertheless the commission found her guilty and condemned her to death. Reluctantly Elizabeth signed the necessary warrant for execution, then entrusted it to her secretary Davison with ambiguous directions as to how he was to proceed with it. Her ministers, acting in urgency and in fear of prolonged hesitations on the part of their sovereign, proceeded to have the warrant carried out. Mary Stuart was accordingly beheaded at Fotheringhay Castle on February 8, 1587.

*   *   *

When Schiller wrote to Goethe that he saw the Mary Stuart theme as "especially adapted for the Euripidean style" he referred to his method of treating this long and complex story only at its final and tragic stage. He would not duplicate the panoramic technique so admirably applied to *Wallenstein;* rather, he would open his drama on the eve of the heroine's death, when her fate had already been decided by her enemies. The eventful biography of the Queen would be evoked only in retrospect. The no less complex political and religious controversies which had brought about the tragic situation would also be placed on the periphery of his drama. The focus would be entirely on the two royal antagonists at the fateful hour. A sure dramatic instinct prompted Schiller to adopt this stand, and the result was his technically finest work.

He began by ignoring the nineteen years of captivity almost entirely. Sufficient time has elapsed since Mary's detention to allow for more than one unsuccessful attempt to liberate her, but she is still young, beautiful, and impetuous, whereas in real life the prisoner had grown corpulent, was obliged to wear a wig to conceal her baldness, and a certain lethargy had replaced the ardor of her youth. Bothwell is left in the remote past, whereas in fact he died about the same time as Mary, a wretched victim of raving madness from the long imprisonment into which the King of Denmark had cast him upon his arrival in that kingdom. The luxury consistently permitted the imprisoned Queen is now transformed into physical privation the better to symbolize Mary's plight. Schiller strenuously rejected the idea that a dramatist was under obligation to produce what we should nowadays call a "documentary work." A poet, he maintained, echoing Aristotle, should be free to manipulate the facts of history in the interests of higher, poetic truth. Hence there is much in the play that derives only from the author's imagination. Yet there is quite as much that is actual fact, and without scrupulous researches it is difficult to identify with confidence what is fact and what is fiction. Elizabeth's bizarre evasions with Davison in the matter of the death warrant are fact; the very plausible interview between the two Queens in Act III, on the other hand, never took place. The fascinating figure of Mortimer is pure fiction, while the less credible figure of Leicester is historical, though his love for Mary is an invention of the dramatist. Catalogues of items could be compiled under the captions of True and False, but such lists would not advance the understanding of the drama at all. Schiller's purpose can be perceived only on the poetic plane.

Mary Stuart is the proper title of the play, for all impulses that animate the work proceed from the Scottish Queen. Nevertheless both Queens are of prime concern, both roles demand actresses of the highest capabilities, and neither role is comprehensible without the other.

Schiller assumed that Mary was guilty of complicity with Bothwell in the murder of Darnley. In her last confession he makes her admit her hatred of Elizabeth and passionate adultery with Bothwell. We ourselves witness her exultant fury when she heaps unpardonable insults upon Elizabeth in Act III. Yet with all her guilt, including even murder, we see the doomed Mary as ardent, human, and lovable. Other characters in the play also find her so. Her attendant women are genuinely grief-stricken at her fate; Mortimer dies for her sake; Leicester wishes he had done so. Elizabeth, on the other hand, is cold, vain, unloving and unloved. Leicester abandons her with horror; the loyal Shrewsbury resigns his office; Burleigh and Davison she herself cashiers. Mary, guilty but worthy of love, is attended in her final hour by as many friends, of both sexes, as are able to penetrate her strictly guarded prison; Elizabeth, free and a Queen, is in her hour of triumph left utterly alone. What makes the sinner beloved despite her sins is the element of Rousseauistic "heart"; what turns everyone away from the technically virtuous Elizabeth is precisely the lack of the same quality. Better, says the author, are ardor and affection with passionate error than cold monotony of egotism posed in the stiff regalia of virtue. The antithetical women represent another striking permutation of the author's basic human opposites, Idealist and Realist, intuitive heart versus calculating rational intellect.

The theme is a great one and Schiller conceived it greatly. As drama the work has proved itself unfailingly stageworthy. The over-all disposition of the matter, however, shows a certain stylization which delights some while eliciting from others the accusation of being so correctly symmetrical as to be contrived. The odd-numbered acts, with the exception of the short final scene, are set at Fotheringhay, the even-numbered acts at West-

minster Palace. Act I is all Mary; II is all Elizabeth; III brings
them together; then, as in a mirror image, Act IV is all Elizabeth, while most of V is again all Mary. The characters too are
disposed with the symmetry of chesspieces. Mary is attended by
women, Elizabeth has only men about her. Each woman is
assigned a lover appropriate to her character-weakness, and
both lovers are dissemblers with two masks each. Mortimer,
the youth of passionate heart, carries his passion to frenzy as
he carries his religion to fanaticism; he is, as it were, a carica-
ture of Mary's love and faith, yet all the time he masquerades as
a frigidly dutiful subject of Elizabeth and as an incorruptible
Protestant. Leicester, parallelwise, is a travesty of Elizabeth's
heartlessness and craft, aspiring to love but suppressing love
for the sake of worldly advantage, yet all the time masquerades
as a man of ardor and devotion. Mortimer, like Mary, perishes;
Leicester, like Elizabeth, survives amid loneliness. On the
other hand the men are contrasted with the female counter-
parts. Mortimer perishes in a gorgeous bit of melodrama,
irrationally and bursting out of all control, while the passionate heart of Mary achieves a noble serenity. Leicester's craft
prompts him finally to flight abroad and loneliness in foreign
lands, while the craft of Elizabeth brings her to final and total
isolation at home; he flees responsibility for his actions, she is
compelled to face her responsibility. Queen Mary's faithful
servant Melvil braves all perils to serve her at the end of her
life; Queen Elizabeth's faithful servant Shrewsbury declines
at the last to serve Elizabeth at all. In this play each move has
its countermove. The total work has about it the quality of
geometric precision as in an intricate classical dance.

Such symmetry and balance are factors commonly accepted
in classical comedy, but their presence is somewhat surprising
in this Shakespeareanizing tragedy. For, despite the "Euripidean" focus on the final stage of the conflict exclusively, the
over-all dramatic treatment, the blank verse, the historical

topic itself, all have about them more of Shakespeare than of Greece. And what is not of Shakespeare is, in turn, more of Racine than it is of Euripides, particularly the muted close, which reminds one of the final scene of *Britannicus*. These statements in themselves betoken Schiller's multiple inspiration. His purpose was to amalgamate the best elements of the three dramatic traditions, ancient Greek, Elizabethan English, and French classical, to add elements of his own German genius to the amalgam, and to create thereby a new drama worthy to stand with the great works of the past and capable of enduring through ages to come.

Into this new art form he infuses much of his own lofty spirit. *Mary Stuart* is by no means a belated example of the play of court intrigue. Its two Queens are grandiose figures of love and of lovelessness, they are conceived as human embodiments of constant antitheses of life, they enact a mighty parable. Over and above this large idea there is furthermore the portrayal of the troubled soul of Mary as it finally eludes its prison,—not the material prison of stones and iron locks, but the prison of its own passions,—and finds ultimate serenity. It is amid a Heaven-shed radiance of martyrdom that Mary goes to execution, a Christian rapture is hers as she welcomes death. She goes to an infinitely better world. Here below, life is dark and full of evil illusion, and it is over such a realm of falsity and loveless shadows that Elizabeth is left at the end as Queen. Assumption into Heaven and eternal damnation in Hell are the true analogies that underlie this fine Romantic play.

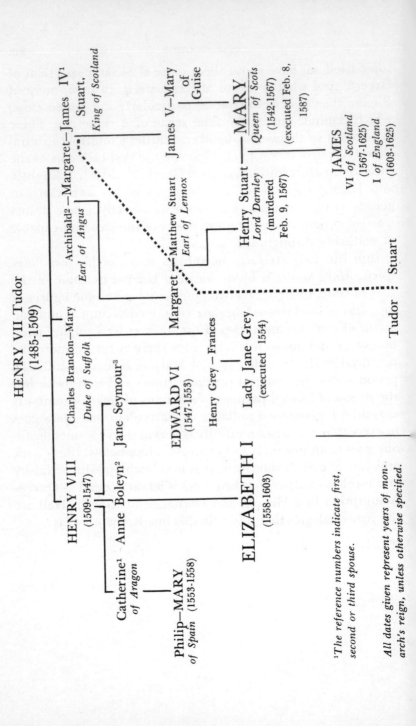

¹The reference numbers indicate first, second or third spouse.

All dates given represent years of monarch's reign, unless otherwise specified.

MARY STUART

CHARACTERS

ELIZABETH, QUEEN OF ENGLAND
MARY STUART, QUEEN OF SCOTLAND, a prisoner in England
ROBERT DUDLEY, EARL OF LEICESTER
GEORGE TALBOT, EARL OF SHREWSBURY
WILLIAM CECIL, BARON OF BURLEIGH, Lord High Treasurer
THE EARL OF KENT
WILLIAM DAVISON, State Secretary
AMIAS PAULET, KNIGHT, Mary's jailer
MORTIMER, his nephew
COUNT AUBESPINE, the French Ambassador
COUNT BELLIÈVRE, Ambassador extraordinary from France
O'KELLY, Mortimer's friend
DRUGEON DRURY, Mary's second jailer
MELVIL, her chief steward
BURGOYN, her surgeon
JANE KENNEDY, her nurse
MARGARET KURL, her lady-in-waiting
The Sheriff of the shire
An Officer of the Bodyguard
French and English gentlemen
Guards
Court servants of the Queen of England
Male and female servants of the Queen of Scotland

Time: February 6, 7, and 8, 1587
Place: England, alternately at the rural Castle of Fotheringhay
and at Westminster Palace in London.

2

ACT I

In Fotheringhay Castle. A room.
Jane Kennedy, the Queen of Scotland's nurse, in vehement dis-
pute with Paulet, who is in the act of opening a cabinet. Drugeon
Drury, his assistant, with a crowbar.

KENNEDY: What are you doing, Sir? More insolence!
  Get back from there!
PAULET: How did this jewel get here?
  It had been thrown down from the upper storey;
  The gardner was supposed to have been bribed
  By means of this—A curse on women's wiles!
  For all my watchfulness, my sharp-eyed search,
  More precious items yet, *more* hidden treasures!
          (going to work on the cabinet)
  Where that was hidden there are more!
KENNEDY: Get back you reckless man!
  Here lie my Lady's secrets!
PAULET: Those are just
  What I am looking for.
          (taking out papers with writing)
KENNEDY: Mere harmless scraps   10
  Of paper, exercises of the pen
  To make the prison's dreary time more short.
PAULET: The Devil thinks up work for idle hands.
KENNEDY: The writing is in French.
PAULET: So much the worse!
  That is the tongue of England's enemies.
KENNEDY: Rough drafts of letters to the Queen of England.
PAULET: I will deliver them.—What glitters here?
      *(He has opened a secret compartment and
      takes out jewels from a hidden drawer.)*

3

A royal tiara, rich with precious stones
And in-wrought with the fleur-de-lys of France!
(He gives it to his companion.)
There, take it, Drury. Put it with the others!   20
(Exit Drury.)
KENNEDY: Outrageous violence that we endure!
PAULET: While she owns anything she can do harm,
For anything in her hands is a weapon.
KENNEDY: Be kind, Sir. Do not take the last adornment
Out of our lives. The piteous creature finds
Delight beholding the magnificence
Of old, for you have robbed us of all else.
PAULET: It will be in good hands. And in due time
It will be scrupulously given back.
KENNEDY: Would anyone who looked at these bare walls   30
Guess that a queen resided here? Where is
The canopy above her chair? Must she
Not set her tender, soft-accustomed foot
Upon the rough and common floor? And at
Her table she is served from ugly tin, —
The humblest noblewoman would disdain it.
PAULET: She served her spouse that way at Sterling Castle
While she drank with her lover out of gold.
KENNEDY: We even lack the mirror's small requirement.
PAULET: As long as she beholds her vain reflection   40
She will not cease to hope and venture plans.
KENNEDY: We lack for books to entertain the mind.
PAULET: She has been left her Bible to improve
Her heart.
KENNEDY: Her very lute has been removed.
PAULET: Because she played her wanton songs upon it.
KENNEDY: Is this a fate befitting one soft-reared,
Who was a queen already from her cradle,
Who at the sumptuous court of Catherine
Of Medici grew up in joy's abundance?
It should have been enough to take away   50
Her power; must you begrudge her these poor trinkets?

A noble heart enures itself to *great*
Misfortune finally, but it is painful
To be deprived of life's small ornaments.
PAULET: They only turn toward vanity the heart
That should, by turning inward, learn repentance.
A wanton, crime-stained life can be atoned
In deprivation and abasement only.
KENNEDY: If tender youth in her once trespassed, let
Her settle that with God and with her heart.   60
There is no judge in England over her.
PAULET: She will be judged where she did her misdeeds.
KENNEDY: Bonds much too tight bind her from all misdoing.
PAULET: And yet from those tight bonds she has been able
To stretch her arm into the world to hurl
The torch of civil war into the realm
And to equip assassin-packs with weapons
Against our Queen, whom God preserve from harm!
Did she not from these very walls stir up
That scoundrel Parry and that Babington   70
To the accursed deed of regicide?
And did these iron bars deter her from
Ensnaring Norfolk's noble heart with love?
The best head in our island fell beneath
The headsman's ax in sacrifice for her—
And did that woeful spectacle scare off
The madmen striving to outdo each other
In plunging into the abyss for her sake?
The scaffolds are filled up because of her
With new and ever newer death-doomed victims,   80
And this will never end till she herself,
The guiltiest of all, is slaughtered there.
—Cursed be the day when the coasts of this country
With hospitality received this Helen.
KENNEDY: England, you say, showed hospitality?
To this unfortunate, who since the day
When she set foot within this country and
As suppliant, as exile dispossessed,

Came seeking harborage with relatives,
Sees herself captive in defiance of   90
The dignity of kings and laws of nations,
Forced to waste lovely years of youth in prison—
Who after all she has gone through, and all
The bitter things imprisonment entails,
Must now like common criminals be haled
Before the bar of judgment and accused
Disgracefully, on pain of death—a Queen!
PAULET: She came here as a murderess, expelled
By her own people, driven from a throne
She had dishonored with a deed of horror.   100
She came, conspiring against England's welfare.
To bring the times of Spanish Mary back,
Those bloody times, make England Catholic
Again, and then betray it to the Frenchman.
Why should she have disdained to sign the Treaty
Of Edinburgh abandoning her claim
To England, which with one stroke of the pen
Would have directly opened her a way
Out of this prison? She preferred to stay
A captive and mistreated rather than   110
Renounce the empty glory of that title.
And why did she do that? Because she trusts
Intrigues and vile arts of conspiracy,
Because she hopes with woven wiles of mischief
To conquer this whole island from her prison.
KENNEDY: You mock us, Sir.—To harshness you add further
Your bitter scorn! Such dreams as these you claim
She fosters, living walled up here alive,
No sound of comfort reaching her, no voice
Of friendship from her homeland coming through,   120
Beholding this long time no human face
Except the sombre mien of jailers, lately
Receiving one more spying watcher in
The uncouth person of your relative,
Perceiving new bars hemming her about—

PAULET: No iron bars protect us from her cunning.
　　How do I know these bars are not filed through,
　　Or that this floor, these walls, apparently
　　Quite sound, have not been hollowed out inside
　　To let in treason while I am asleep?　　　　　　　　130
　　O what a cursed task to fall to me
　　To guard this mischief-plotting, cunning creature.
　　Fear starts me up from slumber; in the night
　　I wander like a ghost in torment, testing
　　The bolts of doors and loyalty of guards,
　　And trembling see each morning come, lest it
　　Should make my fears come true. But happily
　　For me, there is hope that this soon will end.
　　For I would rather have a post beside
　　The gate of hell and guard the legions of　　　　140
　　The damned, before this wily, scheming Queen.
KENNEDY: Ah, here she comes!
PAULET:　　　　　　　　With Christ clasped in her hand,
　　And pride and worldly pleasure in her heart.
　　　　　　(Enter Mary in a veil and with a
　　　　　　　　crucifix in her hand.)
KENNEDY (hurrying toward her):
　　O Queen! They trample us beneath their feet,
　　Of tyranny and harshness there will be
　　No limit, each new day heaps newer sorrows
　　And shame on your crowned head.
MARY:　　　　　　　　　Compose yourself!
　　Now tell me, what new thing has happened?
KENNEDY:　　　　　　　　　　　　Look!
　　Your desk is broken open, and your papers,
　　Your only prize that we had salvaged with　　　　150
　　Such pains, the last of all your bridal jewels
　　From France,—all those are in his hands. You now
　　Have nothing royal left. All has been stolen.
MARY: Compose yourself, Jane. All those trinkets do
　　Not make the Queen. We can be treated basely
　　But they cannot debase us. I have learned

How to put up with many things in England;
This, too, I can get over. Sir, you have
Appropriated forcibly what I
Today intended to surrender to you.   160
Among those papers you will find a letter
Which was to be sent to my royal sister
Of England.—Give me now your word that you
Will faithfully deliver it to her
And not put it in Burleigh's treacherous hand.
PAULET: I will consider what to do about it.
MARY: Sir, you shall know the contents. In that letter
I make request of a tremendous favor—
I ask her for an interview in person,
With her whom I have never seen.—I have   170
Been summoned up before a court of men
Whom I do not acknowledge as my peers,
In whom I cannot put my confidence.
Elizabeth is of my family
And of my sex and rank—to her alone,
The sister, queen, and woman, can I speak.
PAULET: My Lady, you have very often trusted
Your honor and your destiny to men
Who were less worthy of your high esteem.
MARY: I make request of still another favor.   180
Sheer inhumanity alone would fail
To grant it. I have been in prison this
Long time without the Church's consolation,
The benison of sacraments, and she who has
Robbed me of crown and freedom and now threatens
My life itself, will not close Heaven's gate
To me.
PAULET: The local Dean at your request will—
MARY (interrupting him sharply):
I will have nothing of the Dean. It is
A priest of my own Church that I demand.
—I also ask for clerks and notaries   190
To draw up my last will and testament.

Affliction and long misery of prison
Are gnawing at my life. My days are numbered,
I fear, and I now look upon myself
As on a dying woman.

PAULET: You do well
To do so. Those are views befitting you.

MARY: How do I know but that a sudden hand
Will hasten the slow business of my sorrow?
I want to draw my will, make disposition
Of everything that I possess.

PAULET: You have   200
That liberty. The Queen of England does
Not wish enrichment gained from plundering you.

MARY: I have been separated from my loyal
Servants and chamberladies. Where are they?
What is their fate? Their services I can
Forego; but I wish reassurance that
These loyal persons shall not want and suffer.

PAULET: Your servants are provided for.
              (He starts to leave.)

MARY: You leave me, Sir? You leave me once again
Without discharging my tormented heart   210
Of its dread anguish of uncertainty?
I am, thanks to your spiers' vigilance,
Cut off from all the world; no information
Can penetrate these prison walls to reach me;
My enemies hold my fate in their hands.
A painfully long month has now gone by
Since I was taken by surprise by forty
Commissioners who came into this castle,
Set up their court, and with unseemly haste
Called me, without attorney's aid, unready,   220
To come before a tribunal unheard of,
And made me speak off-hand, from recollection,
To grave and deviously worded charges
While I was flustered with surprise and stunned. —
Like ghosts they came and disappeared again.

Since that day every mouth has maintained silence.
I seek in vain to read your looks and tell
Which has prevailed: my innocence, and zeal
Of friends, or evil counsel of my foes.
At long last, break your silence—let me know   230
What I may have to fear, or have to hope for.

PAULET (after a pause):
Settle your account with Heaven.

MARY: Sir,
I have hopes in its mercy—and hopes in
The strict uprightness of my earthly judges.

PAULET: You shall have justice. Have no doubt of that.

MARY: Has my case been decided?

PAULET: I don't know.

MARY: Am I condemned?

PAULET: My Lady, I know nothing.

MARY: They like to do things quickly here. Am I
To be surprised by my assassins too,
As by my judges?

PAULET: Think of it that way,   240
And they will find you more prepared than did
The latter.

MARY: Nothing will amaze me, Sir,
That a Westminster court of justice, guided
By Burleigh's hatred and by Hatton's zeal,
Might now presume to judge.—I do know, though,
What England's Queen is bold enough to do.

PAULET: England's rulers need have fear of nothing
Except their consciences and parliaments.
What Justice has pronounced, Might will perform,
And fearlessly, for all the world to see.   250

    (Enter Mortimer, Paulet's nephew. Without paying any
    attention to the Queen, he says to Paulet :)

MORTIMER: They want you, Uncle.

    (He withdraws in the same manner. The Queen notices
    it with annoyance and turns to Paulet, who is on the
    point of following him.)

MARY: Sir, one more request.
  If *you* have anything to say to me . . .
  I will bear much from you, revering your
  Old age. I will not bear this stripling's brashness.
  Spare me the spectacle of his rude manners.
PAULET: What makes you loathe him so, makes me esteem him.
  He is indeed not one of those weak fools
  Whom a false woman's tear will melt. — And he
  Is traveled. He has been to Rheims and Paris,
  But he brings back his good old English heart: 260
  My Lady, you will waste your wiles on him.
                (Exit.)
       (Reenter Kennedy.)
KENNEDY: O, does the brute dare say that to your face!
  O, that is hard.
MARY *(lost in thought)*:
  Back in the days of our magnificence
  We lent our flatterers an ear too willing;
  It is but just, good Kennedy, that we
  Now harken to Reproach's solemn voice.
KENNEDY: So daunted, so dispirited, dear Lady?
  You used to be so cheerful, used to comfort me;
  I used to have to scold you more about   270
  Frivolity than melancholy.
MARY: I know him.
  It is the gory shadow of King Darnley
  That rises menacing up from his tomb,
  And he will never make his peace with me
  Until misfortune's measure has been filled
  For me.
KENNEDY: What kind of thoughts —
MARY: Jane, you forget —
  But I possess a faithful memory —
  Today the anniversary of that
  Unholy deed has once again come round,
  And that is what I keep with prayer and fasting.   280
KENNEDY: Dismiss that evil ghost to rest at last.

You have atoned for that deed by long years
Of heart's remorse and grievous acts of penance.
The Church, which holds the key of absolution
For every sin, has pardoned you, and Heaven
As well.
MARY: The long forgiven sin fresh-bleeding
  Has risen from its lightly covered grave!
  My husband's vengeance-seeking spirit will
  Not be dismissed into its tomb by any
  Priest-raised Host or bell of acolyte.   290
KENNEDY: You did no act of murder! Others did!
MARY: I knew of it. I let the deed be done,
  And lured him smiling to the toils of death.
KENNEDY: Youth mitigated your misdeed. You were
  Still of such tender years.
MARY: Such tender years—
  Yet burdened my young life with grievous guilt.
KENNEDY: You were provoked to it by brutal outrage
  And by the arrogance of a man whom
  Your love had elevated as a god's
  Hand elevates out of obscurity,   300
  Whom you led through your bridal chamber to
  A throne, and favored with your lovely self
  And with your own hereditary crown.
  Could he forget his splendid lot was only
  The generous creation of your love?
  And yet he did forget, unworthy wretch!
  And with his base suspicion and rude manners
  Committed outrage on your tenderness
  And made himself quite odious to your sight.
  The spell was broken that deceived your gaze,   310
  You fled in anger from the shameless creature's
  Embrace and then consigned him to contempt.—
  And he—did he try to regain your favor?
  Or did he sue for mercy? Did he fall
  Repentant at your feet and promise to
  Improve? The worthless wretch defied you—who

Created him—and tried to play the King.
Before your eyes he had your favorite murdered,
The handsome singer Rizzio.—You merely
Took bloody vengeance for that bloody deed.   320
MARY: And bloodily it will avenge itself
  On me. Consoling me, you speak my doom.
KENNEDY: When you consented to that action, you
  Were not yourself, not mistress of yourself.
  Blind frenzy of desire swept you away
  And held you subjugated to the dread
  Seducer, ill-starred Bothwell.—Over you
  With arrogant male will that artful man
  Held sway, inflaming you with magic philtres
  And hellish tricks that throw the mind into   330
  Confusion—
MARY: His tricks were never anything more than
  His masculinity and my own weakness.
KENNEDY: Oh no, say I! He had to summon all
  The spirits of perdition to his aid
  To weave those fetters over your clear senses.
  For your friend's voice of warning you no longer
  Had ears, nor any eyes for what was seemly.
  Your delicate respect for men's opinion
  Deserted you. Your cheek, which once had been
  The seat of bashful, blushing modesty,   340
  Was flushed with nothing but the fire of passion.
  You cast aside the veil of secrecy.
  The brazen vice of that man overcame
  Your timid shyness; with defiance you
  Exposed your shame before the general view.
  You caused the royal sword of Scotland to
  Be carried through the streets of Edinburgh
  Triumphantly in front of you by that
  Assassin, in whose wake the people's curses
  Resounded; then you ringed your Parliament   350
  With weapons, and within the very temple
  Of justice forced the judges in a farce

To clear the guilty man of murder.—Yes,
You went still further—God in heaven—

MARY: Say it!
And I gave him my hand before the altar!

KENNEDY: O let an everlasting silence cloak
That deed! It is revolting, horrible,
It suits a woman wholly lost—But you are no
Lost woman—I know you, I was the one
Who supervised your childhood. Your heart is   360
Of tender kind, accessible to shame,
And indiscretion is your only crime.
Again I say it: there are evil spirits
Which momentarily in man's unguarded
Bosom make their habitation and
Within us perpetrate these monstrous things,
Then, making their escape to hell, leave horror
Behind them in the heart they have polluted.
Since that deed which put blackness on your life,
You have done nothing reprehensible.   370
I am a witness to your betterment.
Therefore take courage! Make peace with yourself!
Whatever you have to repent, in England
You are not guilty; neither England's Queen
Nor England's Parliament can be your judge.
What overwhelms you here is force. To that
Presumptuous court you may present yourself
With all the courage lent by innocence.

MARY: Who comes?

(Mortimer appears at the door.)

KENNEDY: It is the nephew. Go inside.

(Enter Mortimer timidly.)

MORTIMER *(to the nurse)*:
Withdraw, and keep a watch outside the door.   380
I have things I must speak of to the Queen.

MARY *(with authority)*:
Jane, you will stay.

MORTIMER: Have no fear, my Lady. Learn to know me.
                    (He hands her a card.)
MARY *(looks at it and falls back startled):*
  Ha, what is this?
MORTIMER *(to the nurse):*   Go, Mistress Kennedy,
  Take care my uncle does not take us by
  Surprise.
MARY *(to the nurse, who is hesitating and looking questioningly*
    at the Queen):
              Go! Go! Do as he says.
              (The nurse withdraws with signs of
                    astonishment.)
                          From France,
  And from the Cardinal of Lorraine, my uncle!
                    (reading)
  "Trust in Sir Mortimer who brings you this,
  You have no friend more loyal in all England."
            (looking at Mortimer in astonishment)
  Can it be possible? Not some delusion   390
  That dazzles me? I find a friend so near
  And thought myself abandoned totally—
  Find him in you, the nephew of my jailer,
  Whom I took for my direst enemy—
MORTIMER *(throwing himself at her feet):*
  Forgive me, Queen, this odious disguise
  Which I have had to fight enough to wear
  And yet which I must thank for being able
  To get to you and bring you help and rescue.
MARY: Stand up—You take me by surprise, Sir—I
  Can not arise so fast out of the depths   400
  Of wretchedness to hope—Speak, Sir—Explain
  This stroke of luck to me, so that I may
  Believe it.
MORTIMER *(rises):*   Time is running short. My uncle
  Will soon be here. An odious man is with him.
  Before you are surprised by their dread errand,
  Hear first how Heaven sends you rescue.

MARY: Heaven's
  Omnipotence has wrought this miracle!
MORTIMER: Allow me to begin first with myself.
MARY: Speak, Sir!
MORTIMER: I had achieved the age of twenty, Queen,
  I had grown up amid stern obligations,   410
  Been bred to grim hate for the papacy,
  When irresistible desire impelled me
  To travel to the continent. I left
  The gloomy sermon-rooms of Puritans,
  I left my native land behind me, and
  In rapid journey crossed through France in search
  Of much-praised Italy with hot desire.
    It was the great time of the jubilee,
  The roads were teeming with the throngs of pilgrims,
  Every image wore a wreath, it was   420
  As if mankind were travelling together
  Upon a pilgrimage to heaven—I
  Myself was caught up in the faithful throng
  And borne along into the realm of Rome—
    What feelings swept me, Queen,
  When to my sight arose the splendor of
  Triumphal arch and column, when amazement held me
  Enthralled amid the Colosseum's majesty,
  And when the lofty soul of art enclosed
  Me in a cheerful world of wonders. I   430
  Had never sensed the power of the arts.
  The church that reared me hates the senses' charms,
  It tolerates no image, reverences
  The fleshless Word alone. What feelings swept me
  When entering the churches. Heaven's music
  Descended, and a plenitude of forms
  Arose luxuriant from wall and ceiling,
  And the supreme sublimity was borne
  Quite tangibly past my enraptured senses;
  And then when I beheld those things divine—   440
  The Angel's Salutation, Our Lord's Birth,

The Blessed Mother, the Transfiguration
In glory, the descending Trinity—
And when I saw the Pope himself in splendor
Say Mass and give the nations benediction!
O what is the magnificence of gold
And jewels which adorn the kings of earth!
Divinity encircles *him* alone.
A realm of heaven is his house, indeed,
For those forms surely are not of this world.   450
MARY: O spare me! Speak no more of these things! Cease
Unfurling the fresh tapestry of life
Before me—I am wretched and a captive.
MORTIMER: And so was I, my Queen! And then my prison
Sprang open, and my spirit suddenly
Felt free and welcomed life's resplendent day.
I vowed to hate the narrow, gloomy book,
To wreathe my temples with fresh garlands, and
To mingle joyously among the joyous.
Many noble Scotsmen thronged to me,   460
And jolly companies of Frenchmen too.
And then they took me to your noble uncle,
The Cardinal of Guise—O what a man!
How clear, assured, and manly great!—How wholly
Born to be ruler over human minds!
The model of a royal priest, a Prince of
The Church, the like of which I never saw!
MARY: You have beheld his cherished countenance,
The face of that sublime and much-loved man
Who was the mentor of my tender youth.   470
O speak of him! Does he still think of me?
Does Fortune love him? Does his life still flower?
And does he still stand as the Church's rock?
MORTIMER: The excellent man himself deigned to expound
To me the lofty doctrines of the Faith
And to dispel the doubts that filled my heart.
He showed me how the Reason with its quibbles
Must everlastingly lead man astray,

How human eyes have need of seeing what
The heart is to believe, how the Church must   480
Present a visible head, how the Spirit
Of Truth dwelt in the Councils of the Fathers.
How the illusions of my childish soul
Were all dispelled by his triumphant mind
And by the suasion of his mouth. Thus I
Returned into the bosom of the Church
And there into his hands renounced my error.

MARY: You are one of those thousands, then, whom he,
Like that sublimest Preacher on the Mount,
Has seized on by his eloquence from heaven   490
And brought back to salvation everlasting.

MORTIMER: When duties of his office soon thereafter
Called him to France, he sent me up to Rheims,
Where the Society of Jesus in
Its pious diligence trains priests for England.
And there I found the noble Scotsman Morgan,
Your faithful Lessley too, the learned Bishop
Of Ross, who are all living joyless days
Of banishment upon the soil of France. —
I joined those worthy men in close alliance   500
And strengthened myself in the Faith. — One day
While looking through the Bishop's residence,
A woman's picture fell upon my eyes
Of wondrously affecting charm. It moved
Me powerfully to the depths of my soul,
And there I stood with feelings uncontrolled.
The Bishop said to me: You do quite right
To dwell upon that portrait with emotion.
For that most beautiful of living women
Is also the most miserable of all.   510
It is for our Faith's sake that she endures
And it is your home country where she suffers.

MARY: That upright man! No, all has not been lost
When such a friend is left in my misfortune.

MORTIMER: Then he began describing to me with

Heart-rending eloquence your martyrdom
And the bloodthirstiness of all your foes.
And he referred me to your family tree
And showed me your descent from the high House
Of Tudor and convinced me you alone   520
Should properly be ruler here in England,
Not this pretender of a Queen, conceived
In an adulterous bed, repudiated
By Henry, her own father, as a bastard.
I would not trust his testimony only,
I sought advice from all the learned jurists,
Poured over many books of heraldry,
And all the experts whom I found to ask
Confirmed to me your claim's validity.
By now I realize that your good right   530
To England constitutes your only wrong,
That this realm is your rightful property
In which you languish as a guiltless captive.
MARY: Alas, that right is my misfortune! It
Is the sole cause of all my sufferings.
MORTIMER: Just at that time the information reached me
That you had been removed from Talbot's castle
And been committed to my uncle's charge—
In that contingency I thought I saw
Miraculous deliverance from heaven.   540
It seemed as though Fate clearly summoned me
And made choice of *my* arm to set you free.
My friends with joy agreed, the Cardinal
Gave me his blessing and his counsel and
Taught me the hard art of dissimulation.
The plan was soon contrived, and I set out
Upon my homeward journey to my country
Where, as you know, I landed ten days since.
                    (He stops.)
Then, O my Queen, I saw you—you yourself!
Not just your picture! —O, what treasure is   550
Kept in this castle! This is not a prison!

This is a hall of gods more splendid than
The royal court of England—O how lucky
The man who may breathe this same air with you!
    O she does well to hide you so completely!
For all the youth of England would rise up,
No sword would be left idle in its sheath,
Rebellion with gigantic head would stalk
This peaceful island, if the Briton were
To see his Queen!

MARY: And it is well for her,   560
If every Briton saw her through your eyes.

MORTIMER: If they, like me, were witness to your sorrows,
And to your meekness, and the noble calm
With which you here endure unworthiness.
For do you not emerge from all your trials
Of sorrow like a Queen? Does prison's shame
Deprive you of the glory of your beauty?
You lack all things that make life beautiful,
Yet light and life are ever shed about you.
I never set my foot upon this threshold   570
But that my heart is torn with torments and
Enraptured with the joy of looking at you! —
Yet fearsomely decision nears, and danger
Becomes more menacing with every hour.
I must postpone no longer—must no longer
Conceal the dread news from you—

MARY: Is my sentence
Pronounced? Disclose it frankly. I can hear it.

MORTIMER: It is pronounced. The forty-two high judges
Have brought their verdict: *Guilty;* and the House
Of Lords, the House of Commons, and the City   580
Of London urgently demand the sentence
Be carried out; the Queen alone is still
Delaying—craftily, so they will force her,
Not from compassion or from humane feelings.

MARY *(with composure)*:
Sir Mortimer, you do not take me by

Surprise nor frighten me. For such news I
Have long since been prepared. I know my judges.
After the mistreatment I have suffered,
I realize they cannot grant me freedom—
I understand what they are driving at.   590
They mean to hold me prisoner forever
And thus to bury my revenge and all
My rights and claims in prison darkness with me.

MORTIMER: No, Queen—no, no! They will not stop at that.
This tyranny will not be satisfied
To do its work half way. As long as you
Still live, the Queen of England's fear still lives.
No prison can inter you deep enough,
Your death alone can make her throne quite safe.

MARY: But would she ever dare to lay my crowned   600
Head down in shame upon the headsman's block?

MORTIMER: She will so dare. Make no mistake about it.

MARY: Would she hurl her own majesty into
The dust and all kings' majesty as well?
Does she not fear the vengeance France might take?

MORTIMER: She is now making lasting peace with France
And gives the Duc d'Anjou her throne and hand.

MARY: And will the King of Spain not take up arms?

MORTIMER: She would not fear the whole world up in arms
As long as she has peace with her own people.   610

MARY: Would she give Britons such a spectacle?

MORTIMER: This country has, in recent times, my Lady,
Witnessed several royal women step
Down from the throne to mount upon the scaffold.
This same Elizabeth's own mother trod
That path, and Katherine Howard, and the Lady
Jane Gray wore a crown likewise on her head.

MARY (after a pause):
No, Mortimer! Vain fear has made you blind.
It is your loyal heart's concern for me
That now gives rise to these vain terrors in you.   620
Sir, it is not the scaffold that I fear.

There are quite different means, more quiet ones,
To which the Queen of England can resort
To rid herself of my disturbing claims.
Before a headsman can be found for me,
A paid assassin will be found and hired.
—And *that,* Sir, is what makes me tremble. Never
Do I raise any cup's brim to my lips
But that a shudder courses through me lest
My sister's love should have prepared it for me.   630
MORTIMER: Assassination shall not touch your life
By either public means or secret ones.
Have no fear! Everything has been prepared.
Twelve noble young men of this country are
In league with me; this very morning they
Took their oath on the sacrament to set
You free by force and take you from this castle.
Count Aubespine, the French ambassador,
Knows of the plan and lends us help himself;
We have our place of meeting in his palace.   640
MARY: You make me tremble, Sir—but not with joy.
My heart is touched with evil premonition.
What have you undertaken? Do you know?
Do Babington's and Tichburn's bloody heads
Nailed up on London Bridge not terrify you?
Nor yet the ruin of the countless ones
Who in like risky hazard found their deaths
And only made my chains the heavier?
Unfortunate, misguided youth—flee now!
Flee while there still is time—if that spy Burleigh   650
Is not already on your track, has not
Already set a traitor in your midst.
Flee swiftly from this kingdom! Mary Stuart
Has yet to be fought for without disaster.
MORTIMER: No, Babington's and Tichburn's bloody heads
Nailed up on London Bridge affright me not,
Nor yet the ruin of the countless ones
Who in like risky hazard found their deaths;

They found undying fame as well, and it
Is happiness to perish for your rescue.   660
MARY: All futile! Neither force nor craft can save me.
The foe is sleepless and the power is his.
Not only Paulet and his host of spies
But all of England guards my prison doors.
The free will of Elizabeth alone
Can open them.
MORTIMER: O do not hope for that!
MARY: There does live one man who can open them.
MORTIMER: O name that man to me—
MARY: Count Lester.
MORTIMER (falls back astonished):   Lester!
Count Lester—your bloodthirstiest opponent,
The favorite of Elizabeth—By that —   670
MARY: If I can be saved, only he can save me.
—Go to him. Speak your purpose frankly.
As surety that it is I who send you,
Give him this letter. It contains my picture.
        (She takes a paper from her bosom. Mortimer
    steps back and hesitates to accept it.)
Take it. I long have carried it about me
Because your uncle's steady vigilance
Has barred all means of access to him.—You
Were sent by my good angel—
MORTIMER: Queen—this riddle—
Explain—
MARY: Count Lester will resolve it for you.
If you trust him, he will trust you—Who comes here?   680
        (Enter Kennedy in haste.)
KENNEDY: Sir Paulet with a gentleman from court.
MORTIMER: It is Lord Burleigh. Queen, compose yourself!
Hear what he says with equanimity.
        (He goes out by a side door. Kennedy follows him.
    Enter Lord Burleigh, Lord High Treasurer of
    England and Sir Amias Paulet.)
PAULET: You wished today for certainty about

Your fate. His Excellency, my Lord of Burleigh,
Brings you that certainty. Bear it with meekness.
MARY: With dignity, I trust, befitting innocence.
BURLEIGH: I come as the court's representative.
MARY: Lord Burleigh lent the court his mind before,
He now obligingly lends it his mouth.   690
PAULET: You speak as if you knew the verdict now.
MARY: Because Lord Burleigh brings it, I do know.
—Come to the point, Sir.
BURLEIGH: Lady, you submitted
Yourself before the court of forty-two—
MARY: Forgive my interrupting you, my Lord,
Right at the start—You say that I submitted
To judgment by the court of forty-two?
I never did submit myself to them.
I could not do so—I could not impugn
My rank and dignity so much, nor those of   700
My people, or my son, or of all monarchs.
It is decreed in English law that any
Person brought to trial shall be tried
By sworn men chosen from among his equals.
And who on that Commission is my equal?
Kings are my only peers.
BURLEIGH: You listened to
The articles of accusation and
In court submitted to examination—
MARY: I let myself be lured by Hatton's cunning,
Merely for my honor's sake and trusting   710
The winning power of my arguments,
To hear those articles of accusation
And demonstrate their groundlessness.—I did so
Out of respect for the Lords' worthy persons,
Not for their office, which I must reject.
BURLEIGH: Acknowledge it or not, my Lady, that
Is only meaningless formality
Which cannot hamper the court's operation.
You breathe the air of England and enjoy

The blessings and protection of its laws,   720
And you are subject to its sovereignty!
MARY: I breathe the air inside an English prison.
  Is that in England known as living and
  Enjoying benefaction of its laws?
  I hardly know them. And I never gave
  Consent to keep them. I am not a subject
  Of this realm, but a free Queen from abroad.
BURLEIGH: And do you think your royal name can serve
  As patent to sow with impunity
  Blood-stained dissension in a foreign country?   730
  What would become of the security
  Of states if the just sword of Themis could
  Not reach the guilty brows of royal guests
  As certainly as it does beggars' heads?
MARY: I do not seek escape from justice but
  From judges whom I do not recognize.
BURLEIGH: From judges! What, my Lady? Are they some
  Dredged-up and outcast scourings from the rabble,
  Some shameless shysters for whom truth and justice
  Are cheap, who willingly allow themselves   740
  To be hired out as tools of crass oppression?
  Are they not the first men of this country,
  And of sufficient independence to
  Be upright and be elevated far
  Above base bribery and fear of Princes?
  And are they not the very ones who rule
  A noble people freely and with justice,
  Whose names need but be named to silence all
  Suspicion and all doubt immediately?
  To head the list there is the people's shepherd,   750
  The pious primate of Canterbury,
  Wise Talbot, Keeper of the Privy Seal,
  And Howard who directs the nation's fleet.
  Now tell me, could the Queen of England do
  More than she has done, to select the noblest
  From all her monarchy and to appoint

Them to be judges in this royal quarrel?
Even if it were thinkable that hatred
Of parties could bribe individuals,—
Could forty chosen men agree upon   760
A verdict that involves such passion?

MARY (*after a silence*):
I stand amazed to hear the vehemence
Of lips which always have brought me misfortune—
How shall I, a woman and unlearned,
Compete against a speaker of such skill! —
Ah! if those Lords were such as you describe them,
I should be forced to silence; my case would
Be lost and hopeless if they found me guilty.
But those names which you mention with such praise,
Which are supposed to crush me with their weight,   770
My Lord, I see them play quite different roles
Down through the course of annals of this country.
I see those high aristocrats of England
And that majestic senate of this kingdom
Act like seraglio slaves in flattering
The Sultan's whims of my great-uncle Henry
The Eighth—I see that noble Upper House,
As venal as the venal House of Commons,
Enact laws and revoke them, now dissolve
A marriage, now enforce it, at the mighty   780
Man's bidding, disinherit England's Princesses
Today and shame them with the name of bastards,
And then again tomorrow crown them Queens.
I see those worthy peers with swiftly changed
Convictions *four times* alter their religion
Under *four* regimes.

BURLEIGH: You claim that you
Are unfamiliar with the laws of England
But you are well informed on England's woes.

MARY: Such are my judges! —Lord High Treasurer!
I want to be quite fair with you! Be so   790
Likewise with me.—They say that you are well

Intentioned toward this state, that with your Queen
You are alert, unbribeable, and tireless—
I shall believe that. You are governed not
By your advantage but by what is of
Advantage to your Sovereign and your country.
Do not therefore, my noble Lord, mistake
For justice what is useful to the state.
I do not doubt that other noble men
Are seated there with you among my judges.   800
But they are *Protestants,* men filled with zeal
For England's welfare, and they sit in judgment
On me, the Queen of Scotland and a Papist!
The Englishman can not be just in judging
The Scotsman, goes an ancient saying.—Hence
Tradition has it since times of our fathers:
No Englishman shall testify in court
Against a Scot, nor any Scot against him.
Necessity occasioned that strange law.
Deep meaning lies in those old usages,   810
And one must honor them, my Lord.—These two
Fierce nationalities were cast by Nature
Upon this plank in ocean; this she parcelled
Unequally and bade them fight for it.
The narrow Tweed is all that separates
Those fiery tempers; often in its waves
The blood of fighting men has been commingled.
With hand on sword, they have looked threateningly
Across from both those shores these thousand years.
No enemy has menaced England yet   820
But that the Scotsman joined him as a helper;
No civil war has kindled Scotland's cities
But that the Englishman provided tinder.
Nor will the hatred ever die until
One parliament joins them in brotherhood,
Until one sceptre rules throughout the island.
BURLEIGH: And I suppose a Stuart would afford
    The realm that blessing?

MARY: Why should I deny it?
   Yes, I confess that I had cherished hopes
   Of unifying these two noble nations   830
   Freely in the shadow of the olive.
   I never thought I would become the victim
   Of these two peoples' hatred. I had hoped
   To quench forever their long jealousy,
   The wretched passion of their ancient quarrel,
   And, as my forebear Richmond once united
   Both roses after bloody struggle, wed
   In peace the crowns of Scotland and of England.
BURLEIGH: Then you pursued that goal by evil ways
   When you sought to enflame the kingdom and   840
   Ascend the throne through fires of civil war.
MARY: That I did not seek, by the living God!
   When did I seek that? Where are proofs of that?
BURLEIGH: I did not come to argue here. The matter
   Is past the point of disputation now.
   Decision has been made by forty votes to two
   That you have violated last year's Act
   Of Parliament and have incurred the forfeit.
   It was enacted into law last year:
   "In case disorder shall arise within   850
     The kingdom in the name and to the vantage
     Of any person claiming rights upon
     The throne, that person shall be prosecuted
     By law and, if found guilty, put to death."—
   And since it now is proved—
MARY: My Lord of Burleigh!
   I do not doubt but that a law, expressly
   Drawn up against me, written to destroy me,
   Will be invoked and used against me.—Woe
   To the poor victim, when the very mouth
   That made the law pronounces sentence also!   860
   Can you deny, my Lord, that that same Act
   Referred to was devised for my destruction?
BURLEIGH: It was intended as a warning to you,

You have yourself turned it into a snare.
You saw the pit that opened up before you,
And yet, despite fair warning, you plunged in,
For you were in collusion with the traitor
Babington and his accomplices;
You were informed of everything, and from
Your prison guided the conspiracy.   870
MARY: When do you claim I did that? Let them show
   Me documents to prove it.
BURLEIGH: Those were laid
   Before you only recently in court.
MARY: The copies, written by an unknown hand!
   But let proof be adduced that I dictated
   Those documents myself, and that I did so
   In that precise form in which they were read.
BURLEIGH: Before his execution Babington
   Acknowledged them as those he had received.
MARY: And why was he not brought before my eyes   880
   Alive? And why were they in such a hurry
   Despatching him out of the world before
   He was produced before me, face to face?
BURLEIGH: Your secretaries also, Kurl and Nau,
   Confirmed on oath those were the very letters
   That they had written down from your own mouth.
MARY: I am condemned, then, on the testimony
   Of my domestics! On the basis of
   The faith and trust of those men who betrayed me,
   Their Queen, who broke their faith that very moment   890
   When they bore witness there against me?
BURLEIGH: You once declared the Scotsman Kurl yourself
   To be a man of virtue and of conscience.
MARY: I knew he was—And yet the hour of danger
   Alone can test the virtue of a man.
   It may be that the rack so terrified him
   That he confessed to things he did not know!
   False witness, he imagined, might save him,
   Yet not harm me, a Queen, so very much.

BURLEIGH: He gave his evidence with a free oath.   900
MARY: He did not give it in my presence! —What, Sir?
  Here are two witnesses, both still alive!
  Let them be brought before me, and have them
  Repeat their testimony to my face!
  Why should a favor be refused to me,
  A right, in fact, not kept from murderers?
  I know from Talbot's lips, my former jailer,
  That under date within this very reign
  An Act of Parliament was passed requiring
  Accused to be confronted with accuser.   910
  What? Or did I not hear aright? —Sir Paulet!
  I always have found you an honest man.
  Now prove that. Tell me on your conscience: Is
  That not so? Is there no such law in England?
PAULET: My Lady, it is so. That is our law.
  I must speak what is true.
MARY: Well then, my Lord!
  If I must be so strictly treated by
  Your English law when that law does me harm,
  Why circumvent that very law when it
  Can operate to help me? —Answer me!   920
  Then why was Babington not brought before
  My eyes, as the law stipulates? Why not
  My secretaries, who are still alive?
BURLEIGH: Do not get angry, Lady. Your collusion
  With Babington was not the only thing—
MARY: It is the only thing that lays me open
  To the law's sword, and of which I must clear me.
  My Lord! Stick to the point. Do not evade.
BURLEIGH: It has been proved that you had dealings with
  Mendoza, the ambassador of Spain—   930
MARY (agitatedly):
  Stick to the point, my Lord!
BURLEIGH: —that you laid plots
  To overthrow the state religion here,
  That you had stirred up all the kings of Europe

   To war with England—
MARY: And what if I did?
  I did not do so—Yet supposing that
  I did! My Lord, I am held captive in
  Defiance of all international law.
  I did not come into this country with
  A sword, I came here as a suppliant,
  Asked for asylum, threw myself into   940
  A Queen's arms who is my blood-relative—
  Force apprehended me, put me in chains
  Where I had sought protection.—Tell me now!
  Do I owe anything in conscience to
  This state? Am I in duty bound to England?
  I practice nothing but the sacred right
  Of self-defense in trying to shake off
  These bonds, in turning force by force,
  In stirring up all states to my defense.
  I may quite rightly exercise whatever   950
  Is right and chivalrous in a just war.
  Murder alone, the secret deed of blood,
  My conscience and my pride forbid my doing.
  I would be stained by murder and dishonored.
  I said: dishonored—but in no respect
  Condemned, subjected to a legal sentence.
  For the concern between me here and England
  Is not with justice, but with force alone.
BURLEIGH (pointedly):
  Do not invoke the fearful right of strength,
  My Lady! for it does not favor prisoners.   960
MARY: I am the weak one, she the mighty one—
  So be it! Let her use force, let her kill me,
  Let her slay this victim for her safety.
  But let her then acknowledge that she had
  Recourse to force alone, and not to justice.
  Let her not borrow the law's sword to rid
  Herself of her detested enemy,
  Let her not clothe in holy garb the bloody

Audacity of naked violence.
Deceit like this must not deceive the world!   970
She can assassinate me, but not judge me!
Let her give up combining fruits of crime
With the external holy look of virtue,
And let her seem to be just what she *is!*
(Exit.)

BURLEIGH: So she defies us—will defy us, Paulet,
Right to the scaffold steps!—That haughty heart
Cannot be broken.—Did the sentence take
Her unawares? Or did you see her shed
One single tear? Or even change her color?
She did not play upon our sympathy,   980
She knows the indecision of the Queen
Of England, and our fear makes her courageous.
PAULET: My Lord High Treasurer! This vain defiance will
Soon vanish if the pretext is removed.
There were some improprieties, if I
May be allowed to say so, in this trial.
They should have brought that Babington and Tichburn
To her in person, and her secretaries
Should likewise have confronted her.
BURLEIGH (*quickly*):   No, no,
Knight Paulet! That was much too great a risk.   990
Her power over people's feelings is
Too great, as is her woman's force of tears.
Her secretary Kurl, if he should face her,
And if it came to speaking that one word
On which her life depends, he would back down
Faint-hearted and retract his testimony—
PAULET: But this way England's enemies will fill
The world with their malicious rumors, and
The solemn ceremony of the trial
Will look like nothing but a bold-faced outrage.   1000
BURLEIGH: That is precisely what disturbs our Queen—
Oh, if this instigator of misfortune
Had only died before she ever set

Her foot on English soil!

PAULET: To that I say Amen!

BURLEIGH: If she had died of illness while in prison!

PAULET: That would have saved this country lots of trouble.

BURLEIGH: Yet if some accident of Nature had
    Despatched her—we would still be called assassins.

PAULET: Quite true. For people cannot be prevented
    From thinking what they will.

BURLEIGH: At any rate it could   1010
    Not have been proved, and would have caused less talk that

PAULET: Well, let it cause talk if it will! It is   [way—
    Not loud but righteous blame that can do harm.

BURLEIGH: O! justice in its holiness will not
    Escape blame either, for opinion holds
    With the unfortunate, and envy always
    Pursues the fortunate amid their triumph.
    The sword of judgment, which adorns a man,
    Is odious in a woman's hand. The world
    Does not believe in justice from a woman   1020
    When a woman is the victim. All
    For naught we judges answered by our conscience!
    She has a Queen's prerogative of mercy
    And she must use it! If she lets the law
    Take its strict course, it is intolerable!

PAULET: And so—?

BURLEIGH: So she must go on living? No!
    She must not go on living! Never! That
    Is just the thing that makes our Queen so anxious—
    The thing that drives sleep from her couch—I read
    The struggle of her spirit in her eyes,   1030
    But her lips do not dare pronounce her wishes.
    Her silent glances meaningfully ask:
    Is there not one of all my servants who
    Will save me from the loathesome choice of living in
    Eternal fear upon my throne, or else
    Condemning cruelly this Queeen, my own
    Blood-relative, to death?

PAULET: Necessity will have it so, it can't be helped.

BURLEIGH: The Queen feels that it might indeed be helped
   If only she had more attentive servants.   1040

PAULET: Attentive?

BURLEIGH: Who could take an unexpressed
   Command from her.

PAULET: An unexpressed command?

BURLEIGH: Who, if a poisonous snake were given them
   To keep, would not preserve that enemy
   As if it were a sacred precious jewel.

PAULET *(pointedly)*:
   A good name is a precious jewel, and
   The unsmirched reputation of the Queen,
   Sir, cannot be too carefully protected.

BURLEIGH: When they removed the Lady from the keeping
   Of Shrewsbury and put her in the care   1050
   Of Paulet, the idea was—

PAULET: I hope,
   Sir, the idea was to trust the task
   That was most difficult to hands most clean.
   By God! I never would have taken over
   This bailiff's office if I had not thought
   That it required the best man in all England.
   Do not give me the notion that I owe it
   To anything but my good reputation.

BURLEIGH: It is reported she is in decline,
   Then she gets worse, and finally just dies.   1060
   That way she dies in people's memories—
   While you have your name clear.

PAULET: But not my conscience.

BURLEIGH: If you decline to lend your own hand to it,
   You surely won't object to someone else's—

PAULET *(interrupting him)*:
   No murderer shall step across her threshold
   As long as gods of my roof shelter her.
   Her life is sacred to me; the Queen of England's
   Head is not any more so in my sight.

You are the judges! Judge her! Break the staff!
And when the time comes, have the carpenter   1070
Come up here with his ax and saw and build
The scaffold.—For the sheriff and the headsman
You will find that my castle gates are open.
But now she is entrusted to my keeping,
And you may be assured I will protect her
From doing harm or letting harm affect her.   [1076]

(Exeunt.)

ACT II

The palace at Westminster. [*Morning of the following day.*]
Enter the Earl of Kent and Sir William Davison, meeting.

DAVISON: My Lord of Kent? Back from the tournament
  Already? Is the festival all over?

KENT: Why, didn't you attend the knightly games?

DAVISON: My duties kept me.

KENT: You have missed the finest   1080
  Spectacle that taste has yet devised
  Or noble grace has executed.—For,
  You see, they represented the chaste Fortress
  Of Beauty under siege there by Desire;
  And the Lords Marshal and Chief Justice and
  Chief Steward and ten more knights of the Queen
  Were there to hold the Fortress's defense
  While cavaliers of France rode to attack.
  A herald came up first and bade the castle
  Surrender in a madrigal he sang,   1090
  And from the walls the Chancellor replied.
  Then the artillery came into play
  And precious perfumes and bouquets of flowers
  Were fired from pretty mimic cannon. But
  To no avail; Those making the attack
  Were beaten off; Desire had to retreat.

DAVISON: A sign of evil omen, my Lord Earl,
  Regarding the French match-making.

KENT: Oh well, all that was in fun.—In earnest
  I think, the Fortress will surrender in   1100
  The end.

DAVISON: You think so? I cannot believe it.

KENT: The articles that were most difficult
    Are settled now and France accedes to them.
    Monsieur will be content to have his own
    Religious services in private chapel
    And honor and protect the state religion
    In public.—O you should have heard the jubilation
    Of people when that information was made known.
    That was this country's constant fear, that she
    Might die and leave no issue of her body,   1110
    And England would again wear Papal fetters
    If Mary Stuart should succeed her on
    The throne.
DAVISON: *That* fear can be dismissed.—*She* goes
    To marriage, while the Stuart goes to death.
KENT: The Queen is coming!
       (Enter Elizabeth on the arm of Leicester, Count
     Aubespine, Bellièvre, the Earl of Shrewsbury, Lord
     Burleigh, together with other French and English
     gentlemen, come in.)
ELIZABETH *(to Aubespine)*:
    Count, I regret these noble gentlemen,
    Whom gallant zeal has brought here from across
    The sea, should have to miss the splendor of
    The Court of Saint Germain while at my court.
    I am unable to devise such gorgeous   1120
    Feasts of the gods as does the royal mother
    Of France.—An orderly and happy people
    Who throng with benedictions round about my
    Sedan-chair when I show myself in public,—
    Such is the spectacle that I can show
    With my own pride to foreign eyes. The glory
    Of noble maidens who in Catherine's Garden
    Of Beauty show their loveliness would only
    Eclipse me and my own unlustrous merit.
AUBESPINE: Westminster Court shows but one lady to   1130
    Astonished foreigners,—but everything
    About the charming sex that gives delight

Is gathered and assembled in that one.
BELLIÈVRE: Will Sublime Majesty of England grant
    Permission for us to take leave of her
    And go to bring Monsieur, our royal master,
    The joyous tidings for which he so yearns?
    The hot impatience of his heart would not
    Let him remain in Paris; he is waiting
    In Amiens for messengers of his   1140
    Good fortune, and his post extends right to
    Calais to carry the consent which will
    Be spoken by your royal lips, with all
    The speed of wings to his enchanted ear.
ELIZABETH: Count Bellièvre, do not press me further.
    The present moment, I repeat, is not
    The proper time to light the torch of Hymen.
    Black hang the skies above this country, and
    The mourner's veil of crape would suit me better
    Than pomp and finery of bridal raiment.   1150
    A grievous blow is threatened close at hand,
    Aimed at my heart and at my family.
BELLIÈVRE: Give us no more, Queen, than your promise, and
    Fulfillment will ensue in happier days.
ELIZABETH: Monarchs are mere slaves of their condition,
    They may not follow as their own hearts bid.
    My wish has always been to die unwed,
    And my choice would have been to have my fame
    Consist of this: that on my gravestone people
    Should some day read: "Here lies the Virgin Queen."   1160
    And yet my subjects will not have it so.
    Already they are thinking of the time
    When I shall be no more.—It will not do
    For them to have prosperity right now;
    I must be sacrificed for future welfare
    As well, I must give up my virgin freedom,
    My highest treasure, for my people also,
    And have a lord and master forced upon me.
    They show me in this way that I am only

A woman in their eyes, while I thought I   1170
Had ruled them like a man and like a king.
I realize that God is not well served
When Nature's order is abandoned, and
Those who ruled here before me merit praise
For having closed the monasteries and
Returned a thousand victims of a wrongly
Conceived devotion to the obligations
Of Nature. But a Queen who does not spend
Her days in idle, useless contemplation,
Who prosecutes the hardest of all tasks   1180
Undaunted and unwearying, *she* ought
To be excepted from that goal of Nature
Which has the one half of the human race
Subordinated to the other. . . .

AUBESPINE: You have exalted every virtue, Queen,
Upon your throne, and nothing is left wanting
Except to shine as paragon before
The sex whose glory you embody, in
Its unique merits. Actually, there is
No man alive on earth who would be worthy   1190
Of having you renounce your freedom for him.
But if nobility, and birth, heroic
Virtue, and male comeliness have ever
Made any mortal worthy of that honor,—

ELIZABETH: There is no doubt, my Lord Ambassador,
But that a bond of marriage with a royal
Son of France would do me honor. Yes,
I frankly say, if it *must* be—if there
Is no way but yield to my people's pressure—
And they will prove, I fear, more strong than I—   1200
I do not know of any Prince in Europe
To whom I would with less reluctance yield
My freedom, my most treasured jewel. Let
That statement be sufficient for you now.

BELLIÈVRE: It is a *glorious* hope. But it is only
A *hope*. My master wishes something *more*—

ELIZABETH: What does he wish?

> *(She takes a ring from her finger and looks at it pensively.)*

The Queen has no advantage
Over the wives of common citizens!
An equal token marks an equal duty,
An equal servitude.—From rings come weddings,   1210
Rings also finally make up a chain.
—Accept this gift and take it to His Highness.
It is not *yet* a chain, does not yet bind me;
And yet it can become a bond to bind me.

BELLIÈVRE *(kneels and receives the ring)*:
In his name I accept this gift, great Queen,
And kneel as I receive it, pressing also
The kiss of homage on the hand of my new Princess.

ELIZABETH *(to the Earl of Leicester, at whom she has been looking fixedly during the last speech)*:
My Lord, permit me!

> *(She takes the blue sash from him him and puts it on Bellièvre.)*

With this decoration
Invest His Highness as I here invest
You and accept you in the duties of my Order.   1220
Honi soit qui mal y pense!—Between
Two nations let suspicion disappear,
And let a bond of confidence henceforward
Entwine the crowns of England and of France.

AUBESPINE: Exalted Queen, this is a day of joy!
May it be such for all, and further, may
No sufferer in all this island grieve!
Now mercy gleams upon your countenance.
O! if a glimmer of its cheerful light
Might fall upon a Princess in misfortune   1230
Whose destiny concerns both France and England
Alike—

ELIZABETH: No further, Count! Let us not mingle
Two wholly incompatible affairs.

If France sincerely wishes my alliance,
Then it must also share my cares with me
And not be friendly to my enemy—
AUBESPINE: In your own eyes France would be acting basely
  If she forgot in this alliance that
  Unhappy Queen, her co-religionist,
  The widow of her King.—Humanity   1240
  And honor both require—
ELIZABETH: In that sense I
  Esteem her intercession at its due.
  France will fulfill her duty as a friend;
  Grant me, however, to act as a Queen.
     *(She bows to the French gentlemen, who withdraw
     respectfully with the other Lords.*
     The Queen sits down.)
BURLEIGH: Illustrious Queen! Today you crown the ardent
  Wishes of your people. Not till now
  Have we enjoyed the prosperous days which you
  Confer upon us, for we look no more
  With anxious dread into the stormy future.
  One fear alone besets this country still,   1250
  There is one victim whom all voices cry for.
  Grant us this one thing more, and this day will
  Have founded England's welfare for all time.
ELIZABETH: What more is it my people ask for? Speak,
  My Lord.
BURLEIGH: They want the Stuart's head.—If you
  Wish to assure your people's precious freedom
  And the so dearly purchased light of truth,
  Then *she* must be no more.—If we are not
  To tremble for your precious life forever,
  This enemy must perish! —You well know   1260
  That not all Englishmen hold like opinions.
  The Romish idol-cult still numbers many
  A secret worshipper within this island.
  And all of them still cherish hostile thoughts;
  Their hearts are for this Stuart, and they are

In league with the two brothers of Lorraine,
Irreconcilable foes of your name.
A grim war of annihilation has
Been vowed against you by that rabid party
To be waged with false instruments of hell.   1270
At Rheims, the Cardinal-bishop's see, they have
Their arsenal where they forge thunderbolts.
There regicide is taught—and busily
The missions destined for this island are
Sent out from there, those resolute fanatics
Disguised in every sort of garb.—From there
The third assassin has already come,
And inexhaustibly, forever new
In that abyss breed hidden enemies.
  —In Castle Fotheringhay there sits the Atè   1280
Of that eternal warfare, who is using
The torch of love to set this realm on fire.
For her sake, who cajoles them all to hope,
Young men devote themselves to certain death—
Their watchword is: To liberate her, and
Their purpose is to place her on your throne.
Your sacred right is not acknowledged by
The family of Lorraine; in their eyes you
Are merely a usurper, crowned by chance!
They were the ones who led that foolish woman   1290
To sign herself "the Queen of England". There
Can be no peace with her or with her clan!
You must endure the blow or deal it. Her
Life is your death, and her death is your life!
ELIZABETH: My Lord: It is a dreary post you hold.
I know the upright impulse of your zeal,
I know that sterling wisdom speaks in you.
Yet when that wisdom bids that blood be shed,
I hate it from the bottom of my soul.
Invent a milder counsel.—Noble Lord   1300
Of Shrewsbury! Now tell us *your* opinion.
TALBOT: You paid a fitting tribute to the zeal

That stirs in Burleigh's loyal heart.—I too,
Although my mouth has eloquence less ready,
Have in my bosom a heart no less loyal.
May you live on, O Queen, a long time yet
To be your people's joy and to extend
The benison of peace upon this kingdom.
Such prosperous days this island never has
Beheld since it was ruled by its own rulers.   1310
Let it not purchase happiness at fame's
Expense! Let Talbot's eyes at least have closed
Before a thing like that occurs!

ELIZABETH: Now God forbid that we should stain our fame!

TALBOT: Well, in that case you will devise some other means
To save this kingdom,—for the execution
Of Mary Stuart is an unjust means.
You cannot judge *her* and pass sentence on her
Who is not subject to you.

ELIZABETH: Then my Council
Of State and Parliament are wrong, and all   1320
This country's courts are equally in error,
When they agree that I do have that right—

TALBOT: Majorities are no proof of the right,
England is not the world, your Parliament
Is not a union of the human races.
This England of today is not that of
The future, nor the past one either.—Just
As inclination shifts, so also rises
And falls the changeful wave of world opinion.
Do not say that you were compelled to follow   1330
Necessity and pressure of your people.
Whenever you so wish, at any moment
You can discover that your will is free.
Just try it! Say that you revolt at bloodshed
And that you *want* your sister's life preserved.
To those who would advise you otherwise
Reveal the truth of your most queenly wrath
And you will quickly see Necessity

Displaced and Right converted into Wrong.
And you yourself must judge, and you alone.   1340
You cannot lean upon that shaky reed.
Be guided by your natural clemency.
God did not give severity to woman's
Gentle heart.—The founders of this kingdom,
Who also gave the reins of government
To women, meant that rulers of this country
Were not to make severity a virtue.

ELIZABETH: An ardent advocate is my Lord Talbot
For mine and for this country's foe. But I
Prefer the counsellors who love my welfare.   1350

TALBOT: No advocate has been allowed her; no one
Dares to expose himself to your great ire
By pleading her defense.—Allow me then,
An old man near his grave, who cannot be
Seduced by any hopes this world can offer,
To speak up in behalf of this doomed woman.
O let it not be said that selfishness
And passion had their voices in your Council
Of State while only mercy held its tongue.
Against her everyone united stands,   1360
You never have beheld her countenance,
And nothing in your heart speaks for this stranger.
—Her misdeeds I do not excuse. They say
She had her husband murdered. It is certain
She took the murderer as second husband.
A heinous crime! But it occurred back in
A sinister and evil-fortuned time,
Amid the anxious stress of civil war,
When she was weak and saw herself surrounded
By urgently demanding vassals, and   1370
She threw herself into the strongest, bravest
Man's arms—compelled by what devices, who
Can tell? For woman is a fragile creature.

ELIZABETH: Woman is not weak. There are strong souls
Among the sex.—I will not tolerate

Talk of that sex's weakness in my presence.
TALBOT: Misfortune was a rigorous school to you.
    Life did not turn its joyous side to *you*.
    You did not see a throne far up ahead,
    You only saw the grave before your feet.   1380
    In Woodstock and the Tower you were trained
    For solemn duty by affliction at
    This country's gracious Father's own behest.
    You were not sought by flatterers. While young,
    You went untroubled by the world's vain pomp
    And learned by thought and self-communion how to
    Esteem the true possessions of this life.
    — No god saved that poor creature. As a tender child
    She was removed to France and to the court
    Of thoughtless pleasure and frivolity.   1390
    There in the constant giddy festival
    She never heard the solemn voice of Truth.
    With glittering vice she was bedazzled there
    And swept away by the stream of destruction.
    The futile gift of beauty was her portion,
    Her loveliness eclipsed all other women,
    And in her body no less than her birth—
ELIZABETH: Come to your senses, my Lord Earl of Shrewsbury!
    Recall: we sit here in a solemn council.
    Those must indeed be charms beyond compare   1400
    To stir such ardor in an aged man.
    — My Lord of Lester! You alone are silent?
    What makes him eloquent has tied your tongue?
LEICESTER: Queen, I am silent from astonishment
    To think that they should fill your ear with terrors
    To think these fairy tales, which in the streets
    Of London scare the credulous, should rise
    Up to the cheerful air of your State Council
    To occupy the thoughts of serious men.
    Amazement seizes me, I must confess,   1410
    To think this stateless Queen of Scotland, she
    Who was incapable of holding on

To that small throne she had, the mockery
Of her own vassals, outcast from her country,
Should suddenly in prison terrify you!
—By God Almighty! What should make you fear her?
Because she claims this kingdom? Or because
The Guises won't acknowledge you as Queen?
How can this opposition from the Guises
Invalidate what birth has given you   1420
And Parliament confirmed by resolution?
In Henry's last will was *she* not passed over
In silence? And will England, which rejoices
In the new light with so much satisfaction,
Throw itself into the Papist's arms?
Will they go running off from you, the monarch
Whom they adore, to Darnley's murderess?
What do these clamorous people want, that they
Should so torment you while alive about
An heir; who cannot have you married fast   1430
Enough, to save the State and Church from danger?
Are you not in the flower of your youth
While each day she is withering to her grave?
By God! You will, I hope, walk on her grave
For many years to come, without your ever
Needing to plunge her into it yourself.—
BURLEIGH: Lord Lester did not always think this way.
LEICESTER: It is quite true my vote was given in
    Support of her death sentence at the *trial*.
    —In this State Council I speak otherwise.   1440
    Expediency, not right, is here in question.
    Is this the time to fear a threat from her,
    When France abandons her, her sole protector,
    When you are going to bestow your hand
    Upon the royal Prince, and hope arises
    For a new line of rulers in this country?
    Why kill her then? She is already dead!
    To be despised is death in fact. God save us
    From letting pity bring her back to life!

So here is my advice: we let the sentence   1450
That dooms her to the headsman, stand in full
Force; let her live—but let her live beneath
The headsman's ax. As soon as any hand
Takes up a weapon for her—let it fall.

ELIZABETH (rising):

My Lords, I have heard your opinions now,
And thank you cordially for all your zeal.
With God's assistance, who sheds light and guidance
On rulers, I shall test your reasons and
Select the one which seems to me the best.

            (Enter Knight Paulet and Mortimer.)

Here comes Sir Amias Paulet. Noble Sir,   1460
What news have you?

PAULET: Illustrious Majesty!

My nephew, not long since returned from journeys
Abroad, desires to cast himself before
Your feet and swear to you his youthful oath.
May you receive it graciously and let
Him flourish in the sunlight of your favor.

MORTIMER (genuflecting on one knee):

Long live my royal Lady, and may fame
And happiness sit crowned upon her brow!

ELIZABETH: Arise. And welcome back to England, Sir.

You have made the grand tour, have been to France,   1470
And Rome, and spent some time at Rheims.
Now tell me what our foes are up to now.

MORTIMER: May some god send confusion on them and

Turn back the arrows on their marksmen's hearts
Whom they have dared to send against my Queen!

ELIZABETH: Did you see Morgan and the treason-hatching

Bishop of Ross?

MORTIMER: I made acquaintance with

All of the Scottish exiles who at Rheims
Are forging plots against this island and
I wormed my way into their confidence   1480
To see what I could learn about their schemes.

PAULET: And they entrusted him with secret letters
   In cipher for the Queen of Scotland, which
   He loyally delivered here to *us*.
ELIZABETH: Well, tell me now, what are their latest plans?
MORTIMER: They were all struck as by a thunderbolt
   That France had cast her off and was allying
   Herself with England. Now their hopes are turning
   Toward Spain.
ELIZABETH: So Walsingham has written me.
MORTIMER: Then, too, a bull which recently Pope Sixtus   1490
   Has hurled against you from the Vatican
   Had just arrived at Rheims as I was leaving.
   By the next boat it will come to this island.
LEICESTER: England no longer trembles at such weapons.
BURLEIGH: They can be frightful in fanatics' hands.
ELIZABETH (*looking searchingly at Mortimer*):
   It has been claimed that while at Rheims you went
   Into the schools and disavowed your faith?
MORTIMER: I did give that appearance, I will not
   Deny,—so far went my desire to serve you!
ELIZABETH (*to Paulet, who hands her some papers*):
   What are you giving me?
PAULET: It is a letter   1500
   Directed to you by the Queen of Scotland.
BURLEIGH (*reaching for it quickly*):
   Give me that letter.
PAULET (*gives the paper to the Queen*):
                   Pardon me, my Lord
   High Treasurer! Into my Queen's own hands
   She ordered that this letter be delivered.
   She always says I am her enemy.
   I only hate her crimes. Whatever is
   In keeping with my duty, I will gladly
   Perform for her.
      (*The Queen has taken the letter. While she is
      reading it, Mortimer and Leicester secretly exchange
      a few words.*)

BURLEIGH (*to Paulet*): What can the letter say?
Unfounded protestations which should be
Kept from afflicting the Queen's tender heart.   1510
PAULET: She made no secret of its contents. She
Requests the privilege of speaking with
The Queen.
BURLEIGH (*quickly*): O that must never be allowed!
TALBOT: Why not? What she entreats is not unjust.
BURLEIGH: For her, the favor of the royal presence
Is forfeit, the assassination-plotter
Who thirsted for the Queen's own blood. And no
Man whose intentions toward the Queen are loyal
Could offer such false, treasonable advice.
TALBOT: But if the Monarch wants to make her happy,   1520
Would you hinder mercy's gentle impulse?
BURLEIGH: She has been sentenced! Her head lies beneath
The ax. It is not seemly Majesty
Should see the head that has been doomed to death.
The sentence can no longer be fulfilled
Once she has thus approached the Queen, because
The royal presence is a sign of mercy—
ELIZABETH (*drying her tears after reading the letter*):
O what is man! And what is earthly fortune!
How low this Queen has fallen now, who once
Began with such proud hopes, who once was called   1530
To the most ancient throne in Christendom,
And who at one time had it in her mind
To set three royal crowns upon her head!
How different is her language now from then,
When she assumed the coat-of-arms of England,
And by the flatterers of her court allowed herself
To be named Queen of both Britannic isles!
—Forgive me, Lords, it cuts me to the heart,
A sadness seizes me, and my soul bleeds
To think that earthly things do not stand with   1540
A greater firmness, that the monstrous fate
Of man should pass so close to my own head.

TALBOT: O Queen! God has reached down to touch your heart;
  Obey that heavenly emotion! She
  Has gravely expiated her grave guilt
  And it is time her hard ordeal ended!
  Extend your hand to her, the deeply fallen!
  Go like an angel's form of shining light
  Down to the tomb-like darkness of her prison—
BURLEIGH: Great Queen, be steadfast. Do not let yourself   1550
  Be misled by a laudable and human
  Emotion. Do not rob yourself of freedom
  Of action to perform the necessary.
  You *cannot* pardon her, you *cannot* save her,
  So do not heap yourself with hateful censure
  For having feasted your eyes on your victim
  In a scene of cruelly mocking triumph.
LEICESTER: Let us remain within our bounds, my Lords.
  The Queen is wise, and she does not require
  Advice from us to choose the worthiest thing.   1560
  An interview between the Queens has nothing
  In common with the course of legal justice.
  The law of England, not the Monarch's will,
  Has sentenced Mary. It is worthy of
  The great soul of Elizabeth that *she*
  Should follow where the lovely impulse of
  Her heart leads her, while law takes its strict course.
ELIZABETH: Leave me, my Lords. We shall find seemly ways
  Whereby both things,—what is required by mercy
  And what necessity enjoins upon us,—   1570
  Can be combined. Now—go.
          (*The Lords withdraw. At the door she calls
          Mortimer back.*)
                              Sir Mortimer!
  A word!
          (*after she has scrutinized him searchingly for
          several minutes*)
              You showed courageous daring and
  A self-control rare for one of your years.

One who has practiced young the hard art of
Deception is of age before his time
And has cut short the years of his probation.
—I prophesy that Destiny will call you
To a high course, and, happily for you,
I can myself fulfill my oracle.

MORTIMER: Illustrious Sovereign, all I am and can   1580
 Perform is dedicated to your service.

ELIZABETH: You came to know the enemies of England.
 Their hatred of me is implacable,
 Their schemes of murder inexhaustible.
 Almighty God has saved me up to now.
 And yet the crown upon my head will always
 Be shaky while *she* lives who lends the pretext
 And feeds the hopes of her fanatic zealots.

MORTIMER: As soon as you so bid, she lives no more.

ELIZABETH: Ah, Sir! I thought I saw myself close to   1590
 That goal, and am no further than when I
 Began. I meant to have the law proceed
 And keep my own hand clean of blood. The sentence
 Has been pronounced. And yet, what have I gained?
 It must be *executed*, Mortimer!
 And I must order such an execution.
 The odium of the deed must fall on me.
 I must acknowledge it and cannot save
 Appearances. That is the worst of it.

MORTIMER: What do you care about appearances   1600
 In a just cause?

ELIZABETH: You do not know the world, Sir.
 What one *appears* to be, all people judge;
 But none judge what one *is*. No one will be
 Convinced that I am in the right, hence my
 Concern lest my part in her death be always
 In doubt. With deeds like this of double form
 There can be no defense except in darkness.
 The worst step is the one that one confesses;
 What one does not give up, was never lost.

MORTIMER *(sounding her out):*
The best thing, then, would be—

ELIZABETH *(quickly):*   That *would* be best!   1610
—O my good angel speaks in you. Go on
And do it, worthy Sir! You are in earnest,
You get right to essentials, and you are
A man entirely different from your uncle—

MORTIMER *(struck):*
Have you disclosed your wishes to the Knight?

ELIZABETH: I did, and I regret it.

MORTIMER: You must pardon
The aged man. The years have made him leery.
So hazardous an undertaking needs
The daring verve of youth—

ELIZABETH *(quickly):*   Then I may count
On you to—

MORTIMER: I will lend my hand to you,   1620
Your name you must save as you can—

ELIZABETH: Sir! If
You could some morning wake me with the news:
Your deadly adversary, Mary Stuart,
Last night took leave of life!, then—

MORTIMER: Count on me.

ELIZABETH: When will my head lie down to sleep in peace?

MORTIMER: The next new moon shall lay your fears to rest.

ELIZABETH: Farewell, Sir! Do not be aggrieved because
My gratitude is forced to borrow Night's
Dark veil.—Remember: Silence is the god
Of happy men.—It is the closest bond—   1630
And tenderest—that secrecy creates!
(Exit.)

MORTIMER *(alone):*
Go, hypocritical, false Queen! As you
Deceive the world, so I will you. It is
Quite proper to betray you,—a good deed!
Do I look like a murderer? Did you
Read villainous adeptness on my brow?

Trust *my* arm only, and hold *your* arm back.
Assume the falsely pious look of mercy
Before the world, while secretly you go
On hoping I will help you by this murder, 1640
We shall gain breathing time that way for rescue!
    So you would elevate me—From afar
You hinted at some precious reward—perhaps
Your very self, your favor as a woman!
Who are you, wretch, and what can you give me?
Ambition lures me not to Glory's height!
With her alone is life's delight—
In choirs of joy, gods float eternally
Around her, gods of grace and youthful pleasure,
And at her bosom heavens yield their treasure, 1650
While you hold only lifeless gifts in fee!
The one supreme thing life confers, when plighted
Heart gives to heart, delighting and delighted,
Its very self in sweet forgetfulness,
That womanly crown you never did possess,
No loving man have you with love requited!
    I must wait for Lord Lester and deliver
Her letter to him here. A hateful errand!
I have no stomach for that courtier.
Her rescue I alone can realize,
Be mine the peril, mine the fame and prize! 1660
            (*As he is on the point of leaving
            he encounters Paulet.*)
PAULET: What was the Queen discussing with you?
MORTIMER: Nothing,
    Sir. Nothing—of importance.
PAULET (*fixing an earnest gaze upon him*):
                            Mortimer!
    It is a smooth and slippery path on which
    You have set foot. There is a lure in monarchs'
    Favor; youth craves honors.—Do not let
    Ambition carry you astray!
MORTIMER: Was it not you who brought me to the court?

PAULET: I wish I had not done so now. At court
  The honor of *our* house was not achieved.   1670
  Stand fast, my nephew. Do not buy too dear!
  Do nothing to offend your conscience!
MORTIMER: What are you thinking of? Such apprehensions!
PAULET: However great the Queen may promise now
  To make you—do not trust her flattery.
  She will deny you after you obey her,
  And then, to wash her own name clean, she will
  Avenge the bloody deed that she commanded.
MORTIMER: Did you say "bloody deed"—
PAULET: Enough pretending!
  I know what the Queen expects of you.   1680
  She hopes your youth in its desire for fame
  Will be more pliant than my stiff old age.
  Did you consent to do it? Did you?
MORTIMER: Uncle!
PAULET: If you have done so, I shall curse you,—and
  May God renounce you—
              (Enter Leicester.)
LEICESTER: Worthy Sir, will you
  Allow me one word with your nephew? Our
  Great Queen is well disposed toward him and she
  Desires the person of the Lady Stuart
  Be unreservedly committed to him.—
  She will rely upon his probity—   1690
PAULET: Rely on—Good!
LEICESTER: What were you saying, Sir?
PAULET: The Queen relies on him, and I, my Lord,
  Rely upon myself and my two eyes.
              (Exit.)
LEICESTER *(astonished):*
  What is the matter with the Knight?
MORTIMER: I couldn't say—This confidence the Queen
  Has placed in me so unexpectedly—
LEICESTER *(looking at him searchingly):*
  Do you deserve to be confided in?

MORTIMER *(likewise)*:
  I ask the same of you, my Lord of Lester.
LEICESTER: You wished to tell me something secretly.
MORTIMER: Assure me first that I may dare to do so.   1700
LEICESTER: And who gives me a guarantee for you?
  —Take no offense at my mistrust! I have
  Seen you display two different faces at
  This court.—And of these, necessarily,
  One must be false. But which one is the real one?
MORTIMER: I have observed the same of you, Lord Lester.
LEICESTER: Then which of us will start the confidences?
MORTIMER: The one who has the lesser stake to risk.
LEICESTER: Well, that is you?
MORTIMER: No, you! *Your* testimony
  As mighty Lord whose word is of great weight,   1710
  Can strike me down, where *mine* is powerless
  In opposition to your rank and favor.
LEICESTER: You are mistaken, Sir. In all else I
  Am mighty, but on this one tender point
  With which I am supposed to trust you now,
  I am the weakest man in all this court;
  One wretched testimony can destroy me.
MORTIMER: If the all-powerful Lord Lester stoops
  And condescends as low as to confess
  A thing like this to me, then I may think   1720
  A little higher of myself and set him
  Example by my generosity.
LEICESTER: Your secret first, and I will follow suit.
MORTIMER *(suddenly producing the letter)*:
  The Queen of Scotland sends you this.
LEICESTER *(startled, reaches for it hastily)*:   Speak softly,
  Sir—What is this I see! Her picture! Ah!
          (He kisses it and gazes at it with rapture.)
MORTIMER *(who has been watching him sharply while he read)*:
  My Lord, I now believe in you.
LEICESTER *(after running quickly through the letter)*:
  You know this letter's contents, Mortimer?

MORTIMER: No, I know nothing.

LEICESTER: Well, she doubtless has
Confided to you—

MORTIMER: She confided nothing
  To me. She said that *you* would solve this riddle.   1730
  To me it is a riddle that the Earl
  Of Lester, favorite of Elizabeth,
  Vowed foe of Mary and one of her judges,
  Should be the man from whom the Queen hopes for
  Deliverance in misfortune.—All the same,
  It must be so, because your eyes express
  Too plainly what your feeling for her is.

LEICESTER: First tell me how it happens that you take
  This ardent interest in her destiny,
  And what won you her confidence.

MORTIMER: My Lord,   1740
  That I can tell you in a few brief words.
  In Rome I disavowed my faith and I
  Am in alliance with the Guises. Letters
  Sent by the Archbishop of Rheims gained me
  Accreditation with the Queen of Scotland.

LEICESTER: I know about your changing your religion;
  That was what roused my confidence in you.
  Give me your hand. Forgive me for my doubt.
  I cannot overdo the use of caution,
  For Walsingham and Burleigh hate me, and   1750
  I know that they are laying snares for me.
  You could well be their creature and their tool
  To lead me to their net—

MORTIMER: What little steps
  So great a Lord must measure in this court!
  Lord Earl, I pity you.

LEICESTER: I throw myself
  With joy upon the bosom of a friend,
  Where I at last can lay aside the long
  Constraint. You are amazed, Sir, that I have
  Had such a sudden change of heart toward Mary.

I never hated her in fact,—the pressure   1760
Of the times made me her adversary.
For long years she had been intended for me,
You know, before she gave her hand to Darnley
While sovereignty still smiled in glory on her.
I coldly thrust that happiness aside,
But now in prison, at the gates of death,
I seek her, and at peril of my life.

MORTIMER: I call that acting generously!

LEICESTER: —The shape
Of things has altered in the meantime, Sir.
It was ambition made me feelingless   1770
Toward youth and beauty. Mary's hand I then
Considered was too slight for me, I hoped
For the possession of the Queen of England.

MORTIMER: It is well known that she preferred you over
All men—

LEICESTER: It seemed so, noble Sir.—Now after ten
Lost years of indefatigable wooing
And odious constraint—O Sir, my heart
Cries out! I must vent my long indignation—
I am called lucky—If they only knew
What chains these are for which they envy me—   1780
Now after sacrificing ten long, bitter
Years to the idol of her vanity,
Submitting with a slave's humility
To every change of her Sultana's whims,
The toy of petty, whimsical caprices,
Cajoled at one time by her tenderness
And then again repulsed by proud reserve,
Tormented by her favor and her harshness
Alike, by Argus-eyes of jealousy
Watched like a prisoner, now taken like   1790
A boy to task, now scolded like a servant,—
O, language does not have a word for this
Especial hell!

MORTIMER: I pity you, Lord Earl.

LEICESTER: To have the prize elude me at the goal!
  Another comes to rob me of the fruits
  Of this dear wooing. To a younger husband
  I lose the rights that I have long possessed!
  I am supposed to go down from the stage
  Where I have shone so long as leading man.
  Not just her hand, her favor too, this new   1800
  Arriver threatens to deprive me of.
  She is a woman, he is lovable.
MORTIMER: He is a son of Catherine. He has learned
  The arts of flattery in a good school.
LEICESTER: My hopes are foundering—and now amid
  This shipwreck of my fortunes I am seeking
  A spar to which I can cling fast—My eye
  Turns back again to its first lovely hope.
  Then Mary's image in the splendor of
  Its charms stood once again before me; beauty   1810
  And youth then reasserted their full claims;
  The heart, not cold ambition, now compared,
  And I felt what a treasure I had lost.
  With terror I saw her plunged into deepest
  Misery, and plunged there by my fault.
  Then hope awoke within me and I wondered
  If I could yet deliver and possess her.
  Thanks to a loyal hand I was successful
  In opening to her my altered heart.
  And now this letter that you bring me here   1820
  Assures me she forgives and will bestow
  Herself as prize upon me if I save her.
MORTIMER: And yet you have done nothing toward her rescue!
  You let it come about that she was sentenced
  And even gave your vote that she should die!
  It took a miracle—the light of Truth
  Had to touch me, the nephew of her jailer,
  And Heaven in the Vatican in Rome
  Had to pick out her unexpected savior,
  Or she would not have found a way to you.   1830

LEICESTER: Ah, this has cost me torments, Sir, enough!
　At just that point she was removed from Talbot's
　Castle up to Fotheringhay and placed
　Beneath the stern surveillance of your uncle.
　All access to her was closed off, I had
　To go on persecuting her before
　The world. But do not think I would have let her
　Go passively to death! No, I hoped then,
　And still hope to prevent the ultimate,
　Till means are found of liberating her.   1840
MORTIMER: That means, Lord Lester, has been found. Your noble
　Secret merits a response. I mean
　To set her free. That is why I am here.
　Arrangements have been made. Your powerful
　Assistance will assure us of success.
LEICESTER: What's that you say? You frighten me. Could you—
MORTIMER: I mean to open up her jail by force.
　I have companions, everything is ready—
LEICESTER: You have accessories and confidants!
　Into what hazard are you dragging me?   1850
　And do they also know about *my* secret?
MORTIMER: O have no fear. The plan was made without you,
　Without you it would have been carried out,
　Had *she* not asked to thank *you* for her rescue.
LEICESTER: Can you assure me then quite certainly
　My name has not been mentioned in this group?
MORTIMER: You may depend on that! So dubious,
　Lord Earl, at hearing news that brings you aid?
　You want to save and to possess the Lady,
　You suddenly find friends when least expected,   1860
　The readiest means drop to you from the sky,—
　And you show more embarrassment than joy?
LEICESTER: It is no good, this use of force. The risk
　Is far too dangerous.
MORTIMER:　　　　　So is delay!
LEICESTER: I tell you, Sir, it is not to be risked.
MORTIMER (*bitterly*):

No, not for you, you want to *possess* her!
We only want to *save* her, hence are not
So scrupulous—
LEICESTER: Young man, you are too rash
In such a dangerous and thorny matter.
MORTIMER: You—too discreet in such a case of honor.   1870
LEICESTER: I see the nets that are laid out around us.
MORTIMER: I feel the strength to rip them all asunder.
LEICESTER: Your courage is foolhardiness and madness.
MORTIMER: This prudence is not bravery, my Lord.
LEICESTER: Perhaps you long to end like Babington?
MORTIMER: You don't, to follow Norfolk's noble action.
LEICESTER: Norfolk did not live to marry her.
MORTIMER: He proved that he deserved to do so, though.
LEICESTER: If we are ruined, she is ruined with us.
MORTIMER: If we are chary, she will not be saved.   1880
LEICESTER: You do not think or listen, you will ruin
Everything with blind impetuousness
That had been started on such a good path.
MORTIMER: On the good path, perhaps, that *you* had cleared?
O, when have you done anything to save her?
—Besides, if I had been enough the scoundrel
To *murder* her, as I was ordered by
The Queen just now, as at this moment she
Expects of me,—declare the steps to me
You would have taken to preserve her.   1890
LEICESTER (*astonished*):
Did the Queen give you such a fatal order?
MORTIMER: She was mistaken in me, as was Mary
In you.
LEICESTER: And you agreed to do it? Did you?
MORTIMER: To see that she did not hire other hands,
I offered mine.
LEICESTER: And you were wise to do so.
This will give us a chance. She will rely
Upon your bloody service, the death sentence
Remains unexecuted, we gain time—

MORTIMER (*impatiently*):
  No, we lose time.
LEICESTER: She will be counting on you,
  She will be that much less afraid of making   1900
  A show of mercy out before the world.
  Perhaps by cunning I can talk her into
  Seeing her opponent's countenance;
  A step like that would surely tie her hands.
  Burleigh is right. The sentence can no longer
  Be executed once she has beheld her.
  —Yes, I will try, I will make every effort—
MORTIMER: And what will that accomplish? If she sees
  Herself deceived in me, if Mary goes
  On living—will not everything be as   1910
  Before? She never will be free. The least
  She can expect is life imprisonment.
  You still will have to end by a bold deed,
  So why not start with such immediately?
  The power is in your hands, you can assemble
  An army if you just agree to arm
  The nobles stationed at your many castles!
  And Mary still has many hidden friends;
  The noble houses of the Howards and
  The Percys, though their chiefs have fallen, still   1920
  Are rich in heroes, they are merely waiting
  For some high Lord to set them an example!
  Stop this dissimulation! Act in public!
  Defend your loved one like a paladin,
  Fight a noble fight for her! Whenever
  You like, you are the master of the Queen
  Of England's person. Lure her to your castles,
  She often followed you there. Show yourself
  A man! Speak as her master! Keep her guarded
  Until she sets the Lady Stuart free!   1930
LEICESTER: I am astonished, horrified—Where has
  Your madness brought you?—Do you know this land?
  Or how things stand here at this court, how straitly

This distaff-rule holds minds in bondage here?
Go seek for that heroic spirit which
Once stirred throughout this country.—Everything
Is now subdued beneath a woman's key,
The springs and coils of courage have gone slack.
Take my advice. Risk nothing indiscreet.
—Go! I hear someone coming.

MORTIMER: Mary hopes!   1940
  Shall I go back to her with empty comfort?

LEICESTER: Take her my vows of everlasting love!

MORTIMER: Take them yourself! I volunteered to be
  Her means of rescue, not your love-note bearer!
                          (Exit.)
                    (Enter Elizabeth.)

ELIZABETH: Who left you here just now? I heard some talking.

LEICESTER *(turning around swiftly, startled at seeing her)*:
  It was Lord Mortimer.

ELIZABETH: What is the matter?
  You look so startled.

LEICESTER *(getting control of himself)*:
                        By the sight of you!
  I never saw you look so fascinating.
  I stand here dazzled by your beauty.—Ah!

ELIZABETH: Why do you sigh?

LEICESTER: Do I not have good reason   1950
  To sigh? When I consider all your charm,
  The nameless sorrow is renewed within me
  Of my impending loss.

ELIZABETH: What are you losing?

LEICESTER: I stand to lose your heart, your lovely self.
  You presently will come to happiness
  Within an ardent husband's youthful arms,
  And he will own your undivided heart.
  He is of royal blood, as *I* am not.
  But I defy the entire world to find
  A man alive upon this earthly globe   1960
  Who feels more adoration for you than

Do I. The Duc d'Anjou has never seen you,
He must love only your renown and splendor,
While I love *you*. Had you been born the poorest
Shepherdess and I the greatest Prince
In all the world, I would stoop to your station
And lay my diadem before your feet.

ELIZABETH: Don't scold me, Dudley, pity me! — I could
  Not ask my heart. It would have chosen elsewhere.
  And how I envy other women who   1970
  Can elevate the one they love. Ah, *I*
  Am not so fortunate that I can place
  The crown upon the man who is the dearest
  Of all to me! — The Stuart was permitted
  To give her hand as inclination willed.
  She took all kinds of liberties; she drank
  The brimming cup of pleasure to the lees.

LEICESTER: And now she drinks the bitter cup of sorrow.

ELIZABETH: She paid no heed to anyone's opinion.
  She found life easy, never once did she   1980
  Assume the yoke beneath which *I* have bent.
  Yet I too might have made my claims to taste
  The joy of life and pleasures of the earth,
  But I chose the stern duties of a monarch.
  And yet she won the favor of all men
  Because she only strove to be a woman,
  And young and old are always courting her.
  Men are like that. Voluptuaries all!
  Frivolity they will pursue, and pleasure,
  And set no store by what they must revere.   1990
  That Talbot, didn't he talk like a youngster
  When he got on the topic of her charm!

LEICESTER: Forgive him. He was once her jailer. She,
  The sly one, fooled him with her flattery.

ELIZABETH: And is it true she is so beautiful?
  I've had to hear so much about that face
  I'd really like to know what to believe.
  Descriptions falsify and paintings flatter,

I would put faith in no eyes but my own.
—Why do you look at me so strangely?

LEICESTER: I   2000
Was thinking of you side by side with Mary.
—I won't deny that I would like the pleasure,
Provided it could be arranged in secret,
Of seeing you confronted with the Stuart!
Then you might taste your total victory!
I would not grudge her the humiliation
Of seeing for herself—for jealousy
Does have sharp eyes—and proving to herself
How utterly in nobleness of form
She is surpassed by you, to whom she must   2010
Give way in every other worthy virtue.

ELIZABETH: In years, however, she is younger.

LEICESTER: Younger!
She doesn't look it. Suffering, of course!
She may well have grown old before her time.
And what would make her sorrow bitterer
Would be to see you as a bride-to-be!
She has her lovely hopes for life behind her.
She would see you approaching happiness,
Betrothed, what's more, to France's royal Prince,
While she has always been so proud about   2020
And was forever flaunting her French marriage,
And even now touts France's mighty aid.

ELIZABETH (remarking carelessly):
They keep tormenting me to see her.

LEICESTER (eagerly):   She
Demands it as a favor; grant it as
A punishment! Though you can send her to
The scaffold, that will grieve her less than seeing
Herself obliterated by your charms.
By that means you will kill her, as she once
Wished to kill you.—Once she has glimpsed your beauty,
By modesty close guarded, set in glory   2030
By reputation for a stainless virtue

Such as *she* cast away for wanton loves,
Exalted by the splendor of the crown
And now adorned with bridal winsomeness,—
Destruction's hour will have struck for her.
Yes,—when I cast my eyes upon you now—
You never have been better armed for triumph
In beauty than right now.—When you stepped into
The room just now, you shed a radiance
Upon me like an apparition of   2040
Celestial light.—If you stepped up to her
Right now,—you will not find a better hour—

ELIZABETH: Not now—No—Not now, Lester—I must think
It over first—discuss with Burleigh—

LEICESTER *(eagerly interrupting):*   Burleigh!
He only thinks of your political
Advantage! womanhood has its rights too.
That tender point befits your own tribunal
And not the statesman's.—Statecraft also wants
To have you see her and gain public favor
By this display of generosity!   2050
Though afterwards you may dispose of this
Detested foe in any way you please.

ELIZABETH: To see my relative in shame and want
Would not be seemly for me. I have heard
That her establishment is not quite royal;
The sight of her in want would be reproachful.

LEICESTER: You will not need to cross her threshold.
Here is my plan. Coincidence has managed
Things perfectly. The great hunt is today,
The route leads right past Castle Fotheringhay,   2060
There in the park the Stuart takes a stroll,
And you come riding over quite by chance;
Let nothing seem to have been planned beforehand;
And if it is repugnant to you, do not
So much as speak to her—

ELIZABETH: If I commit
A folly, Leicester, it is yours, not mine.

I shall deny no wish of yours today,
Because of all my subjects I have done
The most today to cause you pain.
> *(looking at him tenderly)*

Let it be no more than a whim of yours.   2070
Affection shows itself when it is moved
To grant requests which it has disapproved.   [2072]
> *(Leicester throws himself at her feet.*
> *The curtain falls.)*

ACT III

*Region in a park. The foreground is planted with trees; at the rear
a distant prospect.* [*Afternoon of the same day.*]
*Enter Mary running swiftly up from beyond the trees. Jane
Kennedy follows slowly.*

KENNEDY: You rush as if you had wings on your shoulders.
    I can't keep up with you. Wait, wait for me!

MARY: Let me delight in freedom new-found
        And be as a child, — O be one too!
        And on the meadows' greensward round
        Let my winged foot now dance on the dew.
        Have I from dark and the grave now arisen,
        Am I no longer a captive in there?   2080
        Let me drink full and a-thirst from my prison,
        Full of the free and the heavenly air.

KENNEDY: O my dear Lady! Close-confining prison
    Is widened for you only by a little.
    You merely do not see the walls that hem
    Us in, because the trees' dense branches hide them.

MARY: O thanks, thanks for this friendly green of trees
    That hide my prison walls by their profusion!
    I want to dream myself to happy ease,
    Why would you wake me from my sweet illusion?   2090
    I rest upon the broad lap of the sky,
    Unfettered now and free, my eye
    Roves through its vast immensities.
    And yonder where the grey mist-mountains rise
    The borders of my realm advance,
    And yonder cloud that toward the south-land flies
    Is searching for the distant shores of France.

Hastening cloud, you sailer in air!
Happy are they who with you may fare!
Greet for me the land of my youth.   2100
I am a captive, in bondage I lie,
No other messenger have I,
Free in air is your highway,
You are not held under this Queen's sway.

KENNEDY: Dear Lady! You are quite beside yourself,
    This long-lost freedom carries you away.

MARY: A fisherman brings in his skiff down there.
          It could mean my rescue, that wretched thing,
          Swiftly to friendly towns we could fare.
          It barely offers the man a living.   2110
          I would heap on him the richest of treasures,
          He would draw such a draft as he never drew,
          In his nets he would find all fortunes and pleasures,
          If his rescuing boat would take me too.

KENNEDY: A waste of wishes! Don't you see that we
    Are followed from afar by steps of spies?
    A cruel prohibition frightens every
    Sympathetic creature from our path.

MARY: No, my good Jane. Believe me, not for nothing
    Have they unbarred my prison doors for me.   2120
    This little favor is the harbinger
    Of greater fortune. I am not mistaken.
    It is love's active hand I have to thank.
    I recognize Lord Lester's mighty arm.
    My prison will be widened gradually,
    I will progress from lesser things to greater
    Until I finally see the face of one
    Who will set loose my bonds for evermore.

KENNEDY: I cannot make sense of this contradiction.
    Just yesterday death was proclaimed for you,   2130
    Now suddenly today they give this freedom.
    The chains are loosed, I have heard tell, for those
    Whom everlasting liberty awaits.

MARY: That hunting-horn! Do you hear it sounding

Mighty of call through field and grove?
O for a steed of spirit bounding
To join the gladsome throng as they rove!
Still more! O, that familiar voice
Full of memories painfully sweet.
Often my ear has heard it with joy,   2140
As when hunters on heaths of the upland deploy
And the race of the hunt is wild and fleet.

(Enter Paulet.)

PAULET: Well, have I finally acted right, my Lady?
  Do I deserve your thanks for once?
MARY: What, Sir?
  Are you the one who got me this reprieve?
  You?
PAULET: Why should I not be the one? I was
  At court, and I delivered what you wrote—
MARY: You did deliver it? You really did?
  And so the freedom that I now enjoy
  Is a fruit of that letter—
PAULET *(significantly)*:   More than that!   2150
  Prepare yourself for something greater yet.
MARY: For something greater, Sir? What do you mean?
PAULET: Well, you have heard those horns—
MARY *(startled, with premonition)*:   You frighten me!
PAULET: The Queen is hunting in this region.
MARY: What!
PAULET: In a few minutes she will stand before you.
KENNEDY *(hurrying to Mary, who is trembling and on the verge of
      fainting)*:
  What is the matter, Lady? You look pale.
PAULET: Well! Was it not right? Was that not your wish?
  It has been granted sooner than you thought.
  You always used to be so quick of tongue,
  Why do you not bring on your speeches now?   2160
  Now is the time to speak!
MARY: O, why did no one give me any warning!
  I am not ready for that now, not now.

What I requested as the highest favor
Now seems quite dreadful, horrible—Come, Jane,
Take me into the house until I can
Compose myself—

PAULET:　　　　　You must wait here for her.
You may well be alarmed, I understand,
At coming up before your judge.

(Enter the Earl of Shrewsbury.)

MARY: O not on that account! My feeling is　　　　2170
Quite different—Noble Shrewsbury! You come
Sent to me like an angel down from Heaven!
—I cannot see her! Save me, save me from
The sight which I detest—

SHREWSBURY: Control yourself, Queen! Gather up your courage.
This is indeed the hour of decision.

MARY: O, I have waited for this—For years on end
I have prepared, said over everything
And written it upon my memory,
How I was going to move her, touch her pity.　　　　2180
Now everything is suddenly forgotten,
Nothing lives within me at this moment
Except the burning sense of sufferings.
My heart within me turns against her in
Fierce hatred, all my good thoughts flee away,
And with their heads of serpent-locks all shaking,
The evil spirits up from hell surround me.

SHREWSBURY: Control your frantic blood in its revolt,
Restrain your bitterness of heart! Good fruit
Will never come of hatred meeting hatred.　　　　2190
However much your inner heart rebels,
Obey the time and the law of the hour!
She is the one in power—so be humble!

MARY: In front of her! No!

SHREWSBURY:　　　　　　Do it anyway!
Speak deferentially, with calm! Invoke
Her generosity, do not insist
Upon your rights now, now is not the time.

MARY: Alas, I have implored my own destruction,
  And as a curse my plea is being granted!
  We never should have seen each other, never!   2200
  No good can ever, ever come of it!
  Sooner could fire and water meet in love
  And sooner could the tiger kiss the lamb—
  I am too deeply hurt—she has offended
  Too grievously—No peace is possible!

SHREWSBURY: But see her first from face to face!
  You know, I saw how she was shaken by
  Your letter, and her eyes were wet with tears.
  She is not feelingless, but you must cherish
  More trust in her.—That is the reason why   2210
  I hurried on ahead so that I could
  Forewarn you and induce a state of calm.

MARY (grasping his hand):
  O Talbot! You have always been my friend—
  Would I had stayed in your mild custody!
  I have been hardly treated, Shrewsbury!

SHREWSBURY: Forget all that now. Only think of how
  You will receive her with complete submission.

MARY: Is Burleigh with her too, my evil angel?

SHREWSBURY: No one is with her but the Earl of Lester.

MARY: Lord Lester!

SHREWSBURY: Have no fear of him. He does   2220
  Not seek your ruin.—It is his work that
  The Queen has now consented to this meeting.

MARY: O, I was sure it was!

SHREWSBURY: What are you saying?

PAULET: The Queen is coming!
          (They all step aside; only Mary remains,
          leaning on Kennedy's bosom.
              Enter Elizabeth, the Earl of Leicester, and
          retinue.)

ELIZABETH (to Leicester):
  What castle is this?

LEICESTER: Castle Fotheringhay.

ELIZABETH *(to Shrewsbury):*
  Send our hunting party on ahead
  To London. People throng the roads too much.
  We shall seek shelter in this quiet park.
          (Talbot dismisses the retinue. She fixes her
          eyes on Mary while she goes on talking to
          Leicester.)
  My people love me far too much. Their joy
  Is quite immoderate, idolatrous.   2230
  God may be honored so, but not mere mortals.
MARY *(who all this time has been leaning on the nurse's bosom,*
      rises now, and her eye encounters the intent gaze of Elizabeth.
      She shudders and throws herself back on the nurse's bosom):
  O God, no heart speaks from that countenance!
ELIZABETH: Who is the Lady?
                    (General silence.)
LEICESTER: —You are at Castle Fotheringhay, my Queen.
ELIZABETH *(pretends to be surprised and astonished and fixes a*
      dark look on Leicester):
  Who has done this to me? Lord Lester!
LEICESTER: Well, it has happened, Queen—And so, now that
  Your footsteps have been guided here by Heaven,
  Let generosity and mercy triumph.
SHREWSBURY: Allow us to entreat you, royal Lady,
  To cast your eye on this unfortunate   2240
  Here overwhelmed before your gaze.
          (Mary collects herself and starts to walk
          towards Elizabeth, then stops half way with a
          shudder; her gestures express the most vehement
          struggle.)
ELIZABETH: What's this, my Lords?
  Who was it then that told me of a woman
  In deep humility? I find a proud one
  No wise subdued by adverse fortune.
MARY: Be
  It so! I shall submit even to this.
  Hence, impotent pride of the noble soul!

I shall forget now who I am and what
I have endured; I shall bow down before her
Who thrust me down to this ignominy.

(She turns toward the Queen.)

Heaven has decided for you, Sister!   2250
Crowned with triumph is your happy brow,
And I adore the deity that raised
You up.

(She kneels before her.)

   Be generous in turn, my Sister!
Let me not lie here in ignominy.
Stretch forth your hand, your royal right hand give
Me now, to raise me up from my deep fall!

ELIZABETH *(stepping back)*:
Lady Mary, you are in your place!
And thankfully I praise the favor of
My God, who did not will that I should lie
At your feet as you now lie here at mine.   2260

MARY *(with rising emotion)*:
Think of the change that comes to all things human!
Gods do exist who punish arrogance!
Revere them, dread them, they are terrible,
And they have cast me down before your feet—
For the sake of these stranger witnesses,
Respect yourself in me! Do not dishonor
Or put to shame the Tudor blood that flows
In my veins as in yours—O God in Heaven!
Do not stand there so inaccessible
And rugged, like a cliff that shipwrecked men   2270
Vainly strive and struggle to attain.
My life, my destiny, my all, now hangs
Upon the power of my words and tears.
Release my heart so that I may touch yours!
When you look at me with that icy glance,
My heart shrinks shuddering and closes shut,
The stream of tears is stopped, and frigid horror
Chokes my words of entreaty in my bosom.

ELIZABETH (*coldly and severely*):
    What do you have to tell me, Lady Stuart?
    You wished to speak to me. I disregard   2280
    My Queenship, my profoundly outraged Queenship,
    So I may do my duty as a sister.
    I grant the solace of beholding me.
    My generous impulse leads me on, and I
    Expose myself to righteous censure by
    Such low descending—for, as you
    Well know, you did attempt to have me murdered.
MARY: Where shall I start, how shall I prudently
    Contrive my words so that they may have their
    Effect upon your heart, yet not offend it!   2290
    O God, lend power to my speech and take
    From it all thorns that could cause any wounds!
    I cannot any way plead for myself without
    Accusing you, and that I do not want.
    —You have dealt with me in a way that is
    Not proper, for I am, like you, a Queen,
    And you have held me as a prisoner.
    I came to you a suppliant, and you,
    Scorning in me the sacred rights of nations
    And sacred laws of hospitality,   2300
    Had me shut up in prison walls; my friends
    And servants were most cruelly removed;
    I was myself left in unseemly hardship;
    I was called up to an outrageous court—
    No more of that! Oblivion shall forever
    Enshroud the cruel things I have endured.
    —See! I shall term those things of fate's contriving,
    You are not guilty, nor am *I* to blame.
    An evil spirit rose from the abyss
    To kindle hot the hatred in our hearts   2310
    That had already split our tender childhood.
    It grew with us, and wicked people fanned
    The wretched flame and blew their breath upon it;
    Insane fanatics armed with sword and dagger

Officious hands that had no right to meddle—
For this is the accursed fate of rulers,
That once they are at odds, they rend the world
And set at large the Furies of all discord.
—There is no alien mouth to come between
Us now,
  (approaching her trustingly and with caressing tone)
    we stand here in each other's presence. 2320
Now, Sister, speak! Name my offense to me
And I will render total satisfaction.
If only you had given me a hearing
When I so urgently besought your eye!
Things never would have gone so far, nor would
There now be taking place in this sad spot
This sorry and unfortunate encounter!
ELIZABETH: My lucky star protected me from putting
 The adder in my bosom.—You should not
 Accuse the fates, but rather your black heart, 2330
 The wild ambition of your family.
 Between us nothing hostile had occurred.
 And then your uncle, that ambition-crazed
 Proud priest that stretches out his impious hand
 To seize all crowns, threw down his challenge to me,
 Befooled you till you took my coat-of-arms,
 Till you assumed my royal title, till
 You entered with me into battle to
 The death—Whom did he not enlist against me?
 The tongues of priests, the swords of nations, and 2340
 The frightful weapons of religious frenzy;
 Here in the peaceful seat of my own kingdom
 He blew the flames of revolution up—
 But God is with me, and that haughty priest
 Has not maintained the field—The blow was aimed
 At my head, but it is your head that falls!
MARY: I stand here in the hands of God. You will not
 Presume so brutally upon your power—
ELIZABETH: Who is to hinder me? Your uncle set

The model for all monarchs of this world   2350
Of *how* to make peace with one's enemies.
The Saint Bartholomew shall be my school!
What is blood-kinship, or the law of nations,
To me? The Church absolves all bonds of duty
And blesses breach of faith and regicide;
I practice only what your own priests teach.
What pledge would guarantee you for me if
I were so generously to set you free?
What lock would I put on your loyalty
Without Saint Peter's key unlocking it?   2360
The only safety lies with force, for with
The breed of serpents can be no alliance.

MARY: That is your sorry, sinister suspicion!
You always looked upon me only as
An enemy and stranger. If you had
Proclaimed me as your heir, as was my due,
Then gratitude and love would have retained
A loyal friend and relative in me.

ELIZABETH: Out yonder, Lady Stuart is your circle
Of friends, your home is with the Papacy,   2370
Your brother is the monk—Proclaim you as
My heir! A treacherous, deceiving snare!
So that you might seduce my people in
My lifetime, so that like a sly Armida
You might entice the young men of my kingdom
By cunning to your nets for paramours—
So everyone could turn to the newly rising
Sun, while I meanwhile should—

MARY: Rule in peace!
All claims upon this kingdom I renounce.
Alas, my spirit's pinions have been lamed,   2380
I am no longer lured by greatness.—You
Have gained your end. I now am but the shadow
Of Mary. Prison's shame has broken my
Proud spirit.—You have done your uttermost
To me, you have destroyed me in my bloom!

—Now, Sister, make an end! Pronounce those words
Which you have come here to pronounce. For never
Will I believe that you have come here to
Make cruel mockery of me as victim.
Pronounce those words! Say to me: "Mary, you   2390
Are free! My power you have felt, but now
You shall revere my generosity."
Say that, and from your hand I shall accept
My life, my freedom, as a gift.—One word,
And all will be as if it never happened.
I wait. O let me not await too long!
And woe to you if you do not close with
Those words! For if you do not leave me now
With blessing, grandly, like a goddess,—Sister!
Not for this whole rich island, not for all   2400
The countries that the sea surrounds, would I
Stand here before you as you stand with me!

ELIZABETH: Do you admit at last that you are beaten?
Are your plots done? No other murderer
Is on his way? Will no adventurer
Attempt his sorry chivalry for you?
—Yes, Lady Mary, all is over. You
Will tempt no more. The world has other cares.
No one is anxious to be your—fourth husband,
Because you kill your suitors as you kill   2410
Your husbands!

MARY (flaring up):   Sister! Sister!
O God! God! Give me self-control!

ELIZABETH (looks at her with a long look of proud contempt):
So these, my Lord of Lester, are the charms
Which no man with impunity has seen,
With which no other woman dares to vie!
Indeed! *This* fame was cheap to come by: it
Costs nothing to become the world-wide beauty
But to have all the world hold one in common!

MARY: That is too much!

ELIZABETH *(with a sneering laugh):*
                   You show your true face now.
  Till now we only saw the mask.   2420

MARY *(with burning anger, though with noble dignity):*
  I erred, but in a human, youthful way.
  I was seduced by power. I did not
  Conceal or make a secret of it. With
  A royal candor I disdained false seeming.
  The world has known the worst of me, and I
  Can say that I am better than my name.
  But woe to you if from your deeds they once
  Rip off the cloak of honor which you use
  To hide the wild heat of your secret lusts.
  It was not chastity your mother left you;   2430
  We all know what the virtue was for which
  Anne Boleyn climbed the scaffold to the block.

SHREWSBURY *(stepping between the two Queens):*
  O God in Heaven! Must it come to this!
  Is this your self-control and your submission,
  Lady Mary?

MARY: Self-control! I have
  Endured all that a mortal can endure.
  Hence and be gone, lamb-hearted resignation!
  Fly up to Heaven, patient tolerance!
  Burst from your bonds at last, and from your cavern
  Come forth, you long-suppressed resentment now!   2440
  And you who gave the angered basilisk
  His murderous glance, lay now upon my tongue
  The poisoned dart—

SHREWSBURY: She is beside herself!
  Forgive this mad and deeply injured woman!
         (Elizabeth, speechless with anger, is darting
         furious looks at Mary.)

LEICESTER *(in the most vehement agitation, tries to lead Elizabeth*
  away):
                         Do

  Not listen to this frenzied woman! Come

Away from this unhappy place.

MARY: A bastard has profaned the throne of England,
The noble-hearted British people has
Been cheated by a crafty, cheap imposter.
—If right prevailed, you would be lying in   2450
The dust before me, for *I* am your King.

> (*Elizabeth swiftly leaves. The Lords follow
> her in the greatest dismay.*)

KENNEDY: What have you done! She goes away in fury!
Now all is lost, and all our hopes have vanished.

MARY (*still completely beside herself*):
In fury! And she bears death in her heart!

> (*falling on Kennedy's neck*)

O Jane, how glad I feel! At last, at last,
Now after years of this humiliation
And grief, one moment of revenge, of triumph!
A mountain's load is taken from my heart,
I plunged the dagger in my foeman's heart!

KENNEDY: Unhappy woman! Madness sweeps you on,   2460
You have offended the implacable.
She wields the lightning bolt, she is the Queen,
You mocked her in the presence of her lover!

MARY: Before Lord Lester's eyes I shamed her! And
He saw it, he was witness to my triumph!
He stood there when I struck her from her height,
It was his presence that gave me the strength!

> (*Enter Mortimer.*)

KENNEDY: O, what an outcome, Sir—

MORTIMER: I heard it all.

> (*He gives the nurse a sign to go to her post,
> then comes closer. His entire being expresses a
> vehement and passionate mood.*)

You won, you won! You trod her in the dust!
You were the Queen, and *she* the criminal.   2470
I am enraptured by your spirit, I
Adore you, great and splendid like a goddess
You now appear to me.

MARY: You did speak with
  Lord Lester, and you did deliver to him
  My letter and my gift—O tell me, Sir!

MORTIMER: O how your noble royal anger shone
  About you, how your charms were all transfigured!
  Most beautiful of women on this earth!

MARY: I beg you, Sir! Allay my great impatience.
  What did he say? Tell me, do I dare hope?   2480

MORTIMER: Who? He? That wretched coward! Hope for nothing
  From him. Despise him and forget him!

MARY: What!
  What are you saying?

MORTIMER: He save you, possess you!
  He, you! Just let him try it! He! With me
  He'd have to fight first, fight me to the death!

MARY: You did not give my letter to him then?
  —Then all is lost!

MORTIMER: That coward loves his life.
  Whoever saves you and then claims your charms
  Must doughtily clasp Death within his arms.

MARY: He will do nothing for me then?

MORTIMER: No more   2490
  Of him! What can *he* do? What need of him
  When I shall save you, I alone?

MARY: O what can you do?

MORTIMER: Do not dream that matters
  Still stand as they stood with you yesterday!
  The way the Queen took leave of you just now,
  The way that conversation ended, all
  Is lost, all avenues of pardon blocked.
  We now need *action*. *Boldness* must decide.
  Let all be risked for all in a bold fight,
  You must be free before the morning light.   2500

MARY: What's this? Tonight! How is that possible?

MORTIMER: Hear what has been decided. I have gathered
  All my confederates in secret chapel.
  A priest heard our confessions and absolved

Us of all sins we ever may have done
And gave us absolution in advance
For any that we might commit henceforth.
And we received the final sacraments
And thus are ready for the final journey.

MARY: O, what a fearful preparation, Sir!   2510

MORTIMER: This castle we shall scale this very night.
I have the keys in my possession. We
Shall slay the guards and wrest you from your chamber
By force. At our hands everyone must die
So not a living soul is left behind
Who might betray the fact of your abduction.

MARY: And Drury, Paulet, and my other jailers?
O they will shed their final blood before—

MORTIMER: My dagger will begin by killing them!

MARY: What? Kill your uncle, kill your second father?   2520

MORTIMER: He shall die by my hand. Yes, I will kill him.

MARY: O monstrous crime!

MORTIMER: All crimes are pardoned in
Advance. I can commit the worst of crimes,
And I intend to do so.

MARY: Monstrous, monstrous!

MORTIMER: And even if I have to stab the Queen,
I took my oath upon the Host to do it.

MARY: No, rather than shed so much blood for me—

MORTIMER: What is the whole of life compared to *you*
And to my love? Let all the bonds of all
The worlds dissolve, and let a second deluge   2530
Roll in engulfing everything that breathes!
—I value nothing any more! Before
I give you up, the end of time may come.

MARY (*falling back*):
My God! What language, Sir,—the way you look!
—You terrify me, frighten me away.

MORTIMER (*with wild looks and with the expression of quiet
madness*):
                        Life is

One instant only; death, too, only one!
—So let them drag me off to Tyburn, tear
Me limb from limb with red-hot iron tongs,
   (advancing toward her vehemently with wide-open arms)
If I embrace you, ardently beloved—

MARY *(falling back)*:
Away from me, you madman! —

MORTIMER: If I clasp   2540
You to this bosom, to this love-breathing mouth—

MARY: In Heaven's name, Sir, let me go inside!

MORTIMER: A man is mad not to clasp happiness
In close and indissoluble embrace
When once a god had put it in his hand.
I'll save you though a thousand lives should stand
To fall. I will, I will, as surely as
God lives! I swear it, and possess you too.

MARY: O, will no god or angel shield me through
My peril? O monstrous fate, to fling   2550
Me on from ghastly thing to ghastly thing.
Was I born to have madness wakened by me?
Do love and hate conspire to terrify me?

MORTIMER: Yes, ardently, the way they hate, I love you!
Their will is to behead you and to sever
With a sharp ax that neck of dazzling white.
O vow unto the god of life's delight
What you must sacrifice to brutal hate!
With all these charms that are no longer yours
Confer joy on your fortunate beloved!   2560
These lovely locks, these locks of silken hair
Are doomed unto the dismal powers of the grave,
Entwine me in them timelessly, your slave!

MARY: O Sir, what language do I hear from you!
To you my grief and my misfortune should
Be holy if my royal head is not.

MORTIMER: The crown has fallen from your royal head,
Of earthly majesty you have no more,
So try it, let your queenly word be said,

And see if any savior is in store.
Nothing but your alluring form remains,
The beauty that with god-like power reigns,
It makes me dare and undertake all things,
It drives me toward the ax the headsman swings—
MARY: O, who will save me from his frenzied will?
MORTIMER: Audacious service claims audacious cost!
In what cause would you have a brave man spill
His blood? Is life not life's supreme worth still?
Whoever squanders it for naught, is mad!
But I want first to rest on its warm breast—   2580
      (He presses her vehemently to him.)
MARY: O, must I call for help against the man
Who wants to rescue me?
MORTIMER: You do have feelings;
The world does not report you as severe
Or cold; the hot appeal of love can sway
Your heart; you made the singer Rizzio happy,
And you let Bothwell carry you away.
MARY: How dare you!
MORTIMER: He was nothing but your bully!
You trembled in his presence when you loved him!
If only terror can control you fully,
Then by the god of hell, you—
MARY: Let me go!   2590
MORTIMER: Shall tremble in my presence too!
KENNEDY *(rushing in)*:
Quick! there are people coming! The whole garden
Is full of men with weapons.
MORTIMER *(starting up and reaching for his sword)*:
                I'll protect you!
MARY: Jane, save me from his hands! I am afraid!
Where can I find a place where I can hide?
To what saint can I turn to plead for aid?
Out here is terror, murder waits inside.
      (She flees to the house; Kennedy follows.)
      (Paulet and Drury rush in in great excite-
   ment. The retinue hurry across the stage.)

PAULET: Lock up the gates. And hoist the draw-bridge up!

MORTIMER: Uncle, what's wrong?

PAULET: Where is the murderess?
Down with her to the darkest dungeon cell!   2600

MORTIMER: What is it? What has happened?

PAULET: It's the Queen!
Accursed hands! Devilish audacity!

MORTIMER: The Queen? What Queen?

PAULET: The Queen of England, Sir!
She has been murdered on the road to London!
                        (He rushes into the house.)

MORTIMER: Am I insane? Did someone not come by
Just now and cry: the Queen was murdered? No,
No, I was only dreaming. To my mind
A fever dream presents as true and real
The very thing that fills my ghastly thoughts.
Who comes? It is O'Kelly. So distraught!   2610

O'KELLY *(rushing in):*
Flee, Mortimer! Flee! Everything is lost.

MORTIMER: What has been lost?

O'KELLY: Don't ask too many questions.
Think of swift flight!

MORTIMER: What is the matter?

O'KELLY: Savage
Has dealt the blow, the madman.

MORTIMER: Then it's true?

O'KELLY: True, true! Make your escape!

MORTIMER: She has been murdered,
And Mary now ascends the throne of England!

O'KELLY: Murdered? Who said that?

MORTIMER: Why, you yourself!

O'KELLY: She is alive! And you and I are dead men.

MORTIMER: She is alive?

O'KELLY: The blow glanced off, her mantle caught it,
And Shrewsbury disarmed the murderer.   2620

MORTIMER: She is alive!

O'KELLY: Alive, to send us all to death!

Come, they are cordoning off the park already.

MORTIMER: Who did this crazy thing?

O'KELLY: The Barnabite,
 That friar from Toulon that you saw sitting
 Sunk in thought there in the chapel when
 The monk was spelling out the bull in which
 The Pope pronounced anathema on the Queen.
 He wanted to seize on the quickest means
 And liberate the church of God with one
 Bold stroke and win himself a martyr's crown. 2630
 But only to the priest did he confide
 His act, and did it on the road to London.

MORTIMER *(after a long silence)*:
 A cruelly malicious fate pursues you,
 Unhappy woman! Now—now you must perish,
 Your very angel broaches your disaster.

O'KELLY: Which way will you direct your flight? I shall
 Go hide amid the forests of the north.

MORTIMER: Go on and flee, and may God guide your flight!
 I stay,—in spite of all to save her head,
 Or else upon her coffin make my bed. 2640

    (They leave in opposite directions.)

ACT IV

SCENE 1

An anteroom. [Early that evening.]
Count Aubespine, Kent, and Leicester.

AUBESPINE: How are things with Her Majesty? My Lords,
    You see me still beside myself with terror.
    How did it happen? How could it have happened
    Right in this loyal nation's midst?

LEICESTER: Our people
    Did not do it. The perpetrator was
    A Frenchman and a subject of your King.

AUBESPINE: A madman surely!

KENT: No, it was a Papist,
    Count Aubespine!

          (Enter Burleigh in conversation
             with Davison.)

BURLEIGH: The execution warrant
    Must be drawn up immediately and have
    The royal seal affixed.—When it is ready   2650
    It should be brought directly to the Queen
    For signing. Go! There is no time to lose.

DAVISON: It shall be done.

              (Exit.)

AUBESPINE *(approaching Burleigh):*
              My Lord, my loyal heart
    Shares in this island's justified rejoicing.
    Praise be to Heaven that the murderer's
    Blow was averted from that royal head!

BURLEIGH: Praise be to Heaven that the malice of
    Our enemies was put to shame!

AUBESPINE: May God
    Condemn the doer of this cursed deed!

BURLEIGH: The doer and the shameless man who planned it. 2660
AUBESPINE *(to Kent):*
   Lord Marshal, will Your Highness deign to take
   Me to Her Majesty so that I may
   Lay the congratulations of my Lord
   And King most dutifully down at her feet?
BURLEIGH: Don't bother, Count Aubespine.
AUBESPINE *(formally):*   I know my duty,
   Lord Burleigh.
BURLEIGH: Sir, your duty is to leave
   This island just as soon as possible.
AUBESPINE *(falling back in astonishment):*
   What! What is this?
BURLEIGH: Your sacred title will
   Protect you yet today, but not tomorrow.
AUBESPINE: And may I ask what is my crime?
BURLEIGH: If I   2670
   Gave it a *name,* it could not be forgiven.
AUBESPINE: I trust my right as an ambassador—
BURLEIGH: Will not protect a traitor.
LEICESTER AND KENT: What was that!
AUBESPINE: My Lord,
   Consider well—
BURLEIGH: A passport, written by
   Your hand, was found in the assassin's pocket.
KENT: Is it possible?
AUBESPINE: I issue many passports.
   I cannot know a person's inner thoughts.
BURLEIGH: The murderer went to confession in
   Your house.
AUBESPINE: My house is open.
BURLEIGH: To the foes
   Of England.
AUBESPINE: I demand investigation.   2680
BURLEIGH: Beware of one.
AUBESPINE: My King is outraged in
   My person. He will break off the alliance.

BURLEIGH: The Queen has broken it already. There
   Will be no marriage now of France with England.
   My Lord of Kent, you will assume the task
   Of furnishing the Count safe conduct to
   The sea. The outraged populace have stormed
   His mansion, where an arsenal of weapons
   Was found; and they are threatening to tear him
   To pieces if he shows himself. Conceal him   2690
   Until their rage is calmed.—You answer for
   His life!
AUBESPINE: I go, I quit this country where
   They trample under foot the rights of nations
   And toy with treaties.—But my King will ask
   A stern accounting—
BURLEIGH: Let him come and get it!
           (Exeunt Kent and Aubespine.)
LEICESTER: So you are now dissolving the alliance
   Which you officiously arranged yourself.
   You have deserved but little thanks from England,
   My Lord, you might have saved yourself the trouble.
BURLEIGH: I meant well. God disposed things otherwise.   2700
   Lucky the man aware of nothing worse.
LEICESTER: We all know Cecil's brow of mystery
   When he is on the hunt for criminals
   Of state.—These are good times for you, Sir, now.
   A monstrous outrage has occurred; as yet
   A mystery surrounds its perpetrators.
   A court of inquisition can now be
   Set up. Now words and glances can be weighed
   And thoughts themselves made to appear in court.
   Now *you* will be the all-important man,   2710
   The Atlas of the state, with all of England
   Upon your shoulders.
BURLEIGH: I acknowledge you
   My master, Sir. Such triumph as you won
   With your fine talk, was never won by mine.
LEICESTER: What do you mean by that?

BURLEIGH: It was you, was it not, who lured the Queen
  Behind my back to Castle Fotheringhay?
LEICESTER: Behind your back? When have my actions ever
  Shrunk from your sight?
BURLEIGH: Did I say you conducted
  The Queen to Castle Fotheringhay? Oh, no!   2720
  In this case there was nothing of the sort!
  You did not take the Queen! —It was the Queen
  Who was so kind as to conduct *you* there.
LEICESTER: What do you mean by that, my Lord?
BURLEIGH: And what
  A noble rôle you had the Queen perform down there!
  A splendid triumph you arranged for her,
  That guileless, trusting lady.—Kindly Princess,
  They mocked you with such shameless impudence,
  They victimized you so relentlessly!
  —That generosity and clemency   2730
  That suddenly came over you at Council!
  So that was why the Stuart was so weak,
  So insignificant a foe that it
  Was not worth while to be stained with her blood!
  A clever plan! And sharpened to a point!
  A shame it was so sharp the point snapped off!
LEICESTER: You scoundrel! Follow me at once! Before
  The Queen's throne you shall answer me for this.
BURLEIGH: You'll find me there.—My Lord, see to it that
  Your eloquence does not desert you there!   2740
                    (*Exit.*)
LEICESTER (*alone*):
  I am discovered, they see through me.—But
  How did that wretched man get on my traces!
  And woe to me if he has proof! If once
  The Queen discovers there had been an understanding
  Between myself and Mary—God! How guilty
  I stand before her! How deceitful my
  Advice will seem, and my unfortunate
  Concern with getting her to Fotheringhay!

She will see herself cruelly mocked by me,
Betrayed to her detested enemy!   2750
O, she can never, never pardon that!
Now everything will look premeditated,
The bitter turn that conversation took,
Her rival's victory and mocking laughter,
Yes, she will think I even put the weapon
In the assassin's hand that intervened
As unexpected, monstrous act of fate!
Escape is nowhere to be seen! Who comes here!

> *(Enter Mortimer at the peak of excitement;*
> *he looks anxiously about.)*

MORTIMER: Lord Lester! Is it you? Are we alone?
LEICESTER: Unhappy man, away! What have you come for? 2760
MORTIMER: They have got on our track, on yours as well;
Be on your guard!
LEICESTER: Away! Away!
MORTIMER: They know
That at Count Aubespine's there was a secret
Meeting—
LEICESTER: What do I care!
MORTIMER: And that the assassin
Was present at it—
LEICESTER: That is your affair!
You reckless fool! Are you presuming to
Get *me* involved in your audacious crime?
Defend your evil actions for yourself!
MORTIMER: At least hear what I tell you.
LEICESTER *(in violent anger)*:   Go to hell!
Why cling to my heels like an evil spirit!   2770
Begone! I do not know you, I have nothing
In common with cheap murderers like you.
MORTIMER: You will not listen. I have come to warn you;
Your actions are betrayed as well, and—
LEICESTER: Ha!
MORTIMER: The Lord High Treasurer came to Fotheringhay
Directly after the unhappy deed had happened.

The Queen's rooms were minutely searched, and they
Discovered—

LEICESTER: What?

MORTIMER: A letter which the Queen
Had started to write you—

LEICESTER: The wretched woman!

MORTIMER: In which she urges you to keep your word,   2780
Renews the promise of her hand to you,
Speaks of the picture which— ·

LEICESTER: Death and damnation!

MORTIMER: Lord Burleigh has the letter.

LEICESTER: I am lost!
        (During the following speech of Mortimer
        he keeps walking back and forth in desperation.)

MORTIMER: Seize the moment now! Anticipate him!
Save both yourself and *her.*—Swear your way out,
Invent excuses, and avert the worst!
I can do nothing more myself. All my
Confederates are scattered and our whole
Alliance has been broken. I shall hurry
To Scotland to enlist new friends up there.   2790
It's up to you now. Try and see what your
Bold front and influence can do!

LEICESTER *(stops with a sudden resolve):* I will!
                (He goes to the door, opens it,
                    and calls.)

Ho, guards!
                (to the officer who comes in with
                    armed men)
                Arrest this traitor to the state
And guard him well! A plot has been discovered,
A plot of the most shameful kind, and I
Shall bring the Queen the news of it myself.
                    (Exit.)

MORTIMER *(at first stands frozen with astonishment, then gets*
    control of himself, and with a look of supreme contempt
    watches Leicester disappear):

The vile deceiving cur! — But I deserve it!
Who ever bade me trust the jackanapes?
And so he walks away above my neck,
My fall builds him a bridge and he escapes.   2800
— Make your escape, then! My lips shall be true.
You will not be involved in my transgression.
I would not even be allied with you
In death. Life is a bad man's sole possession.
                    (to the officer of the guard
                    who steps forward to arrest him)
What do you want, cheap slave of tyranny?
I ridicule you, I am free!
                    (He draws a dagger.)
THE OFFICER: He has a weapon! —Take away his dagger!
                    (They close in on him; he wards
                    them off.)
MORTIMER: And freely in this final moment I
Shall open up my heart and loose my tongue!
A curse and ruination on you, you   2810
Who have traduced your God and your true Queen!
Who from the earthly Mary faithlessly
Have turned away, as from the one in Heaven,
And sold yourselves unto this bastard Queen—
THE OFFICER: You hear his blasphemy! Go on and seize him!
MORTIMER: Beloved! I have failed to set you free
But I set an example by my love.
Holy Mary, pray for me
And take me with you to your life above!
                    (He stabs himself with the dagger and falls
                    into the arms of the guards.)

SCENE 2

The Queen's apartments.
Elizabeth, with a letter in her hand. Burleigh.
ELIZABETH: To take me down there! Make such mockery   2820

Of me! The traitor! To parade me there
Triumphantly before his paramour!
O Burleigh, never was a woman so
Deceived!

BURLEIGH: I   cannot understand it yet,
What power, what magic arts he could have used
To take my Queen's sagacity so wholly
Unawares.

ELIZABETH: O, I shall die of shame!
O, how he must have ridiculed my weakness!
I wanted to shame *her,* and was myself
The object of her mockery!   2830

BURLEIGH: You now see *I* had loyally advised you!

ELIZABETH: O, I have been severely punished for
Departing from your sage advice! But was
I not to trust in him? Was I to fear
A snare in his vows of the truest love?
Whom can I trust if *he* deceives me so?
Whom I made great above all other great,
Who always was the closest to my heart,
Whom I allowed to act as if he were
The King, the very master of this court!   2840

BURLEIGH: And all the time he was deceiving you,
Betraying you to that false Queen of Scotland!

ELIZABETH: O she shall pay me for this with her blood!
—Has the death warrant been drawn up?

BURLEIGH: It is
Laid ready, as you ordered.

ELIZABETH: She shall die!
He shall behold her death, then die himself.
I have expelled him from my heart, my love
Is gone and vengeance occupies it wholly.
Let his fall be as deep as he stood high,
A monument to my severity   2850
As he was an example of my weakness!
Conduct him to the Tower. I shall name
The peers to sentence him. Let him be subject

To the full rigor of the law.

BURLEIGH: He will
Force his way to you, justify himself—

ELIZABETH: How can he justify himself? The letter
Incriminates him, does it not? His crime
Is clear as day!

BURLEIGH: But you are kind and gracious;
The sight of him, before his mighty presence—

ELIZABETH: I will not see him. Never, never! Have   2860
You issued orders to refuse him entrance
If he should come?

BURLEIGH: The orders have been issued.
                    (Enter a page.)

THE PAGE: My Lord of Lester.

THE QUEEN: O, the shameless scoundrel!
I will not see him. Tell him that I will
Not see him.

THE PAGE: I would not dare say that to
The Lord, and he would not accept the statement.

THE QUEEN: This is the way I raised him up, until
My servants fear his orders more than mine!

BURLEIGH *(to the page):*
Tell him the Queen forbids him to come near!
                    (The Page goes out hesitantly.)

THE QUEEN *(after a pause):*
But what if it were possible—What if   2870
He still could justify himself?—Tell me,
Might it not be a trap that Mary set
To make me quarrel with my truest friend?
She is an arrant ruthless jade! What if
She wrote the letter just to cast suspicion
Into my heart and plunge him whom she hates
Into disaster—

BURLEIGH: But, my Queen, consider—
            *(Leicester wrenches open the doors by force
            and enters with an imperious step.)*

LEICESTER: I want to see the shameless man who would

Forbid me access to my own Queen's room.

ELIZABETH: Audacious man!

LEICESTER: To turn me from the door!   2880
  If she can be seen by a Burleigh, then
  She can be seen by me!

BURLEIGH: You are most bold, my Lord,
  To storm your way in here without permission.

LEICESTER: And you most insolent, my Lord, to speak
  At all. Permission? What! At this court there
  Is no one by whose lips the Earl of Lester
  Can be forbidden or allowed!

                  (as he humbly approaches Elizabeth)
                  Now from
  My Queen's own lips I want to hear what she—

ELIZABETH (without looking at him):
  Out of my sight, unworthy, graceless wretch!

LEICESTER: This is not my own kind Elizabeth   2890
  I hear; I hear the Lord, my enemy,
  In these ungracious words.—But I appeal
  To my Elizabeth.—You granted him
  Your ear, now I ask for the same.

ELIZABETH: Speak, wretch!
  And make your outrage worse! Deny you did it!

LEICESTER: Let this unwanted party first retire—
  Withdraw, my Lord.—The things I have to settle
  Here with my Queen do not require a witness.
  Leave us.

ELIZABETH (to Burleigh):
          Stay here. I order you to stay.

LEICESTER: What business have third parties here between us?
  These matters have to do with no one but   [2900
  My worshipped Monarch.—I demand the rights
  That suit my station.—These are sacred rights,
  And I insist upon it that the Lord
  Withdraw!

ELIZABETH: This haughty language well befits you!

LEICESTER: It does indeed. I am the lucky man

To whom your favor gave high preference.
That lifts me over him and over all!
Your heart conferred this haughty rank upon me,
And what love gave, I will maintain, by God!   2910
And will defend it with my very life.
Now have him go—and it will take two minutes
For me to reach an understanding with you.

ELIZABETH: You need not hope to get around me by
   Sly talk.

LEICESTER: The chatterer might get around you,
   But I am going to talk straight to your heart,
   And what I dared, relying on your favor,
   That I will justify before your heart
   Alone.—And I will recognize no other
   Tribunal over me but your affection!   2920

ELIZABETH: You shameless man! That is the first to damn you.
   My Lord, show him the letter.

BURLEIGH: Here it is!

LEICESTER (runs through the letter without losing countenance):
   This is the Stuart's hand.

ELIZABETH: Read and be speechless.

LEICESTER (quietly, after reading):
   Appearance is against me! but I trust
   That I shall not be judged on mere appearance!

ELIZABETH: Can you deny you had an understanding
   In secret with the Stuart, that you had
   Her picture, that you gave her hope for freedom?

LEICESTER: It would be simple for me, were I guilty,
   To disallow the evidence that is   2930
   Presented by an enemy. My conscience
   Is clear, however. I acknowledge that
   She writes the truth.

ELIZABETH: Well, then?

BURLEIGH: His own mouth damns him.

ELIZABETH: Out of my sight! And to the Tower,—traitor!

LEICESTER: That I am not. I erred in that I made
   A secret of the step and kept it from you.

And yet my purpose was sincere. I did it
To sound the enemy and to destroy her.

ELIZABETH: Absurd evasion!

BURLEIGH: What, my Lord? You think—

LEICESTER: I played a daring game, I realize,   2940
And no one but the Earl of Lester could
Have ventured such an action at this court.
The world well knows how much I hate the Stuart,
The rank I occupy, the confidence
With which the Queen has honored me, can not
Help but refute all doubt of my good motives.
The man who is above all others marked
By your good favor may strike out upon
His own way to achieve his duty!

BURLEIGH: Why,
Though, if the cause was good, did you keep silent?   2950

LEICESTER: My Lord, your habit is to talk before
You act, you are your actions' trumpet. *That*
Is *your* way, Sir, of doing things. Mine is to
Act first, and then to talk.

BURLEIGH: You're talking now because you must.

LEICESTER (*measuring him with his eyes proudly and scornfully*):
                                        And you
Are boasting that you managed to achieve
Some great fantastic deed in rescuing
Your Queen and in unmasking treachery.—
You fancy you know everything, that nothing
Can get past your keen eye.—Poor, empty boaster!   2960
Despite your keenness Mary Stuart would
Be free today if *I* had not forestalled it.

BURLEIGH: You claim that you—

LEICESTER: Yes, I, my Lord. The Queen
Had placed her trust in Mortimer, she opened
Her inmost heart to him, she went so far
As to give him a bloody charge against
The Stuart, since his uncle had rejected
A similar commission with abhorrence—

Now, is that not the case?
>   (*The Queen and Burleigh look at each other
>   in astonishment.*)

BURLEIGH: How did you find
That out?

LEICESTER: But is it not true?—Well, my Lord,   2970
Where were your thousand eyes that you should fail
To see that Mortimer was fooling you?
And that he was the Guises' tool, a frantic
Papist, and a creature of the Stuart,
A bold fanatic with determination,
Who came to set the Stuart free and murder
The Queen—

ELIZABETH (*with the utmost astonishment*):
>   This Mortimer!

LEICESTER: It was through him that Mary
Was able to communicate with me.
It was in that way that I came to know him.
She was to be abducted from her prison   2980
This very day, so his own lips revealed
To me just now. I had them place him under
Arrest, but in despair at seeing all
His work undone and frustrate, and himself
Unmasked, he killed himself.

ELIZABETH: O, I have been betrayed
As no one ever was.—This Mortimer!

BURLEIGH: This happened just now, after I had left you?

LEICESTER: I must, for my part, very much regret
That things turned out this way with him. If he
Had lived, his testimony would have cleared   2990
Me fully and relieved me of all guilt.
That's why I turned him over to his judges.
The strictest processes of law should state
My innocence before the world and prove it.

BURLEIGH: He killed himself, you say? Is that so? Or did you
Kill him?

LEICESTER: A base suspicion! Let the guard

Be heard into whose hands I turned him over.
                    (He goes to the door and calls.
                The officer of the bodyguard comes in.)
Inform Her Majesty about the way
This Mortimer came to his death.
THE OFFICER: I was on guard
    Out in the hall when suddenly the door   3000
    Was opened by my Lord, who ordered me
    To seize the knight as traitor to the state.
    Thereat we saw him fly into a rage
    And draw his dagger with a furious curse
    Upon the Queen; before we could prevent him,
    He plunged it in his heart, so that he fell
    Dead to the floor and—
LEICESTER: That will do. You may
    Withdraw now, Sir. The Queen has heard enough.
                    (The Officer leaves.)
ELIZABETH: O what abysses of atrocities!
LEICESTER: Who was it now that rescued you? Was it   3010
    My Lord of Burleigh? Did he know the danger
    Surrounding you? Did *he* avert it from you?
    —Your ever loyal Lester was your angel!
BURLEIGH: Lord Earl! This Mortimer died most opportunely
    For you.
ELIZABETH: I don't know what to say. I do
    Believe you and I don't. I think you're guilty
    And yet are not. That wretched woman, she
    Is causing all this trouble!
LEICESTER: She must die.
    I now vote for her death myself. I once
    Advised her sentence be left in abeyance   3020
    Until a hand was raised again to help her.
    That now has come about—and I insist
    The sentence be invoked without delay.
BURLEIGH: You would advise that! You!
LEICESTER: As much as I
    Recoil before recourse to extreme measures,

I see now and believe the welfare of
The Queen requires this bloody sacrifice.
Therefore I now propose that the command
For execution be applied at once.

BURLEIGH *(to the Queen):*
  Then since my Lord appears to be in earnest,   3030
  I move the execution of the sentence
  Shall be assigned to him.

LEICESTER: To me!

BURLEIGH: To you.
  There is no better way for you to counter
  All the suspicion that still weighs upon you
  Than by your having *her* beheaded whom
  You are yourself accused of having loved.

ELIZABETH *(fixing her eyes on Leicester):*
  My Lord gives good advice. So shall it be.

LEICESTER: The highness of my rank should really free me
  From a commission of such dismal nature,
  Which would in every sense be more becoming   3040
  To Burleigh than to me. A man who stands
  Thus closely to his Queen ought not to be
  Asked to perform such grim unhappy things.
  However, to affirm my readiness
  To give my Queen full satisfaction, I
  Shall waive the privilege of my rank and shall
  Assume this dire responsibility.

ELIZABETH: Lord Burleigh shall divide it with you.
              (to the latter)   Have
  A care the order is enforced at once.
                  (Exit Burleigh.
              A tumult is heard outside.
              Enter the Earl of Kent.)
  What is amiss, my Lord of Kent? What tumult   3050
  Disturbs the town? What is the matter?

KENT: Queen,
  The populace are all around the palace
  Urgently insisting they shall see you.

ELIZABETH: What do my people want?

KENT: There is alarm
  Abroad in London that your life is threatened
  And that assassins are afoot sent by
  The Pope. The Catholics are said to be
  Conspiring to abduct the Stuart from
  Her prison and proclaim her Queen. The mob
  Believes it and is wild. The Stuart's head   3060
  Alone, that must fall yet today, can calm them.

ELIZABETH: Is violence to be employed against me?

KENT: They are determined not to yield until
  You sign the warrant for her execution.

          (*Reenter Burleigh with Davison,*
            the latter with a document in his hands.)

ELIZABETH: What do you bring me, Davison?

DAVISON (*approaching solemnly*):   You ordered
  Me, Queen,—

ELIZABETH: What is it?

          (*As she is about to take the document she*
            shudders and shrinks away.)
                    O my God!

BURLEIGH: Obey
  The people's voice, it is the voice of God.

ELIZABETH (*indecisive, struggling with herself*):
  My Lords! Who will assure me whether I
  Am really hearing my whole people's voice,
  The whole world's voice? O, I am very much   3070
  Afraid that once I have obeyed the people's
  Desire, a wholly different voice will then
  Be heard—and that precisely those who now
  Urge me so vehemently to the deed
  Will sharply blame me when the deed is done!

          (*Enter the Earl of Shrewsbury*
            in great agitation.)

SHREWSBURY: My Queen, they're hurrying you unduly! O,
  Stand firm, be steadfast!

          (*as he perceives Davison with*
            the document)

             Or is it all over?
  Has it already happened? I perceive
  A sorry document there in his hand.
  Do not allow that in my Queen's sight now.   3080
ELIZABETH: O noble Shrewsbury! They're forcing me!
SHREWSBURY: Who can force you? You are the mistress here,
  Now is the time to show your majesty!
  Command those brutish voices to be silent
  Who dare to offer violence against
  Your royal will and govern your high judgment.
  Fear and blind error agitate the people,
  You are yourself exasperated, hurt,
  You are but human, you can not judge now.
BURLEIGH: This was judged long ago. There is no sentence 3090
  To *pass,* but one to *carry out.*
KENT *(who withdrew at Shrewsbury's entrance, now comes back)*:
  The uproar grows, the mob can not be held
  In check much longer.
ELIZABETH *(to Shrewsbury)*:   See how they compel me!
SHREWSBURY: I only ask postponement now. This pen-stroke
  Decides your whole life's peace and happiness.
  You have been pondering this for years; then shall
  The moment carry you away by storm?
  Just brief postponement. Gather up your thoughts
  And wait for a more tranquil hour, my Queen.
BURLEIGH *(vehemently)*:
  Yes, wait, postpone, delay, until the kingdom   3100
  Is all a-flame, until the enemy
  Succeeds at last in really dealing her
  Death-blow. Three times a god has kept you from it;
  It touched you *close* today; to hope for one
  More miracle yet would be tempting God.
SHREWSBURY: The God who has four times preserved you by
  His wondrous hand, and who today gave strength
  To the old man's weak arm to overwhelm
  A raging madman—He deserves your trust!
  I shall not seek to raise the voice of justice,   3110

This is not the time for that, nor could
You hear it for the fury of this tempest.
But hear just this one thing! You tremble now
Before this living Mary. Have no fear
Before the living one. But tremble at
The dead one, the beheaded one. She will
Rise from her grave and stalk your kingdom as
Avenging ghost and goddess of contention
· To turn your people's hearts away from you.
The Briton *hates* this woman whom he fears,   3120
He will *avenge* her when she is no more.
Once he feels pity, he no longer will
Look on her as the adversary of
His faith, but only as his King's granddaughter
And victim of harsh jealousy and hatred.
You soon will find out what a change there is.
Cross London when the deed of blood is done,
Show yourself to the people who once thronged
About you in their jubilation, and
You will behold another England and   3130
Another people, for that splendid justice
That won all hearts for you, will not invest you;
Before you, Fear, that dread concomitant
Of tyranny, will walk with quaking step
And empty every street through which you pass.
You will have done the uttermost; what head
Is safe when once this sacred one has fallen?
ELIZABETH: Ah, Shrewsbury! You saved my life today,
Averted the assassin's dagger from me, —
Why did you not let him pursue his course?   3140
Then all contention would be over, and,
Free from all doubts, unstained by any guilt,
I would be lying in my quiet tomb!
For I am weary of my life and rule!
If one of us two Queens *must* die so that
The other one may live—and I perceive
It cannot well be otherwise—can I

Not be the one to yield? I'll give my people
Their choice, I'll give them back their sovereignty.
God is my witness I have not lived for   3150
Myself, but only for my people's good.
If from this flattering Stuart, and if from
This younger Queen, they hope for better days,
Then I will step down gladly from this throne
And go back to the quiet solitude
Of Woodstock where my unambitious youth
Was lived, where far from trifles of this earthly
Greatness, I found greatness in myself.—
I was not made to be a ruler! Rulers
Have to be stern; my heart is soft. I have   3160
Long ruled this island happily because
I only needed to give happiness.
Now comes the first hard duty of a king,
And I perceive my weakness—

BURLEIGH: Well, by Heaven!
When I hear words as totally unroyal
As these now spoken by my own Queen's lips,
It would be treason to my fatherland
And duty to keep silent any longer.
—You say you love your people more than self.
Then show that now! Do not choose peace now for   3170
Yourself and leave your kingdom to the tempests.
—Think of the Church! Shall the old misbelief
Be reimported to us by this Stuart?
And shall the monk rule here anew? and shall
The Legate come from Rome to close our churches
And to unseat our kings from their own thrones?
—The souls of all your subjects, I demand
Them from you.—Whether they are saved or lost
Depends on how you act on this occasion.
This is no time for wishy-washy pity.   3180
The people's welfare is your highest duty.
Shrewsbury may have rescued you today,
But I shall rescue England.—That is more!

ELIZABETH: Let me be left now to myself. With human beings
    Is neither peace nor counsel in this matter.
    I shall refer it to a higher Judge.
    As He instructs me, I shall do. — Withdraw,
    My Lords!

                    (to Davison)
            You, Sir, are to remain near by.
            (The Lords withdraw. Shrewsbury alone
            remains a few minutes yet before the Queen with
            a meaningful look, then slowly goes out wearing
            an expression of deepest sorrow.)

(alone)
O, slavery of the people's service! Bondage
Of shame. — How tired I am of flattering   3190
This idol that my inmost heart despises!
O, when am I to stand free on this throne!
I must respect opinion, court the mob's
Approval, satisfy a populace
Who can be pleased with charlatans alone.
O, no one is a king who has to please
The world! The only king is he who in his actions
Need ask approval of no man alive.

    To what end have I practiced justice, hated
Capricious despotism all my life,   3200
To find that I have tied my hands in this
First unavoidable deed of sheer force!
The model I myself have set condemns me!
Were I a tyrant like the Spanish Mary,
My predecessor on this throne, I now could shed
The blood of kings without the fear of censure.
But was it, then, my own free choosing to
Be just? Omnipotent Necessity,
Which also forces the free will of kings,
Constrained me to this virtue and compelled me.   3210
    Hemmed in by foes, the people's favor is
All that stays me on this disputed throne.
The continental powers are all trying

To ruin me. Implacably the Pope
In Rome hurls his anathema at my head,
With false fraternal kiss I am betrayed
By France, and on the sea the Spaniard frankly
Prepares a mad war of annihilation.
Thus I, defenseless woman, stand embattled
Against a world! I am compelled to clothe   3220
In lofty virtues my claim's nakedness
As well as that stain on my princely birth
Which my own father cast to my disgrace.
I cover it in vain. — The hatred of
My foes has laid it bare and sets this Stuart
Up as a ghost to threaten me forever.

   No, no, this fear shall have an end!
Her head shall fall. I must and will have peace!
— She is the Fury of my life, a plague
Of torment fastened on to me by Fate.   3230
Wherever I have planted joy or hope,
There lies that serpent out of hell upon
My path. She takes away my lover from me,
She steals my very bridegroom! All misfortunes
That strike me bear the name of *Mary Stuart!*
Once *she* is driven from among the living
I shall be free as air upon the mountains.

             (silence)

With what scorn she looked down on me, as if
Her glance should strike me to the ground like lightning!
Poor, helpless creature! I wield better weapons,   3240
Their stroke is deadly, and you are no more!

     *(walking with rapid step to the table and
     seizing the pen)*

In your eyes, then, I am a bastard? — Wretch!
I am such only while you live and breathe.
The doubt as to my princely birth will be
Wiped out as soon as I have wiped you out.
As soon as no more choice is left for Britons,

My birth shall have been in a bed of wedlock!
>   (*With a quick, firm stroke of the pen she writes
>   her signature, then drops the pen and steps back
>   with an expression of horror. After a pause she
>   rings.*
>   *Enter Davison.*)
Where are the other lords?

DAVISON: They went out to
Bring the excited populace to order.
Their turbulence was quieted as soon   3250
As my Lord Earl of Shrewsbury appeared.
"He is the one," a hundred voices shouted,
"Who saved the Queen! So listen to him now,
The bravest man in England!" Noble Talbot
Then started talking and in gentle words
Reproved the people for their violent
Intention; he spoke so convincingly
That everyone was pacified and stole
Away in silence.

ELIZABETH: O this fickle mob
That shifts with every wind! And woe to any   3260
Who lean upon that reed! —That will do now,
Lord Davison. You may withdraw again.
>   (*when he has turned toward the door*)
O, and this paper—Take it back—I place
It in your hands.

DAVISON (*casts a glance at the paper and starts with alarm*):
                    My Queen! Your signature!
You did decide?

ELIZABETH: I was supposed to sign.
I did so. A mere piece of paper does
Not make decisions, names don't kill.

DAVISON: But *your* name, Queen, upon this document
Decides all matters, kills, and is a bolt
Of lightning winging to its prey. —This piece   3270
Of paper orders the commissioners
And sheriff to betake themselves at once

To Fotheringhay and to the Queen of Scotland
And to announce to her her execution
And to perform it with the coming dawn.
Here there is no postponement: she has lived,
Once I release this paper from my hands.

ELIZABETH: Yes, Sir. God lays a weighty destiny
In your weak hands. Implore Him now in prayer
That He may shed His light of wisdom on you.   3280
I go and leave you to your duty now.

             (She starts to leave.)

DAVISON *(intercepting her)*:
O no, my Queen! I beg you, do not leave me
Before you have made your will clear to me.
Is any other wisdom needed here
Than following your orders to the letter?
— You place this paper in my hands for me
To forward with despatch to execution?

ELIZABETH: Be guided by your *own* discretion—

DAVISON: Not
By mine! O God forbid! Obedience
Is my entire discretion. Nothing should   3290
Be left here for your servant to decide.
A tiny error might mean regicide,
A monstrous and immeasurable disaster.
Allow me in so great a matter to
Be your blind instrument without a will.
Declare your meaning in clear words: What is
To be done with this fatal order now?

ELIZABETH: — Its name makes that quite plain.

DAVISON: Then you wish it to be fulfilled at once?

ELIZABETH *(hesitating)*:
I did not *say* that, and I shudder at   3300
The thought.

DAVISON: You wish me to hold on to it?

ELIZABETH *(quickly)*:
O, at your peril! You will answer for
The consequences!

DAVISON: I? My God! —Speak, Queen!
  What is your wish?
ELIZABETH (*impatiently*):   I wish no further mention
  Be made of this unhappy subject, I
  Wish to have done with it for evermore.
DAVISON: It will cost you a single word. O tell me,
  Decide what is to be done with this paper!
ELIZABETH: I told you. Do not bother me again.
DAVISON: You say you told me? You have told me nothing.   3310
  O, may it please my Queen to recollect.
ELIZABETH (*stamping her foot*):
  This is intolerable!
DAVISON: I beg you to have patience
  With me! I have been only a few months
  In office here. I do not know the language
  Of courts and monarchs.—I grew up amid
  Plain ways and simple customs. Therefore please
  Have patience with your servant! Do not be
  Regretful for a word that will instruct me
  And set me clear as to my duty—
          (*He approaches her in a posture of supplica-
          tion; she turns her back to him. He stands in
          despair, then says in a decisive tone*):
  Take back this paper! Take it back again!   3320
  It turns to burning fire between my hands.
  Do not choose me to serve you in so fearful
  A business.
ELIZABETH: Do the duty of your office!
                    (*Exit.*)
DAVISON: She goes. She leaves me helpless and in doubt
  With this dread document.—What shall I do?
  Am I to keep it? Or deliver it?
                    (*Enter Burleigh.*)
  O good, good that you come, my Lord! You were
  The person who appointed me to office.
  Release me from it now! I undertook it,
  Unconscious of what it entailed. Let me   3330

Return to the obscurity where you
Once found me, I do not belong in this post—

BURLEIGH: What is the matter, Sir? Compose yourself.
Where is the warrant? The Queen summoned you.

DAVISON: She left me in great anger. O advise me!
Help me! Save me from this anguished hell
Of doubt! Here is the warrant—it is signed.

BURLEIGH (hastily):
It is? Then give it here!

DAVISON: I must not.

BURLEIGH: What?

DAVISON: She has not made her wishes plain to me—

BURLEIGH: Not plain! She signed it. Let me have it then.   3340

DAVISON: I am supposed to execute it—yet
Not execute it—God! What shall I do?

BURLEIGH (pressing more urgently):
You execute it right away. So let
Me have it. You are lost if you delay.

DAVISON: I will be lost if I am over-hasty.

BURLEIGH: You are a fool, and mad! Give it to me!
          (He snatches the document from him and
          hurries off with it.)

DAVISON (hurrying after him):
What are you doing? Stop! You'll ruin me!   [3347]

ACT V

SCENE 1

*The scene is the same room as in Act I. [Early morning of the
third day.]*
*Jane Kennedy, dressed in deep mourning, her eyes red from
weeping, and with great but silent sorrow, is busy sealing packages
and letters. Grief frequently interrupts her in her task, and intermittently she is seen praying silently.*
*Enter Paulet and Drury, likewise in black garments. They are
followed by numerous servants carrying gold and silver vessels,
mirrors, paintings, and other valuables, with which they fill up
the rear of the room. Paulet hands the nurse a jewel-box together
with a paper, and indicates to her by gestures that it contains an
itemization of the things he has brought. At the sight of these
luxuries the nurse's grief is renewed. She sinks into profound
sorrow, while the former silently withdraw again.*
Enter Melvil.

KENNEDY (*utters a cry as she catches sight of him*):
  Melvil! You! I see you once again!
MELVIL: Yes, loyal Kennedy, we meet again.
KENNEDY: And after such a long, sad separation!   3350
MELVIL: This is a sad, unhappy meeting, too!
KENNEDY: O Lord, then you have come—
MELVIL: To bid my Queen
  A last farewell for all eternity.
KENNEDY: At last, now, on the morning of her death
  She is allowed the long-missed presence of
  Her people.—O dear Sir, I will not ask
  How things have fared with you, nor will I name
  The grievous things that we have suffered here
  Since you were wrested from among our midst.

III

Ah, some day there will come the hour for that!   3360
O Melvil! Melvil! Why must we have lived
To see the dawning of this day!

MELVIL: Let us
Not make each other weak! As long as I
Have life within me, I shall weep; no smile
Shall ever cheer these cheeks of mine again,
Nor shall I ever lay aside this garment
Of night. I shall mourn everlastingly!
But for today I shall be steadfast.—Promise
Me too, to moderate your grief as well.—
If all the others inconsolably   3370
Give way to their despair, let *us* proceed
Before her with a nobly calm composure
And be her staff along this path to death.

KENNEDY: Melvil, you are mistaken if you think
The Queen has any need of our assistance
In order to walk steadily to death!
She sets us the example of a noble
Composure. Have no fear, Sir. Mary Stuart
Will perish as a Queen and heroine.

MELVIL: Did she receive the death announcement with   3380
Composure? They say she was not forewarned.

KENNEDY: No, she was not. But other terrors did
Distress my Lady. Mary did not tremble
At death but at her would-be liberator.
—We had been promised freedom. Mortimer
Vowed he would take us out of here last night,
And thus between her hope and fear, in doubt
If she should trust her princely person and
Her honor to that reckless youth, the Queen
Had waited for the coming of the morning.   3390
—Then came a tumult in the castle; pounding
Struck fright into our ears, and hammer blows.
We thought we heard the liberators coming,
Hope beckoned, and the sweet impulse of life
Involuntarily and strongly stirred—

And then the door was opened—and it was
Lord Paulet to announce—that—carpenters
Were putting up the scaffold at our feet.
            (She turns aside, seized by violent grief.)
MELVIL: Just God! O tell me, how did Mary bear
    The revelation of that dreadful change?   3400
KENNEDY *(after a pause during which she has somewhat regained
    her composure)*:
    One does not gradually let go of life.
    All of a sudden, swiftly, instantly
    The change must be made from the temporal
    To the eternal. To my Lady God vouchsafed
    The power at that moment to reject
    The hopes of earth with a decisive soul
    And to grasp Heaven with abundant faith.
    No sign of fear, no word of lamentation
    Dishonored my Queen then.—And not until
    She heard about Lord Lester's treachery,   3410
    About the wretched fate of that esteemed
    Young man who sacrificed his life for her,
    And saw that old knight's deep distress for whom
    The final hope had died because of her,
    Then her tears flowed; it was not her own fate, however,
    That forced them from her, but the grief of strangers.
MELVIL: Where is she now? Can you take me to her?
KENNEDY: She passed the night in vigil and in prayer,
    Wrote letters of farewell to cherished friends,
    And drew up her last will in her own hand.   3420
    This last sleep will refresh her.
MELVIL: Who is with her?
KENNEDY: Burgoyn, her house physician, and her women.
            (Enter Margaret Kurl.)
    What word now, Mistress? Has the Lady wakened?
KURL *(drying her tears)*:
    She is already dressed—and asks for you.
KENNEDY: I'll come directly.
            (to Melvil who starts to accompany her)

Do not follow me
Till I prepare the Lady for your coming.
                    (She goes inside.)

KURL: Melvil! Our old steward!

MELVIL: It is I.

KURL: O, this house needs no steward any more!
— Melvil, you come from London; can you tell   3430
Me anything about my husband?

MELVIL: He will be set at liberty, they say,
As soon—

KURL: As soon as the Queen is no more!
O, the detestable, the shameless traitor!
He is this dear Lady's murderer.
They say it was his testimony that
Condemned her.

MELVIL: So it was.

KURL: O, may his soul
Be damned to hell! He gave false testimony—

MELVIL: My Lady Kurl! Consider what you say!

KURL: I will swear to it at the bar of justice,   3440
I will repeat it to his very face,
I will proclaim it to the entire world
That she dies innocent—

MELVIL: God grant she may!
                    (Enter Burgoyn followed by
                    Jane Kennedy.)

BURGOYN *(catching sight of Melvil)*:
O Melvil!

MELVIL *(embracing him)*:
         Burgoyn!

BURGOYN *(to Margaret Kurl)*:   Go prepare a cup of wine
For our dear Lady, Mistress Kurl. And hurry!
                    (Exit Kurl.)

MELVIL: Why, is the Queen not well?

BURGOYN: She feels quite strong.
She is deceived by her heroic spirit
And thinks that she requires no sustenance.

A heavy struggle still awaits her, and
Her enemies shall not boast that her cheeks   3450
Grew pale before the fear of death, not even
If nature does succumb out of sheer weakness.

MELVIL (*to the nurse, who has come back in*):
Will she see me?

KENNEDY: She will be here directly.
—You seem to look about with wonderment
And your eyes ask me what are all these things
Of splendor doing in this place of death.
—O Sir, we suffered want while we still lived,
But now with death this superfluity returns.

> (*Enter two other of Mary's ladies-in-waiting,*
> *likewise dressed in mourning. At sight of Melvil*
> *they burst into loud weeping.*)

MELVIL: O, what a sight is this! And what a meeting!
Gertrude, Rosamund!

SECOND LADY: She sent us out.   3460
She wishes to communicate alone
With God this one last time.

> (*Enter two more female servants, dressed in*
> *mourning like the former ones. They express*
> *their grief in mute gestures.*
>
> *Enter Margaret Kurl. She is carrying a cup*
> *with wine which she sets on the table; pale and*
> *trembling she steadies herself at a chair.*)

MELVIL: What is the matter? What affrights you so?

KURL: O God!

BURGOYN: What is the matter?

KURL: What I saw!

MELVIL: Compose yourself, and tell us what it was.

KURL: As I was carrying this cup of wine
   Just now up the great stair that leads down to
   The lower hall, the door was opened—I
   Glanced in—I saw—My God!

MELVIL: What did you see?

KURL: I saw the walls all draped in black, and from   3470

The floor a mighty scaffold rose, hung with
Black cloth, and in the middle a black block,
A cushion and a gleaming whetted ax
Laid there beside it.—And the hall was full
Of people thronging round that fatal platform
With lust of blood hot in their eyes, awaiting
The sacrifice.

THE LADIES-IN-WAITING: O God, have mercy on our Lady!

MELVIL: Be calm. She comes.

> (*Enter Mary. She is magnificently dressed in
> white; upon a chain of little beads an Agnus Dei
> hangs at her throat; a rosary is suspended from
> her girdle; she has a crucifix in her hand and a
> diadem in her hair, and her great black veil is
> thrown back. At her entrance, those present step
> back on both sides and give expression to the
> most vehement grief. Melvil, with an involun-
> tary movement, has fallen to his knees.*)

MARY (*surveying the whole circle with serene dignity*):
Why are you weeping? Why are you lamenting?   3480
You should be glad with me because my goal
Of grief is reached at last, my fetters fall,
My prison opens, and my joyous soul
On angel wings soars up to everlasting
Liberty. When I was in the power
Of my haughty enemy, enduring
Indignities unseemly for a great
Free Queen, then was the time to weep for me!
—Benignly, healingly, Death comes to meet me,
My earnest friend. And he bedecks my shame   3490
With his black wings.—A human being is
Ennobled by his last, his lowest fate.
I feel the crown upon my head again
And in my noble soul a worthy pride.

> (*as she advances a few steps forward*)

What? Melvil here?—No kneeling, noble Sir!
Arise! You have come here to witness your

Queen's triumph, not her death. Such happiness
Has fallen to my lot as I had never
Hoped for, because report of me is not
In the hands of my enemy entirely,   3500
But one friend, a professor of my faith,
Shall stand as witness to my hour of death.
—Now tell me, noble Sir, how have you fared
In this ungracious, hostile country since
The time when you were wrested from my side?
Concern for you has often grieved my heart.
MELVIL: No want afflicted me except my sorrow
For your sake, and my powerlessness to serve you.
MARY: And what of Didier, my old chamberlain?
O, but that faithful man must long be sleeping   3510
Eternal sleep, for he was far in age.
MELVIL: God has not granted him that mercy. He
Is still alive to bury your fair youth.
MARY: O, if before my death the happiness
Had fallen to me to embrace just one
Beloved head of my dear relatives!
But I must perish in the midst of strangers
And see no tears but yours shed for me here.
—Melvil, my last wishes for my kinsmen.
I shall lay to your true heart's charge: —I now   3520
Bless the Most Christian King, my brother-in-law,
And all the royal house of France;—I bless
The Cardinal of Guise, my holy uncle,
And Henry, Duke of Guise, my noble cousin.
I also bless the Pope, the sacred Vicar
Of Christ, who will return his blessing to me,
And that Most Catholic King who nobly offered to
Become my rescuer and my avenger.—
They all are cited in my will, and they
Will not set slight store by the gifts of my   3530
Affection, be those gifts however poor.
                    (turning to her servants)
You I have recommended to my royal

Brother of France; he will look after you
And find another fatherland for you.
And if you prize my last request at all,
Do not remain in England for the Briton
To glut his haughty heart on your misfortune
And see *those* in the dust who once served *me*.
Now swear to me upon the image of
The Crucified that you will leave this wretched   3540
Country just as soon as I am dead.

MELVIL (*touches the crucifix*):
I swear it in the name of all here present.

MARY: Whatever I, impoverished and despoiled, still own
And over which they grant me disposition,
I have divided up among you, and
I trust that they will honor my last will.
What I now wear upon my path to death
Shall be yours also.—Grant me once again
My earthly splendor on my way to heaven.
                    (*to the young women*)
To you, my Alix, Gertrude, Rosamund,   3550
I give my pearls and all my dresses, for
Your youth still takes delight in fine adornment.
You, Margaret, have the highest claim
Upon my generosity because
I leave you most unhappy of them all.
That I do not avenge your husband's guilt
On you, my will will testify.—But you,
My faithful Jane, find no charm in the value
Of gold or in the worth of splendid jewels;
Your jewel is the memory of me.   3560
Take, then, this cloth. I worked it with my own
Hand for you in the hours of my sorrow,
And wove my burning tears into its pattern.
With this cloth you will bind my eyes for me
When we shall come to that.—That final service
I wish to have performed by my own Jane.

KENNEDY: O Melvil, I can't bear it!

MARY: Come now all
Of you, come and receive my last farewell.
> *(She holds out her hands; one after another*
> *falls at her feet and kisses her extended hands*
> *amid intense weeping.)*

Farewell now, Margaret—Alix, too, farewell—
Thanks, Burgoyn, for your loyal services—   3570
Your lips burn hot, my Gertrude—I have been
Much hated, but I have been much loved also.
O, may a noble husband make my Gertrude
Happy, for this fervent heart needs love.—
Bertha, you have chosen what is best,
You wish to be the unstained bride of Heaven.
O, hasten to fulfill that vow! The goods
Of this earth are deceptive, as you learn
From the example of your Queen! —No more!
Farewell! Farewell! For all of time, farewell!   3580
> *(She turns quickly away from them. All*
> *except Melvil withdraw.)*

I have set all things temporal in order
And hope to leave this world the debtor of
No human being.—But there is one thing
Yet, Melvil, which prevents my burdened soul
From rising up with freedom and with joy.

MELVIL: Disclose it to me and relieve your heart,
Confide your sorrow to your loyal friend.

MARY: I stand at the brink of eternity;
Soon I shall step before the Judge Supreme,
And still I have not made my peace with God.   3590
A priest of my own Church is still denied me,
And I disdain to take the Sacrament's
Angelic food from false priests' hands. I want
To die within the Faith of my own Church,
For it alone can make one blessed.

MELVIL: Set
Your heart at rest. The fervent pious wish
Without the deed will be enough for Heaven.

The tyrant's might can only bind the hands,
The heart's devotion rises free to God.
The word is dead, belief brings us to life.   3600
MARY: The heart unaided, Melvil, cannot be
Sufficient; faith requires an earthly sign
In order to perceive the High Divine.
For that, God took the form of man and closed
Invisible, celestial gifts in mystic
Fashion in the body visible.
—It is the Church, the lofty, holy Church
That builds the ladder for us up to heaven;
Its name: the universal Catholic Church,
For only by the faith of all is Faith   3610
Confirmed. Where thousands worship and adore,
There fervor turns to flame, and there the wingèd
Spirit soars aloft to all the heavens.
—Ah, happy they, whom joyous prayer in common
Assembles in the temple of the Lord!
The altar is adorned, the candles shine,
The bell is sounded, incense is poured forth,
The Bishop stands in stainless vestments clad,
He takes the chalice, blesses it, proclaims
The miracle of transsubstantiation,   3620
And there before the present God the people
Sink down in the conviction of their faith.—
Alas, I am excluded, I alone,
No sign from Heaven penetrates my prison.
MELVIL: Oh, but one does! And it is close at hand.
Trust the Omnipotent.—The withered staff
Can put forth branches in the hand of faith.
And he who struck the water from the rock
Can set an altar for you in your prison,
He can transform *this* chalice and this earthly   3630
Refreshment speedily into divine ones.
                    (*He picks up the cup which stands*
                         on the table.)
MARY: Melvil! Do I grasp your meaning? Yes!

I do! There is no priest here, and no church,
No Eucharist. — But the Redeemer says:
Where two of ye are gathered in *my* name,
I shall be present there among them also.
What consecrates a priest to be the Lord's
Own mouth? A pure heart and a sinless life.
— Thus *you* for me are, though unconsecrated,
A priest, God's messenger, who brings me peace.   3640
To you I now will make my last confession,
And your lips shall pronounce my absolution.

MELVIL: If you feel such a mighty impulse in
Your heart, my Queen, then to your comfort know
That God can work a miracle as well.
You say that there is no priest here, no church,
No body of the Lord? — You are mistaken.
There is a priest here, and God is here present.
        (At these words he uncovers his head; at the
            same time he shows her a Host in a gold case.)
— I am a priest. To hear your last confession,
And to pronounce peace over you upon   3650
Your path to death, I have myself received
The seven holy orders on my head,
And from the Holy Father, who himself
Pronounced the consecration, I bring you
This Host.

MARY: O, must such happiness of heaven
Befall me at the threshold of my death!
As an immortal comes on golden clouds
Descending, as once the Apostle was
Led by an angel out of prison bonds,
No bars preventing him, no keeper's sword,   3660
And walking mightily through bolted doors
Until he stood there radiant in the dungeon,
Just so am I surprised by Heaven's herald
Where every earthly rescuer had failed me!
— And you, *my* servant once, are now the servant
Of Most High God, — you are His holy mouth!

As your knee formerly was bent to *me*,
So I now lie before you in the dust.
    (She falls on her knees before him.)
MELVIL *(as he makes the Sign of the Cross over her)*:
  In the name of the Father, of the Son,
  And of the Spirit! Mary, Queen! Have you   3670
  Searched in your heart, and do you swear and promise
  To speak the truth before the God of Truth?
MARY: My heart is open here to you and Him.
MELVIL: Of what sin does your conscience call you guilty
  Since you were reconciled last time to God?
MARY: My heart was filled with jealous hatred, and
  Thoughts of revenge have raged within my bosom.
  I, as a sinner, hoped for God's forgiveness
  While I could not forgive my enemy.
MELVIL: Do you repent this sin, and is it your   3680
  Sincere resolve to leave this world atoned?
MARY: As truly as I hope, may God forgive me.
MELVIL: What other sin does your heart find upon you?
MARY: Ah, not through *hate* alone, through sinful love
  I have still more offended Highest God.
  My foolish heart felt drawn in its affection
  To one who broke his faith in vile deception.
MELVIL: Do you repent that sin, and has your heart
  Turned from the foolish idol back to God?
MARY: It was the hardest battle I have won,   3690
  But that last earthly bond is now undone.
MELVIL: What further guilt lies still upon your conscience?
MARY: Alas, an early blood-guilt, which I had
  Long since confessed, returns in frightening power
  Now in the reckoning of this final hour
  And blackly washes toward the gates of heaven.
  I caused the King, my husband, to be murdered
  And gave my heart and hand to the seducer.
  I did harsh penance for it by church laws,
  Yet in my soul the conscience-worm still gnaws.   3700
MELVIL: Does your heart still complain of other sin

Which you have not confessed or yet atoned for?

MARY: You now know all that weighs upon my heart.

MELVIL: Think of your nearness to Omniscient God!
Think of the punishments which Holy Church
Imposes for an incomplete confession.
That is a sin unto eternal death,
For it offends against His holy spirit.

MARY: Eternal Mercy grant me triumph then
In this last struggle, as I withhold nothing when   3710
I speak to you.

MELVIL: What? Will you hide from God
The very crime for which mankind condemns you?
You tell me nothing of your bloody share
In Parry's and in Babington's high treason?
For that deed you die temporal death; will you
Die everlasting death for it as well?

MARY: For God's world I am ready. Be it known:
Before the minute-hand in its progression
Moves, I shall stand before my Judge's throne;
But I repeat that I have finished my confession.   3720

MELVIL: Weigh this with care. The heart is a deceiver.
Perhaps with cunning ambiguity
You have got round the *word* that makes you guilty,
Though the *intention* shared in the misdeed.
Be sure that trickery will not deceive
The eye of flame that looks into the heart!

MARY: I did appeal to all the potentates
To set me free from my unworthy bonds,
But never by intention or by deed
Did I plot harm to my opponent's life!   3730

MELVIL: Your secretaries bore false witness, then?

MARY: As I said, so it is. May God be judge
Of what they testified!

MELVIL: You mount the scaffold
In the assurance of your innocence?

MARY: God deems me worthy to atone for youthful grievous
Blood-guilt by a death unmerited.

MELVIL *(makes the Sign of the Cross over her)*:
  Go, then, and by your death atone for it!
  Fall as assenting victim at the altar!
  Blood can atone for what blood once transgressed.
  Only woman's frailty erred in you,   3740
  The weaknesses of flesh will not pursue
  The blessed soul to its transfigured rest.
  But I, by virtue of the power which
  Is vested in me to remit and bind, proclaim
  Remission of your sins in God's high name.
  According to your faith, so be it with you.
                    (He gives her the Host.)
  Receive the body, for you it was slain.
            *(He takes the chalice which is standing on the
            table, consecrates it with silent prayer, and then
            hands it to her. She hesitates to take it and
            pushes it back with her hand.)*
  Receive the blood, for you it was poured forth.
  Receive, I say; the Pope grants you this favor.
  At death you are to exercise this highest,   3750
  This priestly function of the kings of old.
                    (She receives the chalice.)
  As you now in your earthly body are
  Bound mystically together with your God,
  So, yonder in His kingdom of pure joy,
  Where there is no more sin and no more weeping,
  You will, as a transfigured angel,
  Be joined with God in His eternal keeping.
            *(He sets the chalice down. At a noise that is
            heard, he covers his head and goes to the door.
            Mary remains on her knees in silent reverence.)*
  (coming back)
  You still have one hard fight to undergo.
  Do you feel strong enough to conquer any
  Impulse now of bitterness and hatred?   3760
MARY: I do not fear relapse. My hate and love
  Together I have sacrificed to God.

MELVIL: Prepare yourself, then, to receive the Lords
  Of Lester and of Burleigh. They are here.

> *(Enter Burleigh; also Leicester and Paulet.*
> *Leicester remains standing way off to one side*
> *without raising his eyes. Burleigh, who observes*
> *his self-possession, steps between him and the*
> *Queen.)*

BURLEIGH: I have come, Lady Stuart, to receive
  Your last commands.

MARY: I thank you, noble Lord.

BURLEIGH: It is the will of my great Queen that nothing
  Within the bounds of reason be denied you.

MARY: My will contains the list of my last wishes.
  I have put it into Lord Paulet's hands   3770
  And ask that it be followed faithfully.

PAULET: Rely upon it.

MARY: I ask that all my servants be released
  To go unharmed to Scotland or to France,
  Wherever they themselves wish and desire.

BURLEIGH: It shall be as you wish.

MARY: And since my corpse
  Is not to rest in consecrated ground,
  Permit this faithful servant here to carry
  My heart to France and to my family.
  —Ah, it was always there!

BURLEIGH: It shall be done.   3780
  Have you a further—

MARY: To the Queen of England
  Take my sisterly salute.—Tell her
  That I forgive her for my death with all
  My heart, and that I beg her pardon for
  My violence of yesterday.—May God
  Protect her and grant her a happy reign!

BURLEIGH: And have you still not chosen better counsel?
  You still disdain to have the Dean's assistance?

MARY: I have been reconciled to God.—Lord Paulet!
  I have unwittingly caused you much grief,   3790

Deprived you of the prop of your old age—
O, let me hope you won't remember me
With hatred—

PAULET *(gives her his hand):*
May God be with you, Lady. Go in peace.

> *(Enter Jane Kennedy and the Queen's other
> women with expressions of horror. They are
> followed by the Sheriff with a white staff in his
> hand; behind him, through the opened door, are
> seen armed men.)*

MARY: What is the matter, Jane?—Yes, it is time.
Here comes the Sheriff to lead us to death.
It is the time to part. Farewell! Farewell!

> *(Her women cling to her with violent grief.*
> *To Melvil):*

You, worthy Sir, and you, my faithful Jane,
Shall now accompany me on this last walk.
My Lord, do not deny me this last kindness.

BURLEIGH: I do not have authority for that.   3800

MARY: What, Sir? You would refuse me that small wish?
Have some consideration for my sex!
Who is to do these final services
For me? It cannot be my sister's will
To see offense done to my sex through me
And that rude hands of men should touch me now!

BURLEIGH: No woman is permitted to ascend
The scaffold steps with you.—Their cries and wailing—

MARY: She shall not wail! I shall be guarantee
For my Jane's self-possession and calm spirit.   3810
Be kind, my Lord! Do not divide me in
My death from my true nurse and foster-mother!
She bore me into life upon her arms,
Let her lead me with gentle hand to death.

PAULET *(to Burleigh):*
Let it be done.

BURLEIGH: So be it.

MARY: I have nothing

More in this world.—

> (*She takes the crucifix and
> kisses it.*)

My Saviour! My Redeemer!
As on the Cross thou didst spread wide Thy arms
Of mercy, spread them to receive me now.

> (*She turns to go. At this moment her eye
> encounters the Earl of Leicester who had invol-
> untarily started up at her departure and looked
> at her.—Mary trembles to behold him, her knees
> falter, she is on the verge of collapse; where-
> upon the Earl of Leicester seizes her and takes
> her into his arms. She looks at him solemnly for
> a time in silence; he cannot bear her glance.
> Finally she speaks.*)

You keep your word, Lord Earl of Lester.—You
Once promised me your arm to lead me from   3820
This prison, and you lend it to me now.

> (*He stands as though annihilated.
> She goes on speaking in a mild tone.*)

Yes, Lester, and not merely
My freedom did I wish to owe to you.
You were supposed to make my freedom *precious;*
At your hand, and made happy by your love,
I wanted to rejoice in my new life.
And now, when I am on the path departing
From this world to become a blessed spirit
Whom no affection of this earth can tempt,
Now, Lester, now, without the blush of shame   3830
I may confess to you my conquered weakness.—
Farewell, and if you can, live happily.
It was your privilege to woo two Queens:
You have disdained a tender loving heart,
Betrayed it so that you could win a proud one.
Go kneel before Elizabeth! May your
Reward not prove a punishment in store!

Farewell!—On earth I now have nothing more!
> *(She walks out, the Sheriff preceding her, her*
> *nurse at her side. Burleigh and Paulet follow;*
> *the others, wailing, watch her out of sight, then*
> *they withdraw through the other two doors.)*

LEICESTER *(remaining behind alone):*

And I am still alive! I still endure
Existence! Will this roof not fall on me!   3840
Will no abyss cleave open to consume
The wretchedest of creatures! *What* have I
Lost here! And what a pearl I cast away!
What happiness of heaven I have squandered!
—She goes, already a transfigured spirit,
And leaves *me* to the lost hope of the damned.
—But where is that resolve with which I came,
To stifle my heart's voice relentlessly?
To watch the falling of her head unflinchingly?
Does sight of her revive my withered shame?   3850
—Must she in death snare me in love's captivity?
It will henceforth be an ill-suited aim,
You wretch, for any pity to be shown;
Love's happiness lies now beyond your claim;
Let armor made of bronze be made to frame
Your breast, and let your brow be made of stone.
Lest the prize of your shameful deed be lost,
You must see it fulfilled at any cost.
Be silent, Pity! Turn to stone, my eye:
I will be witness, I will see her die.   3860
> *(He walks with determined step toward the*
> *door through which Mary has passed, but stops*
> *midway in his course.)*

In vain! In vain! Hell's anguish seizes me!
I cannot, cannot force myself to see
The ghastly sight, I cannot watch her die—
Hark! What was that?—They are downstairs already—
The dreadful business is now under way
Beneath my feet—I hear their voices—Out!

Out of this house of horror and of death!
> (*He starts to flee by another door but finds it
> locked and reels back.*)

Has some god chained me to this floor? Must I
Hear what I shudder to behold? That is
The Dean's voice now—He is exhorting her—   3870
—She interrupts him—Hark!—She prays aloud—
With a firm voice—Now silence—total silence!
I only hear the women sobbing now—
They are undressing her—They shove the stool up—
She kneels upon the cushion—lays her head—

> (*After he has spoken these last words with
> mounting anguish and stopped for a time, he is
> seen to shudder suddenly with a convulsive
> motion and collapse fainting. Simultaneously
> the muffled sound of voices rises from below and
> continues for a long time.*)

SCENE 2

The Queen's apartments, as in Act IV, Scene 2.
*Elizabeth emerges from a side door; her gait and gestures express
the most intense uneasiness.*

ELIZABETH: No one here yet—No news yet—Will it never
Be evening? Does the sun stand firmly placed
In its celestial course?—Am I to go
On waiting on my rack of expectation!
—Has it been done? Or has it *not*?—I shudder   3880
In either case, yet do not dare inquire!
Lord Lester does not come, nor Burleigh either,
Whom I had named to carry out the sentence.
If they are gone from London—then it has
Been done. The arrow has been shot, it flies,
It strikes, it has already struck. Not for
My kingdom can I hold it back.—Who's there?
> (*Enter a Page.*)

You have come back alone—Where are the Lords?
THE PAGE: My Lord of Lester and the High Treasurer—
ELIZABETH *(in the utmost suspense):*
    Where are they?
THE PAGE: They are not in London.
ELIZABETH: No?   3890
    Then where are they?
THE PAGE: No one was able to inform me.
    Before the break of day both of the Lords
    Had left the city secretly and in
    Great haste.
ELIZABETH *(blurting out):* I am the Queen of England, then!
                    *(pacing back and forth in extreme
                            agitation)*
    Go, call—No, better stay here—She is dead.
    Now I have room at last upon this earth.
    —Why am I trembling? Why does terror seize me?
    The grave will cover up my fear, and who
    Can say I did it? I shall never lack
    For tears to shed for the dead woman's sake!   3900
                    (to the Page)
    Are you still here?—Send instantly and have
    My secretary Davison come here.
    Send for the Earl of Shrewsbury.—Ah, here
    He is!
                    (Exit the Page.)
                    (Enter the Earl of Shrewsbury.)
    Welcome, noble Lord! What do you bring?
    It cannot be a trifling matter that
    Directs your step this way so late.
SHREWSBURY: Great Queen,
    My anxious heart, concerned about your fame,
    Forced me today to journey to the Tower,
    Where Mary's secretaries, Kurl and Nau,
    Are kept in prison; for I wished to test   3910
    Once more the truth of what they had deposed.
    Dismayed, embarrassed, the Lieutenant of

The Tower refused to show the prisoners.
By threats alone I managed to get entry.
O Heaven, what a sight I there beheld!
With hair dishevelled, with the eyes of madness,
Like one tormented by the Furies, lay
The Scotsman Kurl upon his cot.—The wretch
Had barely recognized me when he threw
Himself down at my feet, and shrieking, clutched   3920
My knees; in desperation like a worm
That writhed before me—he kept begging me
And conjuring me to tell him his Queen's fate.
For a report that she had been condemned to death
Had got in through the Tower's crevices.
When I confirmed the rumor as the truth
And added that it was *his* testimony
That caused her death, he jumped up frantically,
Attacked his fellow-prisoner, pulled him
Down to the floor with madman's giant-strength   3930
And tried to strangle him. We barely wrenched
The wretched creature from his frenzied hands.
And then he turned his rage against himself
And beat his breast with frenzied fists, and cursed
Himself and his companion to all devils.
He said he gave false evidence; the letters
To Babington that he called genuine,
Were false; he had put down quite different words
From what the Queen was dictating to him;
The rascal Nau had led him on to do it.   3940
Then he ran to the window, threw it open
By raging force, and screamed down to the streets
For everybody to come up and hear
That he was Mary's secretary and
The scoundrel who had falsely called her guilty,
That he was cursed, that he had borne false witness.
ELIZABETH: You said yourself that he was not in his
  Right mind. The words of raving lunatics
  Prove nothing.

SHREWSBURY: But this madness of itself
   Proves all the more. O Queen, let me entreat   3950
   You to do nothing in excessive haste.
   Command them to investigate anew!
ELIZABETH: I shall do so—because you wish it, Sir,
   Though not because I think my Peers have moved
   With too great haste to judgment in this matter.
   But for your peace of mind let them reopen
   The trial.—Fortunately there is still
   Time left. Not so much as the shadow of
   A doubt shall rest upon our royal honor.
               (Enter Davison.)
   The warrant, Sir, which I entrusted to   3960
   Your hands—where is it?
DAVISON *(in the utmost astonishment):*
                  Warrant?
ELIZABETH: Which I gave
   You yesterday to keep—
DAVISON: Gave me to keep!
ELIZABETH: The people importuned me so to sign it
   That I was forced to do their will, and did so,
   Under duress I did so, and then gave it
   To you to keep. I wanted to gain time.
   Oh, you know what I said! —Well, let me have it!
SHREWSBURY: Do, worthy Sir! Things now stand otherwise,
   We must reopen the investigation.
DAVISON: Reopen?—Everlasting Mercy!
ELIZABETH: Do   3970
   Not take so long. Where is the document?
DAVISON *(in despair):*
   I am undone, I am a dead man!
ELIZABETH *(interrupting quickly):*   Sir,
   Do not lead me to think that—
DAVISON: I am lost!
   I do not have it.
ELIZABETH: What? What?
SHREWSBURY: God in heaven!

DAVISON: It is in Burleigh's hands—since yesterday.

ELIZABETH: Unhappy man! Then you did not obey me?
Did I not strictly order you to keep it?

DAVISON: Oh no, you gave me no such order, Queen.

ELIZABETH: Will you call me a liar, wretch? When did
I bid you give the document to Burleigh?   3980

DAVISON: Not in so many words—but—

ELIZABETH: Worthless creature!
Do you presume to read interpretations
Into my words? to put your own blood-thirsty
Construction on them?—Woe to you if any
Misfortune has come of your arbitrary
Action! You'll pay me for it with your life.
—Lord Earl of Shrewsbury, you see how they
Misuse my name.

SHREWSBURY: I do see—O my God!

ELIZABETH: What did you say?

SHREWSBURY: If this Squire has presumed
To undertake this step at his own peril,   3990
If he has acted here without your knowledge,
He must be summoned up before the judgment
Seat of the Peers, because he has delivered
Your name to the abhorrence of all ages.

                    (Enter Burleigh.)

BURLEIGH (bending on one knee before the Queen):
Long live my royal Lady, and may all
This island's enemies so perish as
This Stuart perished!

                    (Shrewsbury covers his face.
                    Davison wrings his hands in despair.)

ELIZABETH: Tell me now, my Lord!
Did you receive this execution order
From me?

BURLEIGH: Why, no, my Sovereign. I received it
From Davison.

ELIZABETH: Did Davison deliver   4000
It to you in my name?

BURLEIGH: No, he did not.
ELIZABETH: But you went on in haste to execute it
    Without first ascertaining my intention?
    The sentence was a just one, and the world
    Can not blame us. But you improperly
    Forestalled our clemency of heart—and for
    This action you are banished from our sight!
                    (to Davison)
    A sentence more severe shall fall on you
    For overstepping your authority
    And for abusing a most sacred trust.   4010
    Let him be taken to the Tower. I ask
    That he be charged with penalty of death.
    —My noble Talbot! You alone among
    My counsellors have I found to be just,
    And you shall henceforth be my guide, my friend—
SHREWSBURY: O do not banish your most loyal friends,
    Do not throw them in prison, who have acted
    On your behalf and now keep silent for you.
    —But as for me, great Queen, permit me to
    Give back into your hands the seal with which   4020
    You have entrusted me for these twelve years.
ELIZABETH *(taken aback):*
    No, Shrewsbury! You will not leave me now,
    Not now—
SHREWSBURY: Forgive me, but I am too old,
    And this hand is too stiff and straight to set
    The seal upon your newer policies.
ELIZABETH: Can it be that the man who saved my life
    Would leave me now?
SHREWSBURY: It was a small thing that
    I did.—I was not able to preserve
    Your better part. Live and reign happily!
    Your enemy is dead. From now on you   4030
    Have nothing more to fear, no further scruples.
                    (Exit.)
                (Enter the Earl of Kent.)

ELIZABETH *(to Kent)*:
    Send in the Earl of Lester.
KENT: The Lord begs
    To be excused, he has set sail for France.   [4033]
            (She controls herself and stands with quiet
        self-possession.
                The curtain falls.)

THE MAID
OF ORLEANS

INTRODUCTION

No sooner was the manuscript of *Mary Stuart* completed in June of 1800 than Schiller set to work without delay on a new drama, *The Maid of Orleans* (Die Jungfrau von Orleans). The project advanced without hindrance and by April 16, 1801 it was finished. Upon the work in progress as upon the finished product Goethe bestowed warm praise. The première in Leipzig on September 18 was acclaimed a great success by the public, and subsequent productions in various cities of Germany were no less successful. The printed text, issued on October 12, was financially well rewarded by the publisher, enthusiastically purchased, and widely read. The revised version of 1805 was subjected to a minimum of changes by the author in that legacy of plays which Schiller supervised in the final months of his life. For at least two generations *The Maid of Orleans* was admired as a major creation by Germany's greatest dramatist.

Twentieth-century opinion is far less kind. In fact, the modern reader is more likely to feel hostile toward this play. Nor will it suffice, in explanation of this fact, merely to say that tastes change. Tastes do indeed change, and supreme works of art may pass through eras of antipathy. But with still further changes in the climate of aesthetic opinion supreme works of art unfailingly re-emerge to claim the allegiance of good minds. Dante survived the era of Voltaire's disapprobation; the poems of "Ossian," on the other hand, show no signs of regaining their one-time magic. *The Maid of Orleans,* we venture to assert, was, in its totality, admirable only to a certain period, which may be broadly defined as the Romantic Period. Its partial excellence will not redeem the whole. Authentic genius is stamped on more than one page of this text, but the complete drama must be termed an interesting failure.

The reasons for this interesting failure are by no means simple.

First, it may justly be objected that the historical Joan of Arc was a personage much more interesting, more awesomely sublime indeed, than Schiller's heroine. To one who has scrutinized the record of the actual Maid's life and death, the German poet's drama will seem a misrepresentation verging on the absurd, if not on the blasphemous. Yet, to that same modern reader it will be quite as shocking to learn that Schiller was the first literary man to accord dignity and sympathy to Joan. How painful it is to realize that in the eighteenth century this authentic saint was known Europe-wide as a ludicrous trollop who whored her way through whole armies of hoodwinked fools to achieve dubious victories. The unpardonable libel was perpetrated by Voltaire in his narrative poem *La Pucelle*. In France there were at least dim memories and even faint voices to protest to the contrary, but in Germany almost nothing was known about the warrior maiden of almost four centuries ago except the hearsay reputation that derived from the scurrilous French poem. Thus Schiller confronted audiences predisposed to snigger, but sent those audiences away corrected from their error.

A second objection will surely be raised by the historically minded. Could not a writer of a historical play (they will ask) have acquainted himself with the salient facts about the personage being portrayed? Did he not realize that Joan did not die picturesquely on the battlefield but was most cruelly burned alive by her enemies? The answer to this objection is, of course, that Schiller did realize, and that he did do conscientious research for his drama. Joan's era, however, was remote, her history seemed as unrealistic as a legend, and no traditions restricted the author's treatment of his subject. Moreover,

Schiller was ever anxious to assert the supremacy of the poet over the matter of history. Aristotle, the unchallenged authority of many centuries, had expressly stated in his *Poetics:*

"The distinction between historian and poet is not in the one writing prose and the other verse. . . . It consists really in this, that the one describes the thing that has been, and the other a kind of thing that might be. Hence poetry is something more philosophic and of graver import than history, since its statements are of the nature rather of universals, whereas those of history are singulars."

With such warranty for his method, Schiller proceeded with assurance in the manipulation of historical events of a far-off time and place and fashioned from them a drama which was to be sustained by its own poetic truth. Ironically, twenty-five years after his drama was written and partially from interest inspired by that drama, scholars set about elaborate investigations of the long neglected Maid. The nineteenth century public came to know her story well and to revere her profoundly. In the early twentieth century her Church officially canonized her as a Saint.

Joan made her spectacular entrance upon the stage of history in the penultimate period of the Hundred Years' War, and her brief action there reversed the developments of a century. The wretched feud between England and France had begun in 1338. King Edward III of England, already the holder of large sections of French territory by virtue of feudal rights, decided in that year to demand the throne of France itself upon the death of King Charles IV without male heir. Edward claimed to be the rightful heir himself through his mother, who was the sister of the deceased King, though he well knew that the famous Salic Law in France prohibited both rule of that country by a female as well as succession to the throne through a female of the royal line. The French ignored his claim, and, in observance of their law, crowned a distant relative of Charles IV as their new ruler. Edward proceeded to invade French territory. Battles and defeats and victories ensued intermittently for seventy-five years without a clear decision for either side. Around the turn of the century the conflict had settled down into an uneasy lull.

In April of 1415 Henry V of England abruptly broke the lull by renewing the claims of his ancestor and declaring war once again. Success attended his campaign. The major victory at Agincourt was won on October 25, 1415; all of Normandy was taken in 1418-19; and during these events a secret arrangement guaranteed nonparticipation in the conflict by the powerful Duke of Burgundy, who, by rights, should have come to the assistance of his master, King Charles VI of France. By the Treaty of Troyes, May 21, 1420, Charles VI, ineffectual monarch that he was and afflicted by periodical fits of insanity, acceded to terms that were tantamount to full surrender. His daughter Catherine was to marry Henry V of England; his son the Dauphin was to be debarred from succession in favor of the yet unbegotten offspring of Henry and Catherine; he himself was to continue to rule until his death, but Henry was to be designated forthwith as "heir of France." When a son was born to the royal couple in December of 1421, the terms of the treaty seemed guaranteed for fulfillment.

Unexpectedly in 1422 both monarchs died within two months of one another, Charles VI elderly and infirm, Henry V stricken down by fever in his prime. Now English forces, under the guidance of the Duke of Bedford, prosecuted the war in the name of the infant King Henry VI; French generals Dunois and La Hire continued to fight for what seemed a lost cause in the name of the disinherited Dauphin, who was ultimately to become King Charles VII; the Burgundians, infuriated by that same Dauphin's treacherous murder of their Duke (for reasons of personal spite), rallied around their new

Duke, who now openly entered the war on the English side out of motives of personal revenge. By 1428 the English, with Paris and northern France already in their control, laid siege to the city of Orleans. For months the siege went on. On April 29, 1429 Joan of Arc, a seventeen-year-old peasant girl, assumed command of the French armies at Orleans, and within a few short weeks the English were fleeing northwards away from the city.

Born in the village of Domremy on the border of the eastern French province of Lorraine, probably in 1412, this illiterate and untutored girl had spent an unexceptional childhood together with three elder brothers and one elder sister. While pasturing her sheep, celestial voices, she said, had addressed her and bidden her take up arms to save her country. A local nobleman, Robert de Baudricourt in near-by Vaucouleurs, was at first astounded by her claims, then wholly won over to her and to her mission. He and one of her brothers accompanied her to the Dauphin's court for an interview. There she prevailed over the irresponsible Prince as she prevailed over his frivolous courtiers. In a mood mixed of awe, skepticism, and sheer amazement, the would-be monarch granted her permission to lead his forces at Orleans.

Reversal of the tides of war was almost immediate. In their retreat northward the English armies under Lord Talbot suffered a major defeat at Patay in mid-June, though Talbot himself survived the event by many years. By mid-July Joan was able to witness the coronation of her King in the city of Rheims, which her leadership had set free. The French now seemed irresistible. But in an attack on Paris in September they met with more determined opposition and in the same battle Joan herself was wounded. Through the winter of 1429-30 the campaign slowed again to its old pace. Many, including Charles VII, who had eagerly accepted victories as miracles wrought by Joan, now began to doubt her divine authorization. It was on May 23, 1430 that the Maid was captured by a force of Burgundians during a battle near Compiègne. While her Burgundian captors turned her over to the Duke of Bedford and the English in return for a sum of money, the graceless Charles VII took no steps at all to effect her deliverance from her enemies. Her own attempt at escape ended in recapture. In January of 1431 she was transferred to a prison at Rouen, the capital city of English-held Normandy. There she was brought to trial before an ecclesiastical court on charges of witchcraft and heresy. For three months, while military and political leaders fumed at the delay, the ecclesiastical judges methodically questioned her. At one point she wearily signed a declaration of her own guilt, only to disavow the statement almost at once. On May 30, 1431 she was burned alive in the marketplace of Rouen. The inscription on her execution cap read; "Apostate, scismatic, heretic, idolatress." She was nineteen years old.

The war continued beyond her death. The Burgundians broke their alliance with the English in 1435, French generals won more victories for Charles VII, and ultimately the English were forced back to minimal holdings on the French coast. In the course of the 1450's the conflict gradually wore itself out, but it was not until the next generation that an official conclusion was made by diplomats. In 1455 the Pope called for a review of Joan's trial, with the result that the verdict of 1431 was declared null and void and Joan's character and mission were accorded vindication by the Church. Yet for centuries her name hovered between the judgments of benediction and damnation. Nineteenth-century historians, prompted in considerable degree by patriotic motives, took up her cause and in time convinced the world at large of her goodness and of her greatness. In the twentieth century the Church officially canonized her as a Saint.

These historical data were perfectly well known to Schiller, but for reasons already mentioned he chose to rearrange them with the utmost freedom in order to make of his play "a Romantic tragedy," as his subtitle indicates. Most of the persons in his drama actually existed in the early fifteenth century. Many of them actually performed the actions attributed to them here. Yet the drama itself is thoroughly false to history.

With the word "Romantic"—a term of very recent usage in 1801—Schiller designated an excursus into the fanciful, dreamlike world of those "Middle Ages" which since about 1500 had been traditionally judged barbarous and dark, but which in the late eighteenth century were beginning to be admired, under an aspect inspired by Rousseau, as the lovely childhood of European man. Innocence, beauty, simplicity, reverent faith, a nearness to God as in the Garden of Eden, all these good things were deemed characteristic of that remote time, just as they were deemed characteristic of those "noble savages," the South Sea Islander and the American Indian, who were remote in space, and of the European peasant, who was close enough in time and space but removed behind social barriers. Thus Schiller's drama admirably suited the generations who rather wilfully equated poetic beauty with "Romantic mediaevalism."

Within the limits of a transient literary fashion, then, the poet created a dramatic legend about a struggle between Good and Evil. In his play the powers of Light are discovered at a moment when the powers of Darkness seem about to overwhelm them. The personages staunchly range themselves on the one side or the other. The graceless Charles VII of history is now accorded good intentions, sensitivity, and a pardonable boyish helplessness; his mistress, Agnes Sorel, becomes a devoted girl whom dynastic considerations may exclude from marriage but not from utterly selfless love; Burgundy is justly angry but susceptible to persuasion and good example. The English adversaries are abetted by the harridan Isabeau and

led by the atheist-materialist Talbot, the former grotesque in
her unbridled sensuality, the latter grand in his earthbound
despair without hope. These two constitute the negative poles
opposed to love and faith. In the French camp love and faith
still exist, though both are corrupt and sadly impaired. Their
corruption promises to destroy them completely. At this stage
of the deadly struggle Joan intervenes with angelic strength.

Seen in these terms, the play assumes a certain grandeur, and
the reader is disposed to grant Schiller all the poetic license
necessary to work out so extraordinary a poetic notion. Talbot,
it is understood, dies in pagan despair, while Joan in her defeat
achieves victory; her body dies on the battlefield, her spirit
soars to glory. Those final flags strewn upon her corpse constitute a sumptuous gesture, as theatrically effective as it is
poetically fine, that symbolizes the tribute of reverence from
her living followers and from posterity. The latent nationalism
of the symbol is noble-hearted. Once caught up in this spirit,
the modern reader accepts and welcomes the miracles, such as
Joan's triumphant breaking of her chains, and the melodrama
and the pageantry. A mediaeval tapestry come to life in a
crowded splendor of hues: such is the ideal way of conceiving
this drama.

So worthy a concept, supported by the author's unfailing
technical skill, ought to have yielded a masterpiece. The
failure lies with the heroine herself. The Joan of history was a
rugged peasant lass, physically unattractive, entirely unsus-
ceptible to "la belle passion," transfigured by the energy of
faith. Schiller's Joan is an artificially synthesized girl, com-
pounded of the raptures of Klopstock's saints, the melancholy
strangeness of Ossian's maidens, and Rousseau's abstract doc-
trine of rural innocence. She has a leading lady's beauty, she
has the eloquence of a preacher, and she falls in love with the
aplomb appropriate for Juliet but inappropriate for herself.
With her provincial, rural, naive counterpart, the Welsh lad

Montgomery, she exchanges grandiose hexameters, then slays him with the ease and the indifference of a Valkyrie. If this scene is to be accepted as gashed with realistic blood, then the apparition of the Black Knight is all too bloodless a symbol for the force of Evil. If, like Juliet, she experiences love-at-first-sight, she wholly lacks Juliet's spunk and wholesome courage. Her distress over Lionel makes her seem like a convent-girl in panic after a first kiss, whereas the author surely wished us to perceive a tragic earthly pain in a heart winged with angelic zest. Her literary descendant, Wagner's Brünhilde, is far more credible for accepting the mortal Siegfried with joy after she has lost her goddess-status. Joan has the decorum of a well-bred young lady of 1800, a quality unsuitable alike to sheep-pasture and to battlefield. She never existed except in a book.

Her irreality, not her miracles, make the legend unreal, and perversely we find her enemies more vivid than we find her. Talbot and Isabeau catch and hold our imagination's eye; our interest in Joan flickers; her friends we forget soon after closing the book. The strong poetic voice that we hear in the final scene is Schiller's own, speaking through the personage of his heroine. In this play a great dramatist revealed only at moments the genius that was in him.

THE MAID OF ORLEANS

CHARACTERS

CHARLES VII, King of France
QUEEN ISABEAU, his mother
AGNES SOREL, his beloved
PHILIP THE GOOD, Duke of Burgundy
COUNT DUNOIS, the Bastard of Orleans
LA HIRE ⎫ officers of the King
DU CHATEL ⎭
THE ARCHBISHOP OF RHEIMS
CHATILLON, a Burgundian knight
RAOUL, a knight of Lorraine
TALBOT, Commander-in-Chief of the English
LIONEL ⎫ English Generals
FASTOLF ⎭
MONTGOMERY, a Welshman
COUNCILLORS OF ORLEANS
AN ENGLISH HERALD
THIBAUT D'ARC, a rich farmer
MARGOT ⎫
LOUISON ⎬ his daughters
JOAN ⎭
ETIENNE ⎫
CLAUDE MARIE ⎬ their suitors
RAIMOND ⎭
BERTRAND, another farmer
THE APPARITION OF A BLACK KNIGHT
A CHARCOAL BURNER
THE CHARCOAL BURNER'S WIFE

Soldiers and citizens, officers of the crown, bishops, monks, marshals, magistrates, courtiers, and other mute persons in the train of the coronation procession.

Time: 1429-1431.

2

PROLOGUE

A rural region.
Forward on the right a statue of a saint in a chapel; at the left a
tall oak tree.
Thibaut d'Arc; his three daughters; three young shepherds, their
suitors.

THIBAUT: Yes, my dear neighbors, we are Frenchmen yet
  Today, free citizens, and masters still
  Of the old soil our fathers used to plow.
  But who knows who will be our lord tomorrow!
  For everywhere the Englishman sets his
  Victorious banners flying, and his steeds
  Are trampling down the verdant fields of France.
  Paris has already seen him victor,
  And with the ancient crown of Dagobert
  Adorns this scion of an alien race.   10
  The offspring of our kings must wander as
  A fugitive and disinherited
  Through his own kingdom, while against him fight
  His first peer and his nearest cousin in
  The foeman's host, led by his vulture-mother.
  The cities and the towns are burning. Closer
  And closer still the smoke of desolation
  Rolls toward these valleys which are still at peace.
  —Hence I, dear neighbors, have resolved with God,
  Because it is still possible today,   20
  To make provision for my daughters; for
  In war a woman must have a protector,
  And true love helps to lighten all our burdens.
                (to the first shepherd)

3

—Come, Etienne. You seek my Margot's hand.
Our fields have neighborly and common borders,
Our hearts agree as well,—and that makes for
Good marriage ties.

                    (to the second)
                 So silent, Claude Marie?
And my Louison, does she cast down her eyes?
Shall I divide two hearts who love each other
Because I have no treasures I can offer?   30
Who does have treasures now? Our barns and houses
Are prey to fire or closest enemies.—
The loyal heart of a brave man alone
Provides a stormproof roof in times like these.

LOUISON: My father!
CLAUDE MARIE: My Louison!
LOUISON *(embracing Joan)*:   O my dear sister!
THIBAUT: To each I will give thirty acres farmland,
     A flock, a stable, and a barnyard.—God
     Has made me prosper,—may He bless you also.
MARGOT *(embracing Joan)*:
     Take an example from us. Please our father.
     Let this day form three happy bonds of union.   40
THIBAUT: Make ready, then. The weddings are tomorrow.
     The whole town shall join in the celebration.
               (The two couples walk off arm in arm.)
     Jeanette, your sisters will be wed tomorrow,
     I see them happy, they make glad my age,
     But you, my youngest, give me pain and sorrow.
RAIMOND: What are you thinking of! Why scold your daughter?
THIBAUT: This fine lad here, who does not have his equal
     In all the village, first-rate fellow that
     He is, he has turned his affection to you;
     It is three autumns now that he has sought   50
     Your hand with heartfelt suit and quiet wish.
     Reserved and cold, you have rejected him,
     And yet no other of the shepherds all
     Can win a kindly smile from you.—I see you

Resplendent in the fullness of your youth,
Your springtime is at hand, the time of hope,
The flower of your body is in bloom,
And still I wait but vainly for the flower
Of tender love to break forth from the bud
And ripen joyously to golden fruit.   60
O this can never please me, and it shows
A serious aberration made by Nature!
The heart mispleases me that is held coldly,
Severely closed amid the years of feeling.

RAIMOND: O do not worry, father Arc! Just let
Her have her way! My own good Joan's love
Is a sweet, noble fruit of heaven and
The precious thing will ripen gradually.
She now still loves to dwell up in the mountains,
And from the freedom of the heath she dreads   70
Descent beneath the lowly rooves of man
Where narrow cares are the inhabitants.
I often gaze up with astonishment
From my deep valley to where she stands tall
Amid her flock upon an upland meadow
With noble body and with earnest glance
Cast down upon the little lands of earth.
She seems to signify some higher thing, and
I often feel she comes from other ages.

THIBAUT: But that is just the thing that I dislike!   80
She flees her sisters' pleasant company,
She seeks out the deserted mountains, leaves
Her bed before the crowing of the cocks,
And in the hour of fear when human beings
Like most to cling close to their fellow-humans
She steals out like the solitary bird
Into the dread and dismal spirit realm
Of night, down to the crossroads, and there holds
Strange conversations with the mountain air.
Why does she always have to choose *this spot*   90
And always drive her flock precisely here?

I see her sit for hours on end in thought
Down yonder there beneath the Druid tree
That every happy creature shuns for fear.
For it is haunted there: an evil being
Has its dwelling place beneath that tree
And has had since the old grey heathen times.
The old folk in the village often tell
About that tree,—their tales are grim with horror.
An awesome sound of curious voices may   100
Be sometimes heard among its gloomy boughs.
Once I myself, when in the tardy twilight
My pathway took me past that tree, beheld
A ghostly woman seated there close by,
Who from the folds of her voluminous garment
Slowly toward me stretched a withered hand
As though to beckon; but I hastened on,
Commending my soul to the hands of God.

RAIMOND (*pointing to the statue of the saint in the chapel*):
The blessed presence of the statue yonder
Which sheds the peace of heaven round about,   110
Not Satan's workings, brings your daughter here.

THIBAUT: O no, no! It is not for nothing that
It comes to me in dreams and anxious visions.
Three separate times I have beheld her sitting
At Rheims upon the throne-chair of our kings,
A glittering diadem of seven stars
Upon her head, the sceptre in her hand,
From which there flowered three white lilies forth,
And I, her father, and both of her sisters,
And all the Princes, Counts, Archbishops, and   120
The very King himself bowed down before her.
How does such splendor come into my hut?
O that must signify some mighty fall!
This dream of warning represents in symbols
The idle longings that obsess her heart.
She is ashamed of her base birth—because
God has adorned her body with rich beauty

And blessed her with His lofty wondrous gifts
Above all shepherd lasses of this valley.
Thus in her heart she nurses sinful pride,   130
And it was pride for which the angels fell
And by which hellish spirits seize mankind.

RAIMOND: Who cherishes a mind more virtuous
And modest than your daughter? Is she not
The one who gladly serves her elder sisters?
And she is the most gifted of them all,
And yet you watch her like a lowly servant
As she performs the hardest tasks in silence,
And underneath her hands in wondrous fashion
Your flocks and planted fields all thrive and prosper.   140
On everything she undertakes is shed
Incomprehensible, exceeding blessing.

THIBAUT: Yes, blessing, and incomprehensible,
But I feel downright horror at those blessings!
—No more of this. I am and shall be silent,
For am I to accuse my own dear child?
I can do nothing more than warn her, pray
For her! But warn I must—Avoid that tree,
Do not go there alone, and dig no roots
At midnight, brew no potions, and do not   150
Inscribe there any symbols in the sand.—
The spirits' realm is easily rent open,
They lie in wait beneath the thin earth's crust,
And quick of hearing they come storming up.
Be not alone, for in the wilderness
The Evil One approached the Lord Himself.

*(Enter Bertrand, a helmet
in his hand.)*

RAIMOND: Be still! Here Bertrand comes returning from
The city. Look what he is carrying!

BERTRAND: You are astonished at the curious object
I have here in my hand.

THIBAUT: We are. But tell us,   160
Where did you get that helmet, and why bring

That evil thing into this peaceful region?
*(Joan, who during the foregoing scenes has
stood silent and without interest off to one side,
becomes attentive and steps closer.)*
BERTRAND: I hardly know myself how this thing came
Into my hands. I had been purchasing
Some iron implements at Vaucouleurs.
I found a great throng at the market place
For many fugitives had just arrived
From Orleans with bad news of the war.
The whole town in an uproar had assembled,
And as I threaded my way through the crowds   170
A swarthy gypsy-woman with this helmet
Stepped up to me, looked sharp into my eyes,
And said: "You, friend, are looking for a helmet,
I know you are. And here I have one. Take it!
For a mere trifle it is yours to buy."
"Go to the soldiers over there," I told her,
"I am a farmer with no use for helmets."
But she would not desist, and went on saying:
"No man can say for sure he will not need
A helmet. Nowadays a steel roof for   180
The head is worth more than a house of stone."
She followed me that way all through the streets
Pressing on me what I did not want.
I saw how bright and fine the helmet was,
How worthy of a knightly head, and as
I weighed it in my hands there dubiously
And pondered on the strange adventure, from
My sight the woman suddenly had vanished,
The current of the crowd had swept her on,
And there I had the helmet in my hands.   190
JOAN *(reaching for it suddenly and eagerly)*:
Give me the helmet!
BERTRAND: What good will it do you?
This is no ornament for a young girl.
JOAN *(snatching the helmet from him)*:

Mine is the helmet, it belongs to me.
THIBAUT: What is she up to?
RAIMOND: Let her have her way.
This warlike ornament becomes her well,
Her bosom houses a man's heart within it.
Remember how she fought the tigerish wolf,
The wild ferocious beast that ravaged all
Our flocks, the terror of our herdsmen. By
Herself, this lion-hearted maiden beat   200
The wolf and seized away from him the lamb
That he was dragging in his bloody jaws.
However brave a head this helmet decks,
It never will adorn a worthier!
THIBAUT *(to Bertrand)*:
So tell us what new war-disaster has
Occurred? What did the fugitives report?
BERTRAND: May God have mercy on the King and country!
We have been beaten in two mighty battles,
The enemy are in the midst of France,
And right up to the Loire all lands are lost.—   210
And now they have assembled their whole force
With which they will lay siege to Orleans.
THIBAUT: May God protect the King!
BERTRAND: An untold number
Of cannon have been brought up from all sides,
And as the darkling squadrons of the bees
Swarm round the hive upon a summer's day,
As from the blackened air the cloud of locusts
Descends and covers fields for miles around
In multitudes as far as eye can see,
Just so a warrior-cloud of nations has   220
Poured out across the fields of Orleans
And with the languages of dark confusion
The camp reechoes in a hollow roar.
The powerful Burgundian, possessor
Of many lands, has brought up all his vassals,
Men of Liège, and men of Luxemburg,

Men of Hainaut, and from the Namur lands,
And dwellers from the fortunate Brabant,
The wealthy men of Ghent who strut in silks
And velvet, men from Seeland whose towns rise   230
Up cleanly from the waters of the sea,
Herd-milking Hollanders, and men of Utrecht,
And even from the furthest West Friesland
Where they look toward the icy pole,—all follow
The call to arms of the Burgundian
And seek to conquer Orleans by siege.
THIBAUT: O this unhappy, wretched quarrel which
Has turned the arms of France against the French!
BERTRAND: Then she, the old Queen too, is to be seen,
The haughty Isabeau, the Princess of   240
Bavaria, riding clad in steel through camp
And by the poison-barb of words inciting
All peoples to a rage against her son
Whom once she bore within her mother-womb.
THIBAUT: A curse upon her! And may God some day
Destroy her like the haughty Jezebel!
BERTRAND: The fearful Salisbury, the shatterer
Of walls, is the commander of the siege;
With him are Lionel, the lion's brother,
And Talbot who with murderous sword mows down   250
The nations in his battles. With the courage
Of insolence they have sworn to compel
All virgins unto shame and to put all
Who ever wielded swords, unto the sword.
They have erected four high lookout towers
To overlook the city; from their tops
The Earl of Salisbury with murderous gaze
Looks down and counts the walkers in the streets.
Cannon-balls of hundred-weight already
Have been hurled by the thousands at the city,   260
The churches lie in ruins, and the tower
Of Notre Dame has bowed its royal head.
They have dug powder-mines as well, and over

A hellish kingdom stands the anxious city
Expectant any hour that it will
With thunderous explosion burst in flame.
> *(Joan listens with rapt attention and puts
> the helmet on her head.)*

THIBAUT: But where, then, were the valorous champions,
Saintrailles, La Hire, and France's bulwark-wall,
The hero-hearted Bastard, that the foe
Should have pressed forward so all-powerfully?   270
Where is the King himself? Does he watch idly
His kingdom's peril and his cities' fall?

BERTRAND: The King is holding court down at Chinon,
He lacks for men, he cannot hold the field.
Commanders' courage, heroes' arms, what use
Are these when pale fear lames the army?
A terror, as though sent by God, has seized
Upon the bosoms of the very bravest.
In vain the Princes' summoning calls resound;
As sheep will flock together out of fear   280
When howling of the wolves is heard, just so,
Forgetful of his ancient fame, the Frenchman
Seeks nothing but the safety of the castles.
One single knight, as I heard the report,
Has rounded up one feeble troop of men
To bring the King sixteen new companies.

JOAN *(quickly)*:
What is that knight's name?

BERTRAND: Baudricour. But he
Will hardly slip the enemy's attention
When they are on his heels with two full armies.

JOAN: Where is the knight now? Tell me if you know.   290

BERTRAND: Less than a day's ride off from Vaucouleurs.

THIBAUT: But what is that to you? Girl, you are asking
About things which are no concern of yours.

BERTRAND: Because the enemy is now so mighty
And no protection to be hoped for from
The King, they all agreed at Vaucouleurs

To give themselves to the Burgundian.
That way we will not bear a foreign yoke
But stay with the old royal family; —
Perhaps we will revert to the old crown   300
Once Burgundy is reconciled to France.

JOAN *(in a state of inspiration)*:

No compromises! No surrenders here!
The savior nears, he girds himself for battle.
The foeman's luck shall fail at Orleans.
His cup brims full, he is ripe for the harvest.
The virgin with her sickle shall approach
And she shall mow down the grain of his pride.
She shall pull down his fame out of the skies
Where he has hung it high upon the stars.
Flee not! nor falter. For before the rye   310
Is yellow, and before the moon's disc fills,
No English steed shall drink out of the waves
Of the magnificently flowing Loire.

BERTRAND: Ah, miracles no longer happen now.

JOAN: Miracles still happen. — A white dove
Shall fly and with the boldness of the eagle fall on
These vultures that now rend the fatherland.
It will fight down this haughty Burgundy,
This traitor to the kingdom, and this Talbot,
The heaven-stormer of the hundred hands,   320
And Salisbury too, the temple-desecrator,
And all these insolent, bold islanders,
And drive them homeward like a flock of lambs.
God will be with the dove, the God of battles,
He will elect His timorous creature, through
A tender virgin He will manifest
Himself, for He is the Omnipotent!

THIBAUT: What spirit moves the wench?

RAIMOND: It is
The helmet that makes her so warrior-like.
Look at your daughter. In her eye the lightning   330
Flashes and her cheeks blaze fervent fire!

JOAN: Shall this kingdom fall? This land of fame,
  The fairest seen by the eternal sun
  In all its course, this Paradise of countries
  Which God loves like the apple of his eye,
  Shall it bear fetters of a foreign folk?
  —The heathen hosts were shattered here. Here was
  Erected the first cross, the holy image,
  Here rest Saint Louis' ashes, and from here
  The conquest of Jerusalem began.   340
BERTRAND (amazed):
  How wondrously she speaks! Whence has she gained
  Her lofty inspiration?—Father Arc,
  God has bestowed on you a wondrous daughter!
JOAN: Are we to have no more kings of our own,
  No lord and master born of native stock—
  The King who never dies, is he to vanish
  From the world—who guards the sacred plow,
  Who protects the pasture and makes the earth fruitful,
  Who conducts the serf forth into liberty,
  Who disposes cities round his throne in joy,   350
  Who assists the weak and terrifies the wicked,
  Who does not know envy—for he is supreme—
  Who is man and yet an angel of sweet mercy
  Upon the hostile earth—because the throne
  Of kings, all shimmering and golden, is
  The shelter of the shelterless.—There stand
  Both Might and Mercy,—and the Guilty tremble
  Whereas the Just approach in trusting confidence
  And jest there with the lions by the throne.
  This foreign king who comes from lands afar   360
  For whom no sacred bones of ancestors
  Rest in this ground, how can he love this land?
  He who was never young with our young men,
  For whom our speech with alien cadence runs,
  How can he be a father to its sons?
THIBAUT: God grant the King and France protection! We
  Are peaceful countryfolk who know not how

To wield the sword, nor how to wheel the steed
Of war.—Let us with patience wait and see
Whom victory will give us for a king.   370
The fate of battles is God's judgment, and
Our *lord* will be whoever is anointed
And sets the crown upon his head at Rheims.
—So come to work! And let us think of present
Things only. Let the ones of lofty birth
And Princes vie and draw lots for the earth.
We can behold destruction calmly still,
For storm-fast stand the acres that we till.
The flame may burn our towns and all we grew,
Their horses' hooves may trample down our grain,—   380
The new spring brings new seed-time in its train
And our slight huts will quickly rise anew.

(All except the Maid withdraw.)

JOAN (*alone*):

  Farewell, you mountains, you beloved pastures,
Familiar, quiet valleys, fare you well.
Among you Joan will no longer wander,
Forever Joan bids you now farewell.
You meadows that I watered, and you trees
That I have planted, thrive in joyous green.
Farewell you grottoes and cool-flowing springs,
And Echo, lovely voice amid this valley   390
Who often answered songs of mine in turn,—
Now Joan goes, and never to return.

  O all you scenes of pleasures calm and still,
I leave you now behind for evermore.
Disperse, you lambs, upon the heath and hill,
You are a flock without a shepherd, for
To feed another flock is now His will
Upon the field of peril and of war.
Such is the Spirit's summons unto me,
I am not moved by earthly vanity.   400

For He who unto Moses once descended
Amid the burning bush on Horeb's height
And bade him go to Pharao; who extended
Unto the shepherd Jesse His great might
And chose him for the cause to be defended;
Who showed all shepherds favor in His sight;
He spoke out of the branches of this tree:
"Go, testify upon the earth to Me.

In rugged bronze thy body shall be laced,
In steel thou shalt enclose thy tender breast, 410
With man's love thou shalt never be embraced
Nor passion's sinful flame thy heart invest,
Thy hair shall not by bridal wreath be graced,
No lovely child may nestle at thy breast,
But with war's honors I will make thee great
Before all earthly women's fame and fate.

For when the bravest falter in the fight,
When France is on the verge of last defeat,
Then thou shalt hold My Oriflamme upright,
And like the rapid mower in the wheat 420
Cut down the haughty conqueror in his might
And give his fortune's wheel reverse complete.
To sons of France thou shalt deliverance bring
And set Rheims free and therein crown thy King."

God has vouchsafed to guide me by a sign,
He sent the helmet here, it comes from Him,
Its iron touches me with strength divine,
I have the courage of the Cherubim;
I feel swept onward to the battle line,
A storm's force drives me onward, life and limb, 430
I hear the shouting of the battle ground,
The war steed rears, and trumpet fanfares sound. [432]

(Exit.)

ACT I

King Charles's court at Chinon.
Dunois and Du Chatel.

DUNOIS: No, I can't stand it any longer. I
   Renounce this king who so ingloriously
   Deserts himself. My brave heart bleeds within
   My bosom and I could weep scalding tears to think
   That brigands are dividing royal France
   Among themselves with swords, that noble cities
   Which have grown ancient with the monarchy
   Yield up their rusty keys to foemen's hands   440
   While we are squandering the precious time
   For their deliverance here in idleness.
   —I hear of Orleans besieged, I rush
   To come up here from distant Normandy,
   Expecting I would find the King armed like
   A warrior in the forefront of his army.
   I find him—here, surrounded by buffoons
   And troubadours, and guessing subtle riddles,
   And giving gallant parties for Sorel,
   As if deep peace prevailed throughout the kingdom!   450
   —The Constable is leaving, he can't stand
   To see this outrage any longer.—I go too,
   And leave him to his evil destiny.
DU CHATEL: Here comes the King.
                    (Enter King Charles.)
CHARLES: The Constable has sent his sword back and
   Renounces service with me.—In God's name!
   There we have got rid of a surly man
   Who quite unbearably found fault with us.

DUNOIS: In these hard times one man can be most precious.
   I should not like to lose him carelessly.   460
CHARLES: You say that for the fun of contradiction.
   While he was here you never were his friend.
DUNOIS: A proud, cantankerous, ill-tempered fool
   He was, and never could stop talking. — But
   This time he knew when it was time to go,
   When there was no more honor to be gained.
CHARLES: O you are in your usual pleasant humor,
   I won't disturb you in it. — Du Chatel,
   There are ambassadors here from old King
   René,[1] praised masters of the poet's art,   470
   Of wide renown. — They must be entertained
   And to each must be given a gold chain.
                   (to the Bastard)
   What are you laughing at?
DUNOIS: At you, for shaking
   Gold chains out of your mouth.
DU CHATEL: There isn't any
   More money, Sire, left in your treasury.
CHARLES: Then get some. — Noble singers must not leave
   This court of mine without the proper honors.
   They make our withered scepter bloom again,
   They intertwine immortally green boughs
   Of life in sterile crowns; their art acquires   480
   Them power till they take an equal place
   With kings; but they build thrones of light desires,
   Their harmless realms do not exist in space;
   Thus kings and poets share an equal mind,
   For both dwell on the peaks of human kind.

---

[1] René the Good, Count of Provence, of the House of Anjou. His father and brothers were Kings of Naples, and after his brother's death he himself laid claim to that Kingdom, but failed in the enterprise. He tried to restore the old Provençal poetry and the *Cour d'Amour*, and set up a *Prince d'Amour* as supreme judge in matters of gallantry and love. In the same romantic spirit he turned himself and his spouse into shepherds.
                                  (Schiller's note.)

DU CHATEL: My royal Master, I have spared your ear
  As long as there was help and counsel left,
  But now Necessity has loosed my tongue.
  —You have no more to give, alas, you do
  Not have the wherewithal to live tomorrow.   490
  The high flood of your riches has receded
  And it is ebb-tide in your treasury.
  The soldiers have not yet received their pay,
  They threaten, grumbling, to desert.—I scarcely
  Can manage to maintain your royal household
  With barest needs, but not in princely style.
CHARLES: Then put my royal taxes into pawn
  And have the Lombards lend some money to us.
DU CHATEL: Sire, your crown revenues and taxes have
  Already been pawned three years in advance.   500
DUNOIS: And meanwhile pledge and land are being lost.
CHARLES: And many rich and fine lands still remain.
DUNOIS: As long as God and Talbot's sword so please!
  Once Orleans is taken, you can go
  And pasture sheep down with your King René.
CHARLES: You always turn your wit against that king,
  And yet it was that landless Prince who gave
  Me royal gifts this very day.
DUNOIS: But surely
  He did not send the crown of Naples to you?
  Not that, in Heaven's name! For it is up   510
  For sale, I hear, since he is herding sheep.
CHARLES: That is a jest, a happy game, a party
  That he gives for himself and for his heart
  To found a pure and sinless world amid
  This harsh and barbarous actuality.
  But what he does want, great and royal, is—
  He wants to have the olden times restored,
  When tender love prevailed, when the devotion
  Of knights uplifted great heroic hearts,
  When noble ladies sat in arbitration   520
  With tender judgment judging all things fine.

The kind old man still dwells amid those times,
And as they used to live in olden songs,
So he would like to have them, like a city
Of heaven in the golden clouds, on earth. —
He has set up a Court of Love to which
All noble knights are meant to come as pilgrims,
And where chaste ladies are supposed to throne
In splendor, where pure love is to return,
And he has chosen me as Prince of Love.   530

DUNOIS: I am not yet quite so degenerate
That I disdain the masterdom of Love.
I take my name from her, I am her son,
And in her kingdom lies my patrimony.
My father was the Prince of Orleans,
He found no woman's heart invincible
But neither did he find the forts of foes
Too strong. If you want to deserve the name
Of Prince of Love, then be the bravest of
The brave! — The way *I* read those olden books,   540
Love always was linked with the lofty deeds
Of knights, and heroes, I was always taught,
Not shepherds, sat about the Table Round.
Whoever cannot bravely fight for Beauty
Does not deserve her golden prize. — Here is
The field of battle! Go and fight for your
Ancestral crown. With knightly sword defend
Your property and noble ladies' honor. —
And when from rivers of opponents' blood
You have won your hereditary crown,   550
Then it will be the time and seemly as
A Prince to crown yourself with Love's green myrtles.

CHARLES (*to a Page who has just entered*):
  What is it?
THE PAGE: Councillors from Orleans request
  A hearing.
CHARLES: Show them in.
                    (*Exit the Page.*)

                              They'll ask for help—
And what can I do, helpless as I am?
                    (Enter three Councillors.)
Welcome to my loyal citizens
Of Orleans! How do things stand with my good city?
Is it resisting still with wonted courage
The enemy who is besieging it?

A COUNCILLOR: Alas, Sire, supreme peril presses us, and by   560
The hour destruction swells against the city.
The outer bulwarks are demolished and
The enemy gains new ground with each sally.
The walls have been stripped bare of their defenders,
For, fighting restlessly, the men drop out.
But few of them will see the gates of home.
The plague of hunger also haunts the city.
Therefore the noble Count of Rochepierre,
Who has command there, has in this dire peril
Compacted with the enemy according   570
To ancient usage to surrender in
Twelve days unless an army strong enough
To save the city has appeared before that.
                    *(Dunois makes a vehement gesture
                              of anger.)*

CHARLES: The time is short.

THE COUNCILLOR: And we are now here with
An escort from the enemy to beg
Your princely heart to show your city mercy
And send us help before the time is up,
Or else he will surrender in twelve days.

DUNOIS: And could Saintrailles give his consent to such
A shameful treaty?

THE COUNCILLOR: No, my Lord! As long   580
As that brave man was still alive, there could
Be no talk of surrender or of peace.

DUNOIS: Then he is dead!

THE COUNCILLOR: The noble hero fell
Beside our walls and died for his King's cause.

CHARLES: Saintrailles is dead! In that one man I lose
  An entire army!

     (A knight enters and speaks a few words
     softly to the Bastard, who starts back in surprise.)

DUNOIS: Even that!

CHARLES: What is it?

DUNOIS: Lord Douglas has sent word the Scottish troops
  Are in revolt and threaten to desert
  If they do not receive their pay today.

CHARLES: Du Chatel!

DU CHATEL *(shrugging his shoulders)*:

             Sire, I don't know what to do.   590

CHARLES: Pawn everything you have, half of my kingdom—

DU CHATEL: It will not help. They have been promised for
  Too many times.

CHARLES: They are the best troops in
  My army and they must not leave me now!

THE COUNCILLOR: O King, help us! Remember *our* distress!

CHARLES *(in despair)*:

  Can I stamp up an army from the ground?
  Do grain fields grow in the palm of my hand?
  Tear me to pieces, tear my heart out, and
  Mint it for coin instead of gold! I do
  Have blood yet, but no silver and no soldiers!   600

     (He sees Sorel coming in and hurries toward
     her with outstretched arms.

      Enter Agnes Sorel with a little box in her
     hand.)

  O Agnes, my beloved and my life!
  You come to snatch me out of sheer despair!
  I still have you and I flee to your bosom,
  And nothing has been lost while you are mine.

SOREL: O my dear King!

     (looking around with anxious, inquiring
        glance)

        Dunois! Can it be true?

  Du Chatel?

DU CHATEL: Alas!

SOREL: Are we in such distress?
  We lack for pay? The troops mean to desert?

DU CHATEL: Yes, it is so, alas!

SOREL *(pressing the little box upon him):*

                              Here, here is gold!
  And here are jewels—Melt my silver down—
  Go sell or pawn my castles—Borrow on   610
  My own Provence estates—Turn everything
  To money till the troops are satisfied.
  Go! No time must be lost!

                    (She pushes him away.)

CHARLES: Well, Dunois? Well, Du Chatel? Am I still
  Too poor for you when I possess this crown
  Of womankind?—She is as nobly born
  As I, the royal blood of the Valois
  Itself is not more pure. She would adorn
  The first throne in the world—but she disdains it.
  She only wants to be my love and known   620
  As such. When has she taken any gift
  From me of greater value than a flower
  In winter or rare fruit? She will accept
  No sacrifice from me, yet for me makes
  Them all. She risks all her possessions and
  Wealth generously in my declining fortunes.

DUNOIS: Yes, she is quite as mad as you, and casts
  All that she owns into a burning house,
  And fetches water in the leaky vessel
  Of the Danaides. She will not save you   630
  But only drag herself down—

SOREL: Don't believe
  Him. He has ten times risked his life for you
  And now is irked that I should risk my gold.
  Have I not gladly sacrificed all things
  For you, things valued more than gold and pearls?
  Should I keep back my happiness now for
  Myself? Come, let us cast away all life's

Superfluous adornments! Let me set
You an example in renunciation!
 Transform your royal household into soldiers,   640
Your gold to iron; everything you have
You will cast resolutely with your crown!
Come, we will share together want and danger!
And let us mount the steed of war, expose
Our bodies to the burning arrows of
The sun, accept the clouds above us for
A roof, and take a stone to be our pillow.
Rude warriors will patiently endure
Their own woes when they see their King in want,
Enduring hardships like the least of them!   650

CHARLES (*smiling*):
Now is fulfilled for me an ancient word
Of divination which a nun in Clermont
Declared to me once in prophetic mood.
A woman, so the nun proclaimed, would make
Me victor over all my enemies
And win back my ancestral crown for me.
I sought her in the foeman's camp afar,
I hoped to reconcile my mother's heart—
Here stands the heroine who will lead me
To Rheims! I shall win by my Agnes' love!   660

SOREL: You will win by the brave swords of your friends.

CHARLES: I also hope much from my enemies'
 Dissentions, for I have sure information
That everything is not just as it was
Between these haughty Lords of England and my cousin
Of Burgundy,—and so I have despatched
La Hire with messages for my Lord Duke
To see if I could bring that angry Peer
Back to his former loyalty and duty.—
I now expect him here at any hour.   670

DU CHATEL (*at the window*):
The knight is riding in the gate right now.

CHARLES: O welcome messenger! Now we shall soon

Learn whether we shall triumph or surrender.
> *(Enter La Hire.*
> *Charles goes to meet him.)*

La Hire! Do you bring hope or none? Deliver
Your message briefly. What must I expect?

LA HIRE: Nothing but what your own sword can do.

CHARLES: The haughty Duke would not be reconciled.
But tell me, how did he receive my message?

LA HIRE: Above all things, before he would so much
As grant you ear, he says that he demands   680
That Du Chatel be given up to him,
Whom he declares his father's murderer.

CHARLES: And what if we refuse those shameful terms?

LA HIRE: Then the alliance is dissolved before
It started.

CHARLES: Did you challenge him then as
I bade you do, to fight me on the bridge
At Montereau right where his father fell?

LA HIRE: I threw your glove down at his feet and said
That you would set aside your majesty
And as a knight do battle for your kingdom.   690
But his reply was that he had no need
To fight for something that he had already.
But if you hankered so for battle, you
Would find him out in front of Orleans
Where he was of a mind to go tomorrow.
Then with a laugh he turned his back on me.

CHARLES: But was the pure and lovely voice of Justice
Not raised at all, then, in my Parliament?

LA HIRE: It has been silenced by the rage of parties.
And a decree of Parliament declared   700
The throne was forfeit to you and your line.

DUNOIS: The insolence of citizens turned Lords!

CHARLES: And you attempted nothing with my mother?

LA HIRE: Your mother!

CHARLES: Yes! What sentiments did she express?

LA HIRE *(after he has reflected for a few moments):*

When I came into Saint Denis it happened
To be the coronation festival,
And the Parisians were decked out as for
A triumph. Arches rose in every street,
And under them the King of England passed.
His way was strewn with flowers, and the mob,   710
In jubilation as though France had fought
Its finest triumph, thronged about his carriage.

SOREL: In jubilation—that they now could trample
  Upon the gracious, gentle King's own heart!

LA HIRE: I saw young Harry Lancaster, the boy,
  Installed upon Saint Louis' royal seat,
  And there beside him stood his haughty uncles,
  The Duke of Bedford and the Duke of Gloster,
  And at the throne Duke Philip knelt and swore
  The oath of fealty for all his lands.   720

CHARLES: O Peer unprincipled! Unworthy cousin!

LA HIRE: The lad was timid, and he tripped as he
  Was going up the steep steps to the throne.
  "An evil omen!" all the people murmured,
  And there arose resounding laughter. Then
  Up stepped the old Queen, she who is your mother,
  And—it provokes me just to tell about it!

CHARLES: Well?

LA HIRE: And she clasped the lad into her arms
  And set him in your father's seat herself.

CHARLES: O Mother! Mother!

LA HIRE: The Burgundians   730
  Themselves, the fierce and murder-hardened bands,
  Blushed red with shame beholding such a sight.
  She noticed it, and turning to the people
  Cried out in a loud voice: "Thank me, you Frenchmen,
  For thus ennobling the sick tree with stock
  Clean grafted and preserving you thus from
  The crazy father's misbegotten son.

  (*The King covers his face. Agnes hurries to
  him and takes him into her arms. All present
  express their revulsion and horror.*)

DUNOIS: The she-wolf! O the frenzy-snorting shrew!

CHARLES *(after a pause, to the Councillors):*
  You now have heard how matters stand. Therefore
  Delay no longer, but to Orleans   740
  Return and to my loyal city say
  That I release them from their oath to me.
  They should weigh their own welfare and surrender
  To the Burgundian and ask his mercy—
  His nickname is "the Good," he will be human.

DUNOIS: What, Sire! Would you abandon Orleans?

COUNCILLOR *(kneeling):*
  My royal Lord, do not withdraw your hand
  From us! Do not desert your faithful city
  And let it fall to England's harsh dominion.
  It is a noble jewel in your crown,   750
  And none has kept its faith more sacredly
  Unto the kings, your ancestors.

DUNOIS: Have we
  Been beaten? Dare we leave the field before
  A sword-stroke has been struck for this town's sake?
  With nothing but a word, before the shedding
  Of any blood, would you consider plucking
  The finest city from the heart of France?

CHARLES: Enough of blood has flowed and all in vain!
  The heavy hand of Heaven is against me,
  My army has been beaten in all battles,   760
  My Parliament renounces me, my people,
  My capital receive my enemy
  With jubilation, and my closest kin
  Desert me and betray me.—My own mother
  Suckles this alien brood at her own breast.
  —We shall withdraw beyond the Loire and yield
  Before the mighty hand of Heaven which
  Is only with the Englishman.

SOREL: O God forbid that we, despairing of
  Ourselves, should turn our backs upon this kingdom!   770
  Those words do not come out of your brave heart.

Your mother's harsh unnatural act has broken
My King's heroic heart. But you will once
Again regain your manly self-control,
With noble courage counter Destiny
That fiercely fights against you now.

CHARLES (*lost in gloomy thought*):   Is it not true?
A dark and dreadful destiny pervades
The line of the Valois; it is forsaken
By God; my mother's vicious actions have
Brought down the Furies on this House; my father   780
Lay twenty years in madness, and before me
Three elder brothers were mowed down by Death.
Thus it is Heaven's own decision that
This House of Charles the Sixth shall be destroyed.

SOREL: It will arise in you rejuvenated!
Just have faith in yourself. — O not for nothing
Have you been spared by gracious Destiny
From all your brothers, you, the youngest of them,
And summoned to the throne you never hoped for.
Within your gentle bosom Heaven has   790
Prepared the surgeon who shall bind all wounds
That rage of factions ever dealt this land.
You will put out the flames of civil war,
You will sow peace, my heart assures me, and
You will be the French kingdom's new creator.

CHARLES: Not I. The harsh and tempest-troubled time
Requires a helmsman gifted with great strength.
I could have made a peaceful nation happy;
A wild rebellious one I cannot tame.
I cannot open with my sword those hearts   800
Which hostilely are closed to me in hatred.

SOREL: This nation is struck blind and numbed with madness,
And yet this frenzy nonetheless will pass.
The love for its ancestral king will wake
Anew, the day is not far distant now,
The love deep planted in the Frenchman's heart,
And jealousy will wake, and ancient hatred

That cleaves both nations hostilely forever.
His own good fortune will destroy the victor.
Therefore do not desert the field of battle   810
With too great haste, fight for each foot of ground,
Defend this Orleans as you would shield
Your very heart. Let all the ferries rather
Be sunk and all the bridges be burned down
That carry you across this kingdom's border,
Across the Stygian waters of the Loire.

CHARLES: What I could do, I have already done.
I offered to appear in knightly combat
For my crown's sake. — But that has been refused.
I waste my people's lives for nothing and   820
My cities are collapsing in the dust.
Shall I, like that unnatural mother, let
My child be cloven with the sword in twain?
No, it shall live, and I shall give it up.

DUNOIS: What, Sire? Is this the language of a king?
Would anyone give up a crown this way?
The worst man of your nation stakes his life
On his opinion, on his hates and loves.
All things turn partisan once civil war
Has hung its bloody ensign on display.   830
The plowman leaves his plow, the housewife leaves
Her distaff; children and old men take weapons,
The citizen burns his own city down,
The farmer with his own hands burns his fields,
To do you harm or do you good, whichever,
And thereby to assert his heart's desire.
He shows no quarter and expects no quarter
When once he hears the call of honor, when
He once gets fighting for his gods or idols.
Therefore away with all this weak compassion   840
Which ill befits a royal bosom. — Let
The war rage out its course as it began,
It was not you who set it recklessly
Aflame. A people has to suffer for

Its king, such is the earthly fate and law.
The Frenchman knows not, wills not otherwise.
Of no worth is the nation that will not
Stake everything, and gladly, for its honor.

CHARLES *(to the Councillors):*
Await no other answer. God be your
Protection. I can do no more.

DUNOIS: Then may   850
The god of triumph turn his back on you
As you turn yours upon your kingdom. You
Desert yourself, and I desert you likewise.
Not Burgundy's and England's might combined,
But your faint heart will hurl you from your throne.
The kings of France have all been heroes born,
But you were all unwarrior-like begotten.
                    (to the Councillors)
The King may give you up for lost, but I
Shall go to Orleans, my father's city,
And fighting find my grave beneath its ruins.   860
            *(He starts to leave. Agnes Sorel
                    detains him.)*

SOREL *(to the King):*
O do not let him leave you thus in anger!
His mouth has spoken harshly but his heart
Is true as gold; it is the one that loves
You warmly and has often bled for you.
Come now, Dunois, confess that it was heat
Of noble anger that led you too far. —
And you forgive your friend his angry words!
O come, come! Let me quickly reconcile
Your hearts before the hasty vehemence,
Unquenchable, destructive, bursts in flame!   870
        *(Dunois fixes his gaze on the King and seems
            to be waiting for an answer.)*

CHARLES *(to Du Chatel):*
We shall cross over the Loire. Have my
Equipment loaded onto boats.

DUNOIS (*quickly to Sorel*):   Farewell!
                    (*He turns quickly and leaves.
                        The Councillors follow.*)
SOREL (*wringing her hands in desperation*):
  O if he leaves us, we are lost entirely!
  —Go follow him, La Hire. Try to appease him.
                    (*Exit La Hire.*)
CHARLES: Is my crown a possession so unique?
  Is it so very hard to part with it?
  I know of something harder far to bear:
  To let oneself be domineered by souls
  Of truculence, to live dependent on
  The mercy of imperious, haughty vassals,   880
  That is the hard thing for a noble heart
  And bitterer than succumbing to one's fate!
            (*to Du Chatel who is still hesitating*)
  Go do as I commanded!
DU CHATEL (*throws himself at his feet*):
                    O my King!
CHARLES: I have made my decision. No more words!
DU CHATEL: Conclude peace with the Duke of Burgundy!
  I see no other rescue for you now.
CHARLES: You so advise me, and it is your blood
  Which I would have to shed to seal that peace?
DU CHATEL: Here is my head. In battles I have risked
  It often for your sake. I lay it now   890
  With joy upon the scaffold for your sake.
  Appease the Duke. Deliver me unto
  His anger's full severity and let
  My flowing blood atone his ancient hate.
CHARLES (*gazes at him for a time touched and silent*):
  Then it is true? Things stand so ill with me
  That friends of mine whose eyes see through my heart
  Propose the way of shame as my deliverance?
  Yes, now I see how deeply I have fallen,
  For confidence is forfeit in my honor.
DU CHATEL: But think—

CHARLES: Not one word more! Do not arouse me! 900
　Though I must turn my back upon ten kingdoms
　I will not save myself with a friend's life.
　—Go do as I commanded. Have my army's
　Equipment loaded on the ships.
DU CHATEL: It shall
　Be done at once.

(He rises and leaves. Agnes Sorel
weeps violently.)

CHARLES *(taking her hand)*:   Do not be sad, my Agnes.
　Beyond the Loire there lies another France.
　And we go to a land more fortunate.
　A halcyon and cloudless sky laughs there,
　And lighter breezes blow, and gentler customs
　Receive us; Song is in its homeland there,   910
　And there both life and love more fairly bloom.
SOREL: That I should live to see this day of sorrow!
　My King must go to banishment, the son
　Must quit his father's house to fare at large
　And see his cradle with his back. O sweet
　And lovely land from which we now depart,
　We shall not tread your ways again with joy.

(Re-enter La Hire.)

　You come alone? You have not brought him back?

(as she looks at him more closely)

　La Hire? What is it? What does your glance say?
　A new disaster has occurred!
LA HIRE: Disaster   920
　Has spent itself, and sunshine has returned!
SOREL: What is it?
LA HIRE *(to the King)*: Call back the ambassadors
　From Orleans!
CHARLES: Why? What has happened?
LA HIRE: Call
　Them back. Your luck has turned. There has been an
　Engagement, and—you are victorious.
SOREL: Victorious! The word has Heaven's music!

CHARLES: La Hire, you are deceived by fabled rumors.
I can no more believe in victories.

LA HIRE: You will believe in greater marvels soon.
—Here comes the Archbishop. He brings the Bastard   930
Back to your arms again—

SOREL: O lovely flower
Of victory which straightway bears the fruits
Of peace and reconciliation!

            (Enter the Archbishop of Rheims, Dunois,
            and Du Chatel with Raoul, a knight in armor.)

THE ARCHBISHOP *(leads the Bastard to the King and joins their*
    hands):

                        Embrace,
You Princes, let all rage and discord vanish,
For Heaven itself has now declared for us.

            (Dunois embraces the King.)

CHARLES: Relieve me of my doubts and my amazement.
What does this solemn earnestness portend for me?
What brings about this sudden change?

THE ARCHBISHOP *(leads the knight forward and places him before*
    the King):

                            Speak up!

RAOUL: We had recruited sixteen companies,
Men of Lorraine, to reinforce your army;   940
The knight of Baudricour from Vaucouleurs
Was their commander. When we reached the heights
Near Vermanton and were descending to
The valley through which flows the Yonne, there stood
The enemy before us on the plain,
And weapons glittered where we looked to rearward.
We saw ourselves surrounded by both armies,
There was no hope for victory or flight.
Then sank the bravest hearts, and everyone,
Despairing, started to lay down his weapons.   950
While the commanders were debating what
To do and still could not decide—lo, there occurred
A wondrous miracle before our eyes!

For suddenly out of the woodland depths
A maiden stepped, a helmet on her head,
And like a warrior-goddess beautiful
Yet terrifying to behold. About
Her neck her dark hair fell in ringlets; round
Her stately form there seemed to shine a splendor
Of heaven as she lifted up her voice 960
And spoke: "Why fear, brave Frenchmen? At the foe!
And were his numbers more than sands beside
The sea, God and the Blessed Virgin lead you!"
And quickly from the ensign-bearer's hand
She seized the flag, and at the column's head
She strode with might and dauntless dignity.
Mute with astonishment, ourselves unwilling,
We followed flag and bearer and straightway
Made our attack upon the enemy.
He, utterly amazed, stood motionless 970
With fixed and round-eyed wonder staring at
The miracle displayed before his sight. —
But suddenly, as if the fear of God
Had struck him, he reversed his course
To flee, and casting weapons to the winds,
The entire army scattered on the field.
Then no command, no leader's shout availed;
Without a backward glance and wild with terror
Man and steed plunged to the river's bed
And let themselves be slain without resistance; 980
It should be termed a slaughter, not a battle!
Two thousand enemy bestrewed the field,
Not counting what the river swallowed up,
And of our forces not a man was lost.
CHARLES: By Heaven, strange! most wonderful and strange!
SOREL: You say a maiden wrought this miracle?
Where is she from? Who is she?
RAOUL: Who she is
She will disclose to no one but the King.
She calls herself a seeress and a God-

Appointed prophetess, and promises 990
To save Orleans before the moon has changed.
The men have faith in her and thirst for battle.
She walks behind the troops and soon will be here
Herself.

> *(Bells are heard and a clatter of weapons being struck against each other.)*

      You hear the peals of bells, the uproar?
She comes, the people welcome her God-sent.

CHARLES *(to Du Chatel):*
Have her brought in—

> *(to the Archbishop)*

        But what am I to think!
A maiden brings me victory, and now,
When nothing but an arm of God can save me!
This is not in the course of Nature.—Bishop,
Dare I, dare I trust a miracle? 1000

MANY VOICES *(offstage):*
Hail to the rescuer, hail to the maiden!

CHARLES: She comes!

> *(to Dunois)*

      Now take my place, Dunois, sit here,
And we shall put this maiden to the test.
If she is sent by God and if she is
Inspired, she will identify the King.

> *(Dunois sits down; the King stands at his right, with Agnes Sorel beside him and the Archbishop opposite him with the others, so that the middle area is clear.*
>
> *Enter Joan, accompanied by the Councillors and many knights, who fill up the rear of the stage. With noble dignity she advances and scrutinizes those standing about, one by one.)*

DUNOIS *(after a profound and solemn silence):*
Are you the one, O wondrous maiden—

JOAN *(interrupts him, gazing at him with dignity and clear eyes):*
Bastard of Orleans! Would you tempt God!

Arise from that seat which does not befit you,
For I am sent unto this greater one.
> (*With decisive step she walks up to the King,
> genuflects before him, rises again at once, and
> steps back. All present express their astonish-
> ment. Dunois leaves his seat and a space is
> cleared before the King.*)

CHARLES: You see my face for the first time today;   1010
From whence have you acquired this knowledge?
JOAN: I
Saw you when no one else, save God, saw you.
> (*She approaches the King and
> speaks confidentially.*)

Do you remember, in the night just past
When everything was buried in deep slumber,
How you got up and left the couch where you had lain
And then addressed an ardent prayer to God?
Have *them* withdraw, and I will tell you now
The purport of your prayer.
CHARLES: What I confided
To Heaven I need not conceal from men.
Reveal to me the purport of my plea,   1020
And I shall doubt no more that God inspires you.
JOAN: Three prayers there were that you addressed to God,
Mark well now, Dauphin, if I name them to you.
You pleaded thus in your first prayer to Heaven:
If property unjust clung to this crown,
If any other grievous sin not yet
Atoned and dating from ancestral times
Had summoned forth this war so rife with tears,
To take you as a victim for your people
And to pour forth upon your head alone   1030
The total vials of its wrath.
CHARLES (*recoils in fright*):
Who are you, mighty being? And from whence?
> (*Everyone expresses astonishment.*)

JOAN: To Heaven you addressed this second plea:

If its sublime will and decision was
To wrest the scepter from your family line,
To take from you all that your ancestors,
The monarchs of this kingdom, had possessed,
But three possessions you implored it to
Retain for you: a heart that knew contentment,
Your friend's affection, and your Agnes' love.   1040

    (The King covers his face, weeping violently.
    A great stir of excitement among those present.
    After a pause.)

Shall I now tell you what your third prayer was?

CHARLES: Enough! I do believe in you. No mortal
  Can do thus much. Almighty God has sent you.

THE ARCHBISHOP: Who are you, holy and most wondrous maiden?
  What happy country bore you? Speak. Who are
  The parents blessed by God who gave you birth?

JOAN: Reverend Sir, my name is Joan. I am
  The lowly daughter of a shepherd merely,
  And live in my King's hamlet Dom Remi
  Within the churchly benediction circle   1050
  Of Toul, and from my childhood I have tended
  My father's flocks.—And much and often I
  Have heard about the foreign island-people
  Who had come over sea to make us bondmen
  And to impose a master alien-born
  On us and one who does not love our people,
  How they had captured our great city Paris
  Already and seized power of the kingdom.
  Then I implored God's holy Mother to
  Avert from us the shame of alien chains   1060
  And to preserve for us our native King.
  Outside the village of my birth there stands
  An ancient statue of the Virgin to
  Which many pious pilgrimages came,
  And there beside it stands a sacred oak tree
  Famed for the power of many miracles.
  And in the shadow of the oak I loved

To sit while herding flocks,—my heart so prompted.
And if a lamb was lost among the mountains,
A dream would always show me where it was   1070
While I slept in the shadow of that oak.
—One time when I had sat a long night through
In reverent piety beneath that tree
And had resisted sleep the entire time,
Up stepped the Holy One before me, bearing
A sword and banner, otherwise, however,
Dressed as a shepherdess like me, and said:
"Rise, Joan. It is I. And leave your flocks.
The Lord has called you to another mission.
Take up this banner. Gird this sword around you,   1080
Destroy your people's enemies with it,
And guide your master's son up to the city
Of Rheims and crown him with the royal crown."
But I replied: "How can I bring myself
To do a thing like that, a tender maiden
Entirely ignorant of deadly combat?"
She answered then: "A virgin without stain
May bring to pass all wondrous things on earth
If she will but withstand all earthly love.
Behold *me* now. A virgin chaste, as you are,   1090
I gave birth to the Lord, the Lord divine,
And am myself divine!"—And then she touched
My eyelids, and when I looked up again,
There was the heaven full of angel youths
All carrying white lilies in their hands,
And lovely music floated in the air.
—And in this way three nights one after one
The Blessed One appeared and cried: "Arise now, Joan,
The Lord has called you to another mission."
And when upon the third night she appeared   1100
Then she was angry, and reprovingly she said:
"Obedience is woman's obligation
On earth, endurance is her grievous fate;
Through service strict she gains clarification;

Who has served here, will there above be great."
And speaking thus she shed her garments of
A shepherdess and as the Queen of Heaven
I saw her in the sunlit splendor stand;
Then golden clouds uplifted her and bore her
Slowly fading to the blissful land.   1110

> (*Everyone is moved. Agnes Sorel, weeping
> vehemently, hides her face upon the King's
> bosom.*)

THE ARCHBISHOP (*after a long silence*):
An attestation so divine compels
All doubts of earthly subtlety to silence.
Her deed assures us that she speaks the truth,
For God alone can work such miracles.
DUNOIS: I trust her eyes before her miracles,
Her guileless purity of countenance.
CHARLES: Am I, a sinner, worthy of such grace!
Unerring and all-searching eye, you see
My inmost soul and know my heart is humble!
JOAN: The humbleness of great ones lights the sky.   1120
You bowed, and He has raised you up on high.
CHARLES: And so I shall resist my foemen's host?
JOAN: I shall lay conquered France before your feet.
CHARLES: And Orleans, you say, will not be lost?
JOAN: Loire waves will sooner flow back in retreat.
CHARLES: Shall I reach Rheims in triumph over woes?
JOAN: I'll lead you there despite a thousand foes.

> (*All the knights set up a din with their lances
> and shields and give signs of their courage.*)

DUNOIS: Set us this maiden at the army's head
And where the godlike girl will lead us, we
Shall blindly follow. Her prophetic eye   1130
Shall guide us and my brave sword shall protect her!
LA HIRE: We will not fear an entire world in weapons
If she walks at the head of our battalions.
The God of victory walks at her side,

Let her in battle be our mighty guide.
> *(The knights raise an immense din of weapons*
> *and step forward.)*

CHARLES: Yes, holy maiden, be the leader of
My army, and its leaders shall obey you.
This sword of highest military power
Which the commander for the Crown in anger
Sent back to us, has found a hand more worthy.   1140
Accept it, holy prophetess, and be
Henceforward —

JOAN: No, not so, my noble Dauphin!
Not through this instrument of earthly power
Is victory given to my Lord. I know
Another sword through which I shall achieve
The victory. And I shall show it to you
Just as the Spirit taught me. Send and have
Them fetch it.

CHARLES: Name it, Joan.

JOAN: Send to the ancient
Town of Fierboys, there in Saint Catherine's churchyard
There is a vault where much old iron lies   1150
Heaped up from victory spoils of long ago.
The sword that shall serve me is in among it.
It may be recognized by three gold lilies
Which are engraved upon its blade. Send down
To fetch that sword. By that one you will be triumphant.

CHARLES: Let someone go and do as she has said.

JOAN: And let me also carry a white banner
Edged with a seam of purple round about.
And on this banner let the Queen of Heaven
Be seen with the Child Jesus in His beauty   1160
Hovering above an earthly globe,
For thus our Holy Mother showed it to me.

CHARLES: It shall be as you say.

JOAN *(to the Archbishop):*   My Reverend Bishop,
Lay your priestly hand upon me and
Pronounce a blessing on your daughter's head.
> *(She kneels.)*

THE ARCHBISHOP: You have appeared among us to dispense
  Blessings, not receive them.—Go with God.
  We are ourselves unworthy men and sinners.
                    (She rises.)
A PAGE: A Herald from the English field commander.
JOAN: Have him come in, for it is God who sends him.   1170
                (The King beckons to the Page,
                      who goes out.)
                  (Enter the Herald.)
CHARLES: What do you bring us, Herald? State your errand.
THE HERALD: Who here is spokesman for Charles of Valois,
  Count of Ponthieu, for whom I have a message?
DUNOIS: Base herald! Scoundrel without principle!
  Are you so impudent as to deny
  The monarch of the French on his own soil?
  Your herald's coat protects you, or you would—
THE HERALD: France recognizes one King and no other,
  And that one lives within the English camp.
CHARLES: Be quiet, Cousin! State your errand, Herald.   1180
THE HERALD: My noble field commander, grieved by all
  The blood already shed and still to be shed,
  Still keeps his warrior's sword within its sheath,
  And now before the fall of Orleans
  Would offer you a friendly compromise.
CHARLES: Set forth his message.
JOAN *(steps forward):*   Sire, let me reply
  In your stead to this Herald.
CHARLES: Do so, Maiden.
  Decide which it shall be now; peace or war.
JOAN *(to the Herald):*
  Who sent you and who speaks here through your mouth?
THE HERALD: The British field commander, Salisbury.   1190
JOAN: Herald, you lie! That Lord does not speak through
  You. Only living persons speak, not dead men.
THE HERALD: My general lives in total health and strength,
  And lives for the destruction of you all.
JOAN: When you left he was still alive. A shell

From Orleans this morning laid him low
While he was watching from La Tournelle tower.
—You laugh because I tell you far-off things?
Do not believe my words, believe your eyes!
You will encounter the procession with   1200
His corpse when your feet carry you back home.
Now, Herald, speak, deliver your commission.
THE HERALD: If you are able to reveal things which
   Are hidden, you know this before I tell it.
JOAN: I do not need to know it. Listen now,
   However, to what I tell you, and take
   These words back to the Prince who sent you here.
   —King of England, and you, Dukes of Bedford
   And Gloster who administer this kingdom,
   Give reckoning unto the King of Heaven   1210
   For all the blood that has been spilled by you.
   Surrender up the keys of all the cities
   That you against the will of God have conquered.
   The Maiden has come from the King of Heaven
   To offer you peace or bloody war. Choose now!
   For I say unto you that you may know it:
   Fair France has not been destined by the Son
   Of Mary to be yours,—but rather Charles,
   My Lord and Dauphin to whom God assigned it,
   Will make a royal entry into Paris   1220
   Attended by all nobles of his kingdom.
   —Now, Herald, get you gone from us in haste;
   Before you can reach camp in urgency
   With this report, the Maiden will have placed
   In Orleans her flag of victory.

(She leaves. Everyone is in commotion.
The curtain falls.)

ACT II

A region enclosed by cliffs.
Talbot and Lionel, the English commanders. Philip, Duke of
Burgundy. Knight Fastolf and Chatillon with soldiers and banners.

TALBOT: Beneath these cliffs here let us make a halt
    And pitch a camp well fortified and see
    If we can rally our retreating troops again
    Who fled and scattered in their first dismay.
    Have sentries posted, occupy the heights.   1230
    Night will insure us from pursuit, and if
    The enemy does not have wings as well,
    I do not fear attack.—And yet we do
    Have need of caution, for we have a foe
    To deal with who is bold, and we are beaten.
           (Exit Knight Fastolf with the soldiers.)
LIONEL: Commander, do not mention that word "beaten"
    Again. I must not think of how the Frenchman
    Beheld the backs of Englishmen today.
    —O Orleans! Orleans! Grave of our fame!
    On your fields England's honor has been slain.   1240
    Disgracefully ridiculous defeat!
    Who will believe it in the coming ages?
    The conqueror of Poitiers, Crécy,
    And Agincourt is routed by a woman!
BURGUNDY: Our consolation must be that we were
    Not conquered by a mortal but a devil.
TALBOT: The devil of our folly.—Burgundy!
    Does this ghost of the mob scare Princes also!
    Your superstition is a wretched cloak
    For cowardice.—Your troops fled first today.   1250

42

BURGUNDY: No one stood fast. The rout was universal.

TALBOT: No, Sir! It was in your wing that the rout
　Began. You rushed into our camp and shouted:
　"Hell is abroad, the Devil fights for France!"
　And therewith threw our men into confusion.

LIONEL: You can't deny it. Your wing was the first
　To break.

BURGUNDY: 　　　Because the first attack was there.

TALBOT: The Maiden knew the weak point of our camp,
　She knew where cowardice was to be found.

BURGUNDY: So Burgundy is blamed for the disaster?　　1260

LIONEL: We Englishmen, if we had stood alone,
　By God! we never would have lost Orleans!

BURGUNDY: No—then you never would have seen Orleans!
　Who paved the way for you into this kingdom,
　Held out the faithful hand of friendship to you,
　When you first landed on this foreign coast?
　Who crowned your Henry King in Paris and
　Subdued the hearts of Frenchmen to his cause?
　By God! if this strong arm of mine had not
　Led you inside, you never would have seen　　1270
　Smoke rise from any chimney here in France.

LIONEL: If big talk could accomplish it, Lord Duke,
　You would have conquered France all by yourself.

BURGUNDY: You are disgruntled now because you have
　Lost Orleans and vent your anger's gall
　On me, your friend and your ally. Why did we
　Lose Orleans, if not through greed of yours?
　It was all ready to surrender to me;
　You and your envy have prevented it.

TALBOT: It was not for your sake that we besieged it.　　1280

BURGUNDY: Where would you be if I withdrew my army?

LIONEL: No worse, I fancy, than at Agincourt,
　Where we had worsted you and all the rest of France.

BURGUNDY: And yet you found our friendship badly needed;
　The Regent paid a costly price for it.

TALBOT: Yes, costly, costly, with our honor, have

We paid for it today at Orleans.

BURGUNDY: Do not press this too far, my Lord, you might
  Regret it! Did I leave my lord's just banners,
  Bring down the name of traitor on my head,   1290
  To put up with the like of this from strangers?
  What am I doing, fighting here against
  My country? If I must serve thankless people
  I want to do so for my native King.

TALBOT: You have negotiated with the Dauphin,
  We know you have. But we will find a way
  To guard ourselves from treason.

BURGUNDY: Death and Hell!
  Is this the way you treat me? — Chatillon!
  Tell my troops to get ready for departure;
  We're going back to our own country.

(Exit Chatillon.)

LIONEL: Prosperous journey!   1300
  The Briton's fame was never more resplendent
  Than when, relying on his own good sword
  Alone, he fought without assistants. Let
  Each man fight his own battle for himself.
  For it remains forever true: French blood
  And English blood can never mix with honor.

(Enter Queen Isabeau
accompanied by a Page.)

ISABEAU: What do I hear, Commanders! Cease this quarrel!
  What brain-distorting planet has confused
  Your healthy senses in this way? Right now,
  When nothing else but harmony can save you,   1310
  Will you break up in hatred, and by making
  War on each other, force your own destruction?
  — I beg you, noble Duke, take back that rash
  Command. — And you, illustrious Lord Talbot,
  Appease your friend now swept away by anger.
  Come, Lionel, and help me pacify
  These haughty souls and get them reconciled.

LIONEL: Not I, my Lady. I am quite indifferent.

This is my thought: whoever cannot stand
Together would do best to separate.   1320

ISABEAU: What? Does the trickery of Hell, that proved
   Disastrous to us in the battle, go
   On working here thus to befool our minds?
   Who began this quarrel?—Noble Lord!
            (to Talbot)
   Were you the one who so forgot his own
   Advantage as to hurt your worthy ally?
   What would you achieve without that arm?
   He built your King his throne, and still sustains it,
   And he can overthrow it if he wishes;
   His army makes you stronger, still more his name.   1330
   All England, if it poured its citizens
   All forth upon your coasts, would not be able
   To force this country, if it stood together;
   Only France could ever conquer France.

TALBOT: We well know how to honor a true friend.
   To ward a false one off is wisdom's duty.

BURGUNDY: Who faithlessly forgets his gratitude
   Will not lack for a liar's shameless face.

ISABEAU: What, noble Duke? Could you so totally
   Deny your sense of shame and princely honor   1340
   As to put your own hand into the hand that slew
   Your father? Can you be so mad as to
   Believe in honest reconciliation
   With that same Dauphin whom you have yourself
   Hurled to the very brink of his destruction?
   So near his fall you want to hold him back
   And thus undo in madness your own work?
   Here stand your friends. And your salvation rests
   With fast alliance now with England only.

BURGUNDY: My mind is far from treating with the Dauphin.   1350
   But this contemptuousness and insolence
   Of haughty England I can not endure.

ISABEAU: Come! Overlook a rash word on his part.
   Hard are the griefs that weigh on a commander,

And bad luck, as you know, makes one unjust.
Come! Come! Embrace, and let us quickly heal
This breach before it proves to be eternal.
TALBOT: Well, Burgundy, what do you think? A heart
That's noble readily accedes to Reason's
Victory. The Queen has spoken words   1360
Of wisdom. Let this handclasp heal the wounds
Inflicted by my overhasty tongue.
BURGUNDY: Madame has spoken prudently, and my
Just anger yields before necessity.
ISABEAU: Well said! Now seal this newly formed alliance
With a fraternal kiss, and let those words
Exchanged before be scattered on the winds.
          (Burgundy and Talbot embrace.)
LIONEL *(observes the group; aside)*:
Good luck to the peace founded by this Fury!
ISABEAU: Commanders, we today have lost a battle,
Luck was against us; but for all of that   1370
Your noble courage should not fail. The Dauphin
Despairs of God's protection now and summons
The arts of Satan to his aid. But he shall have
Surrendered to damnation all in vain,
And Hell itself shall not suffice to save him.
A victory maiden leads the foeman's army,
I will lead yours, and *I* will stand you in
The stead of maiden and of prophetess.
LIONEL: Madame, go back to Paris! Here we want
To win with proper weapons, not with women.   1380
TALBOT: Go! Everything has gone downhill since you
Came to this camp. No virtue is in our weapons.
BURGUNDY: Your presence can accomplish nothing good.
The warrior is scandalized by you.
ISABEAU *(looks in astonishment at one after another)*:
What! You too, Burgundy? You side against me
And favor these ungrateful Lords?
BURGUNDY: Go! Go!
The soldiers find their courage leaving them

When they think they are fighting for your cause.

ISABEAU: I barely finish making peace between you
  And you already league yourselves against me?   1390

TALBOT: Go, go with God, Madame. Once you are gone
  There will be no more devils that we fear.

ISABEAU: But am I not your true confederate?
  Is your cause not the same as mine?

TALBOT: But yours
  Is not the same as ours. We are engaged
  Here in an honorable and worthy struggle.

BURGUNDY: I here avenge a father's brutal murder
  And filial duty makes my weapons sacred.

TALBOT: To be quite frank, your treatment of the Dauphin
  Is neither good in men's sight nor just in   1400
  The sight of God.

ISABEAU: Ten generations' curse
  Upon him! He has wronged his mother's head.

BURGUNDY: He merely was avenging spouse and father.

ISABEAU: He set himself up as judge of my morals!

LIONEL: And that was disrespectful in a son!

ISABEAU: He even had me sent to banishment.

TALBOT: He only carried out the public verdict.

ISABEAU: If ever I forgive him, curse befall me!
  What's more, before he rules his father's kingdom—

TALBOT: You will sacrifice his mother's honor!   1410

ISABEAU: You do not know, weak souls,
  What an offended mother's heart can do.
  I love whoever does me good, and hate
  Whoever does me harm, and if that is
  The very son I bore, so much the worse.
  I gave him life and I will take it from him
  If he with reckless pride of insolence
  Offends the very womb that carried him.
  You who are waging war against my son
  Have neither right nor reason to despoil him.   1420
  What grievous guilt against you has the Dauphin
  Incurred? What duties has he failed you in?

Ambition goads you, vulgar jealousy.
I can detest him, for I gave him birth.
TALBOT: Yes, by the vengeance he can feel his mother!
ISABEAU: You sorry hypocrites, how I despise you,
    Deceivers of yourselves as of the world!
    You Englishmen stretch out your brigands' hands
    To seize this France of ours where you have neither
    The right nor valid claim to so much earth   1430
    As one hoof of a horse can cover.—And this Duke,
    Who lets himself be termed "the Good," sells out
    His country and hereditary realm
    To foreign masters and his country's foes.—
    Yet every other word of yours is Justice.
    —I scorn hypocrisy. The way I am,
    That is the way the world shall see me.
BURGUNDY: True!
    You staunchly have maintained *that* reputation.
ISABEAU: I do have passions and warm blood like any
    Other woman, and I came to live   1440
    As Queen, not just to seem one, in this country.
    Was I to give up joy because the curse
    Of destiny had yoked my vivid youth
    Together with a madman of a husband?
    More than my life I love my freedom, and
    Whoever wounds me on that score . . . But why
    Should I dispute with you about my rights?
    The sluggish blood flows thickly in your veins,
    Of pleasure you know nothing, only fury.
    And this Duke, who has hovered his life long   1450
    Between the parts of Good and Evil, can not
    Hate from his heart, nor from his heart feel love.
    —I'll go to Melun. Let me have this fellow,
            (pointing to Lionel)
    Who pleases me, for company and pleasure,
    And then do as you please. I care no further
    About Burgundians or Englishmen.
        (She beckons to her Page and starts to leave.)

LIONEL: You may be sure that we shall send to Melun
    The handsomest French lads that we can capture.

ISABEAU *(returning)*:
    It suits you well to hack away with swords,
    The French alone command the grace of words.   1460
                 (Exit.)

TALBOT: Ah! What a woman!

LIONEL: Your opinion now,
    Commanders! Shall we flee still further, or
    Shall we turn back and wipe out by a bold
    And sudden stroke the shame of this day's battle?

BURGUNDY: We are too weak, our forces have been scattered,
    The army's terror is still far too new.

TALBOT: Blind terror only got the best of us,
    The swift impression of a single moment.
    This phantom of our startled fancy will,
    Once viewed more closely, vanish into nothing.   1470
    Hence my advice is that we lead the army
    At break of day across the river again
    Against the enemy.

BURGUNDY: But think—

LIONEL: With your
    Permission. There is nothing here to think
    About. We must recoup our losses quickly
    Or else we shall forever be disgraced.

TALBOT: It is decided. We shall strike tomorrow.
    And to destroy this phantom of a terror
    That dazzles and unmans our troops, let us
    Engage this devil of a maiden in
    A hand-to-hand encounter. If she stands
    And meets our trusty swords, all well and good:
    She will have seen the last time she has hurt us;
    And if she does not, be assured, she shuns
    A serious fight, the army's spell is broken.

LIONEL: So be it then! Assign to *me*, Commander,
    This easy joust where no blood is to flow.
    For I intend to take this ghost alive,

And there before the Bastard's eyes, her lover,
I'll carry her locked in these arms, and for   1490
The troops' delight, into the British camp.
BURGUNDY: Don't make too big a boast.
TALBOT: If *I* get at her,
I don't intend to clasp her quite so gently.
Come now, and give exhausted Nature some
Refreshment in the way of gentle slumber,
And then to break our camp with morning's dawn.
                    (Exeunt.)
          (Enter Joan with her flag, in helmet and
          breastplate but otherwise in women's clothes;
          with her Dunois, La Hire, knights, and soldiers.
          They are seen above on the cliff-path, then they
          move silently across it, and immediately there-
          after appear on the stage.)
JOAN *(to the knights who surround her, while the march above*
    continues):
The wall is scaled and we are in their camp!
Now cast the cloak of silent night away
That kept your soundless march concealed, and make
Your fearful presence known to the enemy   1500
By your loud battle cry—God and the Maiden!
ALL *(cry aloud amid a wild din of weapons)*:
God and the Maiden!
                (Drums and trumpets.)
SENTRY *(offstage)*:   The foe! The foe! The foe!
JOAN: Bring torches here! Cast fire into their tents!
The frenzy of the flames shall multiply
Their fear and death close menacingly round them!
                (Soldiers rush off; she starts
                    to follow them.)
DUNOIS *(holds her back)*:
You have done your part, Joan. You have led
Us right into the middle of their camp
And put the enemy into our hands.
But now you should stay back out of the battle

And leave the bloody outcome up to us.   1510
LA HIRE: Appoint the way of victory for the army
   And bear the flag in your pure hand before us,
   But do not take the deadly sword yourself
   And do not tempt the fickle god of battles,
   For blindly, without mercy, he prevails.
JOAN: Who here presumes to bid me halt! Or dictate
   Unto the Spirit guiding me? The arrow
   Must fly where the hand of the marksman speeds it.
   Wherever danger is, there Joan must be;
   My fate is not to die *here* or *today*.   1520
   I have to see the crown on my King's head.
   No foe will take my life till I am through
   Performing the high work God bade me do.
(*Exit.*)
LA HIRE: Come on, Dunois! On with this heroine,
   We'll lend our doughty breasts to be her shield!
(*Exeunt.*)
(*English soldiers flee across
the stage.*)
THE FIRST ONE: The Maiden! Right in the camp!
THE SECOND: Impossible! How could she get inside the camp?
THE THIRD: Through the air! The Devil helps her!
THE FOURTH AND FIFTH: Flee! Flee! We are all of us dead men!
(*Exeunt.*)
(*Enter Talbot.*)
TALBOT: They will not hear.—I cannot make them stand.   1530
   All bonds of their obedience are broken.
   As if Hell had spewed forth its legions of
   Accursed spirits, crazed delusion sweeps
   The brave man and the coward senselessly
   Away. I cannot get one tiny band
   To stem the flood-tide of the enemy
   Now rolling, ever swelling, into camp!
   —Am I the only sober man while all
   The rest around me rave in fever heat?
   To flee this way before these weakling Frenchmen   1540

Whom we have beaten in a score of battles! —
Who is she who is thus invincible,
This terror-goddess who all of a sudden
Reverses battle fortunes and transforms
A shy and coward pack of deer to lions?
Can an imposter learn a heroine's role
And play it to strike terror in real heroes?
A woman robs me of my victor's fame?

A SOLDIER *(rushes in)*:
    The Maiden! Flee, Commander!
TALBOT *(cuts him down)*:   Flee yourself
    To Hell! This sword shall pierce the man   1550
    Who talks to me of fear and coward flight.
                    (Exit.)
        *(The prospect opens. The English camp is
        visible in total flame. Drums, flight and pursuit.
        After a time enter Montgomery.)*

MONTGOMERY *(alone)*:
    Where shall I flee? On all sides enemies and death!
    Here the enraged Commander who with brandished sword
    Blockades all flight and drives us on toward death;
    There the awful Maiden dealing deadly blows about her
    Like the fury of the fire. — And all around no bush
    To hide me, nor a cave with room to keep me safe!
    If only I had never crossed the seas to come
    Here, luckless wretch! A vain illusion led me on
    To seek for easy fame here in the wars in France,   1560
    And now I am led by a ruinous destiny
    Into this deadly battle. — If I only were
    Far off at home still by the Severn's fertile shore,
    Safe in my father's household, where my mother stayed
    Behind in sorrow, and my gentle, lovely sweetheart.
                (Joan appears in the distance.)
    O woe! What do I see? There comes the awful Maiden!
    Out of the flames there, darkly gleaming, she arises
    As from the jaws of Hell a spirit of the night
    Comes forth. — Where can I run? Already she has caught

Me with her eyes of fire and from afar   1570
Casts her unerring net of glances out to catch me.
Around my feet the magic tangle tight and tighter
Entwines itself till she denies me flight, caught in
These toils! And I must look, however much my heart
Rebels against it, at that shape of dreadful death.
            (Joan takes a few steps toward him,
                    then stops again.)
She comes! I will not wait until the deadly being
Attacks me first! I will embrace her knees and beg
In supplication for my life—she is a woman—
And see if I perhaps can move her by my tears!
            (As he starts to walk toward her
            she advances swiftly upon him.)
JOAN: You are a dead man! For a British mother gave you birth.
MONTGOMERY *(falls at her feet)*:   [1580
    Forbear, you awesome being! Do not cut me down,
    A man defenseless! Sword and shield I cast away,
    Unarmed, imploring, I fall down before your feet.
    Leave me the light of life, accept a ransom fee.
    Rich in possessions lives my father still at home
    Off in the lovely land of Wales, where through green meadows
    The winding Severn rolls its stream of silver waves,
    And fifty villages acknowledge him their lord.
    He will with rich gold ransom his beloved son
    If he hears I am alive still in the Frenchmen's camp.   1590
JOAN: You fool, lost and deluded! You have fallen now
    Into the Maiden's hands, the fatal Maiden's hands,
    From whom no rescue or escape is to be hoped.
    Had your misfortune put you in the power of
    The crocodile or in the spotted tiger's claws,
    If you had robbed the lioness of her young brood,
    You might perhaps have found some mercy or compassion,—
    But it is fatal to have come upon the Maiden.
    For a dread and binding compact obligates me to
    The Spirit Realm, the Realm severe, inviolable,   1600
    To slaughter with my sword all living things despatched

To me death-consecrated by the god of battles.

MONTGOMERY: Dreadful is your speech, and yet your glance is soft,
You are not terrible to look at close at hand,
I feel my heart attracted to your lovely form.
O by the gentle nature of your tender sex
I beg you and implore: Have mercy on my youth!

JOAN: Do not invoke my sex! Do not call me a woman!
Like spirits incorporeal that do not woo
In earthly wise, so I belong to no race of   1610
Mankind, nor does this armor cover any heart.

MONTGOMERY: O by the holily prevailing law of love
To which all hearts do homage, I implore you now.
At home I left behind a lovely bride-to-be,
As beautiful as you and in the bloom of youth.
She weeps and waits for her beloved's coming.
O if you ever hope yourself to love and hope
To joy in love returned, do not in cruelty
Divide two hearts which sacred bonds of love conjoin!

JOAN: You call on nothing more than alien earthly gods   1620
Who are not holy nor revered by me. Of love's
Alliance by which you implore me I know nothing
Nor shall I ever come to know its idle service.
Therefore defend your life, for death sends you its call.

MONTGOMERY: O then at least have mercy on my sorrow-burdened
Whom I have left at home. For surely you have also   [parents
Left parents who are harried with concern for you.

JOAN: Unhappy youth! And you remind me of how many
Mothers of this country have been rendered childless,
How many tender children fatherless, how many   1630
Affianced brides have been made widows just through you!
Now England's mothers also may learn of despair
And come to know the tears that have been shed
By sorrow-stricken wives throughout the realm of France.

MONTGOMERY: O it is hard to die unmourned in foreign lands.

JOAN: Who called you to this foreign land to lay waste to
The blooming industry of fields, to drive us from
Our native hearths, and cast the fiery brand of war

Into the peaceful sanctuaries of our cities?
You had dreamed in the vain illusion of your hearts   1640
Of plunging freeborn Frenchmen into shame of bondage
And tying this great country like a tiny boat
Behind your high and mighty ocean-going ship!
You fools! The royal coat-of-arms of France hangs by
The throne of God. You will more easily tear out
A star of the Celestial Wain than any town
Out of this kingdom one and indivisible! —
The day of vengeance is at hand. Alive you shall
Not measure back your way across the sacred sea
That God has set between us as a demarcation   1650
And which in your impiety you overstepped.

MONTGOMERY *(lets go her hand):*
O I must die! Death's terror seizes me already.

JOAN: Die, friend! Why should you tremble timidly at death,
The fate that cannot be avoided? Look on *me!*
I am no more than a mere girl, a shepherdess
By birth; my hand is unaccustomed to the sword,
It wielded nothing but the harmless shepherd's staff;
Yet wrested from the pastures of my native place
And from my father's, from my sisters' loving bosoms,
I must here, I must—the voice of gods compels me, not   1660
My own desires—with bitter woe to you, and with
No joy to me, a phantom of sheer terror, slay,
Spread death abroad, and finally die as its victim!
I shall not see the day when I with joy come home.
To many of your people I shall yet bring death,
Make many widows yet, but in the end I shall
Myself be killed and thus fulfill my destiny.
—Fulfill yours likewise. Therefore take your sword in hand
And let us fight now for the precious prize of life.

MONTGOMERY *(rises):*
If you are mortal now as I am, and if arms   1670
Can wound you, it is possible my arm can send
You down to Hell and put an end to England's woes.
Into the gracious hands of God I put my fate.

Accursed creature, call your hellish spirits up
To give you their assistance, and defend your life!
> (*He seizes shield and sword and attacks her;
> martial music resounds in the distance; after a
> brief fight Montgomery falls.*)

JOAN (*alone*):
Your foot conducted you to death. — Farewell.
> (*She steps apart from him and stands
> in thought.*)

Exalted Virgin, you have wrought great things through me!
My arm unwarlike you endow with strength, and with
Implacability you steel this heart of mine.
My soul melts with compassion and my hand shrinks back,   1680
As though it forced an entry to a sacred shrine,
From doing harm to my opponent's youthful body.
I shudder at the very sight of naked steel,
But when it is required, strength straightway comes to me,
And never erring in my trembling hand, my sword
Moves of itself, as though it were a thing alive.
> (*Enter a knight with closed visor.*)

THE KNIGHT: Accursed witch! Your hour has come! I have
Looked for you up and down the battlefield,
You deadly phantom of delusion! Back
With you to Hell from which you first arose!   1690

JOAN: Who are you that your evil angel sends
To me? Your bearing is that of a Prince,
And you do not look like an Englishman,
For you are marked with the Burgundian colors,
Before which the point of my sword bows down.

THE KNIGHT: You wanton trollop, you do not deserve
To die at the hand of a noble Prince.
The headsman's ax should sever your accursed
Head from your body, not the doughty sword
Of the king's-blooded Duke of Burgundy.   1700

JOAN: Then you are that exalted Duke himself?

THE KNIGHT (*raises his visor*):
I am. Therefore, wretch, tremble and despair!

Satanic arts will not protect you now.
You never conquered anyone but weaklings.
Here stands a man before you.
(Enter Dunois and La Hire.)
DUNOIS: Turn and fight
With men there, Burgundy, and not with maidens.
LA HIRE: We shield the Prophetess's sacred head,
Your sword will have to pierce this bosom first—
BURGUNDY: This wanton Circe does not scare me, nor
Do you, whom she has changed so shamefully.   1710
Blush, Bastard; shame confound you too, La Hire,
For prostituting bravery to the arts
Of Hell and making a contemptible
Shield-bearer Page out of a devil's strumpet.
Come here! I challenge all of you! Whoever
Flees to the Devil has lost faith in God.
(They make ready for combat.
Joan steps between them.)
JOAN: Stop! Stop!
BURGUNDY: You tremble for your paramour?
Before your eyes he shall—
(He lunges at Dunois.)
JOAN: Stop, both of you!
Part them, La Hire! —No French blood must be shed!
Swords shall not arbitrate this fight. It has   1720
Been otherwise decided in the stars.—
Apart, I say.—Hear and respect the Spirit
That has come over me, that through me speaks!
DUNOIS: But why do you arrest my upraised arm
Preventing the decision by the sword?
The steel is drawn, the blow will be delivered
That will avenge and reconcile all France.
JOAN *(stands in the middle and separates both parties by a wide*
interval; to the Bastard):
Step to one side!
              (to la Hire)
              Stand there and do not move.

I have things that I must say to the Duke.

(after they are all quiet)

What are you doing, Burgundy? Who is   1730
The foe your glances murderously seek?
This noble Prince is a son of France like you,
This brave man is your countryman and comrade-
In-arms, I am myself your country's daughter.
We all, whom you are trying to destroy,
Belong to your own people;—and our arms
Are open to receive you, and our knees
Prepared to do you reverence;—and our swords
Have no sharp tip against you. Venerable,
Cased even in the foeman's helmet, is   1740
The face that bears our King's beloved features.

BURGUNDY: So with cajoling tone of honeyed talk
You fancy, Siren, you will lure your victim.
You will not fool me, thing of guile. My ear
Is proof against the pitfalls of your speech,
And all the fiery arrows of your eye
Glance off from the good armor of my breast.
To your weapons, Dunois!
With blows and not with words let us do battle.

DUNOIS: Words first, and then to blows. Are you afraid   1750
Of words? That too is cowardice
And the betrayer of a worthy cause.

JOAN: Imperative necessity does not
Force us down at your feet. We are not here
As suppliants before you.—Look about you.
In ashes lies the English army's camp,
And it is your dead that bestrew the field.
You hear the Frenchmen's martial drums resound.
God has decided. Victory is ours.
The lovely laurel's freshly gathered branches   1760
We are prepared to share with our good friend.
—O come to us! Come, noble fugitive!
Come over where Right is, and Victory.
I, who am sent by God, extend to you

A sister's hand. I mean to rescue you
And pull you over to our sinless side! —
All Heaven is for France. Its angels — that
You do not see — are fighting for the King,
And all of them with lilies are adorned.
Snow-pure, as is this banner, is our cause,   1770
And the pure Maiden is its spotless symbol.

BURGUNDY: The words of falsehood are a tangled snare,
But her speech is as simple as a child's.
If evil spirits lend her words, then they
Have counterfeited innocence superbly.
I will not listen further. To your weapons!
My ear, I feel, is weaker than my arm.

JOAN: You have termed me a witch, accused me of
The arts of Hell. — Is making peace, appeasing
Hate and discord, the affair of Hell?   1780
Does harmony rise from the everlasting
Abyss? What is good, innocent, and holy,
If not the struggle for the fatherland?
Since when is Nature so in conflict with
Itself that Heaven will desert the upright cause?
And devils will engage in its defense?
But if what I have said to you is good,
Where else but from on high could I derive it?
Who would have come to me up there amid
My mountain pasture to initiate   1790
The childlike shepherdess in kingly matters?
For never had I stood before high Princes,
The art of speaking is strange to my lips.
But now that I have need of it to stir you,
I have the skill and insight of high things.
The destinies of kings and countries lie
In sun-bright clarity before my eye,
And from my mouth the jagged lightning springs.

BURGUNDY (*intensely agitated, raises his eyes to her and contem-*
plates her with wonder and emotion):
What has come over me? Is it a god

That turns my heart within me to remorse?   1800
—She is not false when she so sways my mind.
No! No! If I am dazzled by the force
Of *magic,* then it is of Heaven's kind.
My heart tells me: from God she takes her course.
JOAN: O he is touched! He is! And I have not
Implored in vain. The storm-cloud of his anger
Is melting from his brow as tears of dew,
And from his eyes now radiant with peace
Breaks forth the golden sun of his emotion.
—Put up your weapons—let heart press on heart.—   1810
He weeps, he is won over, he is ours!   [1811]

>   *(Sword and banner fall from her hands, she*
>   *hastens to him with outstretched arms and em-*
>   *braces him with passionate vehemence. La Hire*
>   *and Dunois drop their swords and hasten to*
>   *embrace him also.)*

ACT III

SCENE 1

The King's court at Châlons-sur-Marne.
Dunois and La Hire.

DUNOIS: We have been bosom friends and soldier comrades,
    For one and the same cause we raised our arms,
    Through thick and thin we have stuck close together.
    Do not let love of women break the bond
    That has endured through every turn of fate.

LA HIRE: Prince, listen to me!

DUNOIS: You are in love with the Maiden
    And I am well aware what you are thinking.
    You mean to go straight off now to the King
    And make request of him to be awarded   1820
    The Maiden as a gift.—He cannot well
    Refuse your bravery that deserved reward.
    But you should know—before I see her in
    Another's arms—

LA HIRE: Prince, hear me!

DUNOIS: It is not
    The sudden, fleeting pleasure of the eyes
    That draws me to her. Never has a woman
    Stirred my unvanquished mind until I saw
    This wondrous Maiden whom God's providence
    Assigned to be this kingdom's savior and
    My wife. And at that instant I swore by   1830
    A sacred oath to bring her home my bride.
    For only a strong woman can be loved
    By a strong man. This ardent heart of mine
    Yearns to repose upon an equal bosom
    That comprehends and can endure its strength.

61

La Hire: Prince, how could I presume to measure my
　Weak merits with your name's heroic fame!
　When Count Dunois once enters in the lists,
　Competitors must all withdraw before him.
　But still a humble shepherdess can not   1840
　Stand worthily beside you as your wife;
　The royal blood that fills your veins can not
　Do otherwise than spurn so base a mixture.

Dunois: She is the child divine of holy Nature,
　As I am, and of equal birth with me.
　Would she dishonor the hand of a Prince,
　She who is like a bride of sinless angels,
　Whose head is circled with a god-like halo
　That shines more brightly than an earthly crown,
　Who sees all great and lofty things that this   1850
　Earth offers lying small beneath her feet!
　For all the thrones of Princes piled one on
　Top of the other to the very stars
　Would not reach to the height where *she* now stands
　In her angelic majesty.

La Hire: Let the King decide.

Dunois:　　　　　　　　No, she must make
　Her own decision! She has made France free,
　And free herself, she must bestow her heart.

La Hire: Here comes the King.

　　　(Enter Charles, Agnes Sorel, Du Chatel, the
　　　Archbishop, and Chatillon.)

Charles *(to Chatillon)*:   1860
　He's coming here! To recognize me as
　His King, you say, and do me homage too?

Chatillon: Right here, Sire, in your royal city of
　Châlons the Duke, my master, means to throw
　Himself before your feet. — He bade me greet
　You as my Lord and King, and say he follows
　Hard on my heels and will be here directly.

Sorel: He comes! O lovely sunshine of this day
　That brings such joy and peace and amity!

CHATILLON: My Lord will have two hundred knights with him,
   And he will kneel in homage at your feet;   1870
   But he expects that you will *not* permit it
   And that you will embrace him as your cousin.
CHARLES: My heart burns to feel his heart beat with mine.
CHATILLON: The Duke requests that at this first encounter
   No mention be made of our ancient feud
   So much as by one word.
CHARLES: The past shall be
   Forever sunk in Lethe. We intend
   To look on bright days only in the future.
CHATILLON: All those who fought for Burgundy shall be
   Included in this reconciliation.   1880
CHARLES: My kingdom shall be doubled in this way.
CHATILLON: Queen Isabeau shall be included in
   This peace if she is willing to accept it.
CHARLES: She has waged war on *me,* not I on *her.*
   Our dispute is over as soon as she ends it.
CHATILLON: Twelve knights shall serve as hostage for your word.
CHARLES: My word is sacred.
CHATILLON: The Archbishop shall
   Divide a Host between you two as pledge
   And seal of honest reconciliation.
CHARLES: By my share in salvation everlasting,   1890
   My heart and handclasp are at one on this.
   What further pledge does the Duke still request?
CHATILLON *(with a glance at Du Chatel):*
   I see a person here whose presence could
   Embitter the initial greeting.
        (Du Chatel walks silently away.)
CHARLES: Go,
   Then, Du Chatel, until the Duke can bear
   The sight of you, you shall remain concealed.
     *(He follows him with his eyes, then
     hurries to overtake him and embraces
     him.)*
   You once were ready to do more than this

For my peace, upright friend!
>   *(Du Chatel goes out.)*

CHATILLON: This document sets forth the other points.

CHARLES *(to the Archbishop)*:
>   Arrange it. We assent to everything.   1900
>   No price can be too costly for a friend.
>   Dunois, go take a hundred noble knights
>   With you to meet the Duke in friendly fashion
>   And be his escort. All the troops shall crown
>   Themselves with branches to receive their brothers.
>   And let the entire city be adorned
>   As for a festival, have all bells sound
>   Proclaiming France and Burgundy are bound
>   Anew in friendship.
>> *(Enter a Page. Trumpets are heard.)*
>>   Hark! What are these trumpets?

THE PAGE: The Duke of Burgundy has made his entry.   1910
>   *(Exit.)*

DUNOIS *(goes out with La Hire and Chatillon)*:
>   Come on! We'll meet him!

CHARLES *(to Sorel)*:
>   You're weeping, Agnes? My strength almost fails
>   Me too, preparing to endure this meeting.
>   How many victims had to fall in death
>   Till we could meet again so peaceably.
>   But every storm at last abates its fury,
>   Day follows after densest night, and in
>   Good time the tardiest of fruits will ripen.

THE ARCHBISHOP *(at the window)*:
>   The Duke can scarcely manage for the press
>   Around him. They are lifting him off from   1920
>   His horse. They kiss his mantle, kiss his spurs.

CHARLES: They are a kindly people, quick to flare
>   Up in their love as in their anger. — How
>   Soon they forget it was this very Duke
>   That slew their fathers and their sons. The moment
>   Consumes and makes up for a total lifetime!

—Control yourself, Sorel. Your vivid joy
Might also be a briar in his side.
Nothing shall shame him here or make him sad.

> *(Enter the Duke of Burgundy, Dunois, La
> Hire, Chatillon, and two other knights of the
> Duke's retinue. The Duke stops at the entryway.
> The King moves toward him, Burgundy simul-
> taneously approaches, and at the moment when
> he is about to fall upon one knee the King
> receives him in his arms.)*

You took us by surprise. — We had intended   1930
To come to meet you. — You have faster horses.

BURGUNDY: They were returning me to duty.

> *(He embraces Sorel and kisses her
> on the brow.)*
>   Cousin,

With your permission. Such, at Arras, is
Our privilege; no pretty woman may
Refuse the custom.

CHARLES: Your court is, they say,
The seat of Love, the market place as well
Where everything of beauty is in stock.

BURGUNDY: My King, we are a commerce-minded people,
Delicious things that grow in all the climates
Are all displayed for seeing and enjoyment   1940
In Bruges, our market town. The highest, though,
Of all commodities is women's beauty.

SOREL: The loyalty of women comes still higher,
But it is never seen out on the market.

CHARLES: You have a wicked reputation, Cousin,
For your disdain of women's finest virtue.

BURGUNDY: This heresy most harshly punishes
Itself. And you are fortunate, my King!
Your heart taught you quite early what my wild
Life taught me late.

> *(He notices the Archbishop and
> gives him his hand.)*

Ah, reverend man of God,   1950
Your blessing. You are always in the right place.
One needs but walk the righteous path to find you.
THE ARCHBISHOP: Now let my Master call me when he will,
My heart is filled with joy, I can depart
In peace now that my eyes have seen this day.
BURGUNDY *(to Sorel):*
They tell me that you robbed yourself of your
Own jewels to convert them into weapons
Against me? Are you then so warrior-minded?
It meant that much to you to ruin me?
But now our strife is past, and everything   1960
Will be recovered that was lost, for even
Your jewels have found their way back to you.
They were intended to make war against me,
Receive them from my hand, a sign of peace.
> *(From one of his attendants he takes the jewel*
> *casket and presents it to her, open. Agnes Sorel*
> *looks at the King in perplexity.)*
CHARLES: Accept the gift, it is a precious double pledge
Of love to me and reconciliation.
BURGUNDY *(as he puts a jewelled rose in her hair):*
O why is it not France's royal crown?
Then I would fasten it with equally
Devoted heart upon this lovely head.
> *(taking her hand in a*
> *meaningful way)*
And—count on me if ever you should have   1970
Need of a friend!
> *(Agnes Sorel breaks into tears and steps aside.*
> *The King too struggles with a strong emotion.*
> *All present look with feeling at both Princes.)*
BURGUNDY *(after looking at each one in turn, throws himself into*
the King's arms):
> O my good King!
> *(Simultaneously the Burgundian knights rush*
> *to Dunois, La Hire, and the Archbishop and*

embrace them. Both Princes remain speechless
for a time in each others arms.)
How could I hate you! How could I renounce you!
CHARLES: Be still! Be still! No more of that!
BURGUNDY: How could
  I crown that Englishman and to that foreigner
  Swear homage, plunging you, my King, in ruin!
CHARLES: Forget it! Everything has been forgiven.
  This moment cancels everything. It was
  A destiny, or some ill-fortuned star.
BURGUNDY *(takes his hand):*
  Believe me, I shall make it good. I shall!
  All your sorrows shall be compensated for!   1980
  And you shall have your entire kingdom back—
  And not a single village shall be missing.
CHARLES: We are united. I fear no more foes.
BURGUNDY: Believe me, with light heart I do not fear
  The weapons used against you. If you knew . . .
  O why did you not send *this* lady to me?
            (pointing to Sorel)
  I surely could not have withstood her tears!
  —But now no power of Hell shall separate
  Us who have clasped each other heart to heart!
  I now have found my true and rightful place,   1990
  My wanderings have ended at this breast.
THE ARCHBISHOP *(stepping between them):*
  You are united, Princes! France arises
  As a rejuvenated Phoenix from
  The ashes, promising a splendid future.
  The country's grievous wounds will heal again,
  The desolated towns and cities will
  Arise more gloriously out of their rubble,
  The fields will deck themselves in newer green.—
  But those who fell as victims of your quarrel,
  The dead will not arise again; the tears   2000
  Shed for your strife have been shed and remain so.
  The coming generation will bloom, but

Not so the one that was a prey to ruin.
The luck of grandsons will not wake their fathers.
Such are the fruits of your fraternal strife.
Let this serve you as guidance: Fear the divine
Lord of the sword before you wrest it from
Its sheath. The mighty may unleash a war;
Not trained, however, as the falcon is
That flies back from the air to huntsmen's hands,   2010
This wild god will not come at human call.
The hand of rescue from the clouds will not
Come twice at the right moment as today.
BURGUNDY: O Sire! You have an angel at your side.
  —Where is she? Why do I not see her here?
CHARLES: Yes, where is Joan? Why is she not with
  Us at this splendid solemn moment which
  She has made possible?
THE ARCHBISHOP: The holy Maiden,
  Sire, does not love the ease of idle courts,
  And when divine behest does not command   2020
  Her to appear before the world, she shuns
  In modesty the gaze of vulgar eyes.
  She surely is communing with her God
  If she is not in action for the welfare
  Of France; for blessing follows all her steps.
          (*Enter Joan in armor but without a helmet,*
            and wearing a wreath in her hair.)
CHARLES: Have you come, Joan, thus adorned as priestess
  To consecrate the friendship that you founded?
BURGUNDY: How terrifying this girl was in battle,
  And how peace shines in grace around her now!
  —Well, Joan, have I kept my word? Are you   2030
  Content? Do I deserve your approbation?
JOAN: You did the greatest favor for yourself.
  You shimmer now in blessed light whereas
  You hung in dark and blood-red glow before,
  A moon of terror in this sky of ours.
          (*looking about*)

I find here many noble knights assembled
And all their eyes are gleaming with bright joy.
I did meet *one,* however, who is sad,
Who has to hide when all the rest rejoice.

BURGUNDY: And who is conscious of such grievous guilt   2040
  That he must give up hope of our good favor?

JOAN: May he approach? O tell me that he may!
Achieve full merit! A reconciliation
Is none at all that does not wholly free
The heart. One drop of hate left in the cup
Of joy will turn the blessed drink to poison.
—Let no wrong be so black that Burgundy
Will not forgive it on this joyous day.

BURGUNDY: I get your meaning!

JOAN: And you will forgive?
You will, Lord Duke?—Come in, then, Du Chatel!   2050
    (She opens the door and leads Du Chatel in;
    the latter stops some distance away.)
The Duke is reconciled with all his foes,
And with you too.
    (Du Chatel comes a few paces nearer and tries
    to read the Duke's expression.)

BURGUNDY: What are you doing to
Me, Joan? Do you know what you are asking?

JOAN: A kindly master opens up his gates
For all the guests to come, he shuts none out.
Free as the firmament that spans the world
A pardon must include both friend and foe.
The sun dispenses equally its rays
To all the spaces of infinity;
In equal measure heaven sheds its dew   2060
Upon all living things that thirst. Whatever
Is good, whatever comes from up above
Is universal and without reserve;
But in the hidden folds, there darkness dwells.

BURGUNDY: O she can do with me just as she pleases,
  My heart in her hands turns to pliant wax.

—Embrace me, Du Chatel. I do forgive you.
Shade of my father, do not rage if I
Now clasp in amity the hand that slew you.
And hold it not against me, gods of death,　　　　　2070
That I now break my awesome vow of vengeance.
Down where you house in everlasting night
No heart beats, everything is everlasting,
Immoveable,—but it is otherwise
With things up here above beneath the sunlight.
Man, the living, feeling creature, is
The easy victim of the mighty moment.

CHARLES (to Joan):
What all I do not have to thank you for,
High Maiden! How well you have kept your word!
How quickly you have changed my destiny!　　　　2080
First reconciled my friends with me, then plunged
My enemies into the dust, and wrested
My cities from an alien yoke.—All this
You did alone.—Now how shall I reward you?

JOAN: Be ever human in good fortune, Lord,
As in adversity.—On greatness' summit
Do not forget the worth of friends in need.
You found that out in your humiliation.
Do not deny your justice or your mercy
To the least of your subjects; forth from flocks　　2090
God summoned your deliverer.—You will
Assemble all of France beneath your scepter
And be the ancestor of famous Princes;
Those who come after you will shine more brightly
Than those who came before you on the throne.
Your race will bloom as long as it maintains
Its people's love within its heart,
And only pride can bring it to its fall.
Out of the lowly huts from whence has come
Your savior now, destruction direly threatens　　2100
Your progeny who will be stained with guilt.

BURGUNDY: Prophetic Maiden whom the Spirit moves,

If your eyes penetrate into the future,
Speak to me also of my race. Will it
Spread splendidly afar as it began?
JOAN: You, Burgundy, have raised your seat on high,
Up to a throne's height, and still higher strives
Your proud heart to uplift the daring structure
Into the clouds.—A hand, however, from
On high will bring its growth to sudden halt.   2110
Yet do not fear the fall of your great house.
It will live on in splendor through a daughter,
And scepter-bearing monarchs, shepherds of
Their peoples, will arise out of her womb.
They will hold sway upon two mighty thrones,
Prescribe laws unto the known world and also
Unto a new one which the hand of God
Has yet concealed beyond untravelled seas.
CHARLES: O tell us, if the Spirit will disclose it,
Will our alliance which we have renewed   2120
As friends unite our most remote descendants?
JOAN (after a silence):
You kings and rulers! Have a fear of discord!
Do not arouse dissension from its cavern
Where it lies sleeping now, for, once awakened,
It will be long before it is new-tamed.
It breeds a progeny, an iron race,
And from brands burning kindles further brands.
—Desire to know no more! Enjoy the present,
And let me draw a veil in silence over
The future.
SOREL: Holy Maiden, you have fathomed   2130
My heart. You know if it is seeking idle greatness.
Grant me a cheerful oracle as well.
JOAN: The spirit shows me only world events.
Your destiny lies in your private heart.
DUNOIS: But your own destiny, what will it prove
To be, exalted Maiden loved of Heaven?
The fairest happiness on earth will surely

Be yours, who are so holy.

JOAN: Happiness
Dwells in the bosom of eternal God.

CHARLES: Your happiness shall henceforth be your King's   2140
Concern, for I will magnify your name
In France. The furthest future generations
Shall call you blessed.—This I shall fulfill
Immediately.—Kneel!

> (*He draws his sword and touches her*
> *with it.*)
                              And rise up again
A noblewoman! I, your King, hereby
Raise you out of the dust of your dark birth.—
Your forebears I ennoble in their graves.—
Your coat-of-arms shall bear the lily-flower,
And you shall be the equal of the best
In France. None but the royal Valois blood   2150
Shall be more noble than your blood. And let
The greatest of my great consider they
Are honored by your hand. It shall be my
Concern to wed you to a noble husband.

DUNOIS (*steps forth*):
My heart chose her when she was still but lowly.
This recent honor that shines round her head
Makes neither my love nor her merit greater.
Here in the presence of my King and of
This Holy Bishop I extend my hand
To her to be my princely spouse, if she   2160
Considers I am worthy to receive her.

CHARLES: Resistless Maiden, you add miracle
To miracle. I now believe that to
You nothing is impossible. Here you
Have conquered this proud heart which heretofore
Mocked Love's omnipotence.

LA HIRE (*steps forth*):   But Joan's finest
Adornment is her modesty of heart.
She merits homage from the greatest, but

She never will lift her desire that high.
She does not strive for giddy heights of earth,   2170
The true affection of an honest heart
Will be enough for her, a tranquil lot
Such as I offer to her with this hand.

CHARLES: You too, La Hire? Two noble suitors, equal
In heroes' virtue and the fame of war!
—But will you, who have reconciled my foes
And made my kingdom whole, now rob me of
My dearest friends? For only one can have her,
And I esteem both worthy of the prize.
Speak, then, for your heart must make this decision.   2180

SOREL (steps closer):
I see the noble Maiden is surprised
And modest shame is coloring her cheeks.
Let her have time to ask her heart, confide
In her good friend, and loose the seal upon
Her tight-locked heart. The moment has now come
When even I may venture to approach
The austere Maiden like a sister and
Lend her a bosom filled with loyal trust.
Allow us first as women to consider
The matters that concern a woman, then   2190
See what we may decide.

CHARLES (starting to leave):   So shall it be.

JOAN: Not so, Sire! What has lent my cheeks their color
Was my confusion, not a bashful shame.
I have no confidences to this noble lady
That I would be ashamed to tell where men
Are present. These knights' choice does me much honor,
But I did not give up my shepherd's pasture
To gain an idle, worldly eminence,
Nor did I put this iron armor on
So I might twine a bride's wreath in my hair.   2200
I have been summoned for a different task
Which no one but a maiden can perform.
I am a warrior of highest God

And may not be the wife of any man.

THE ARCHBISHOP: To man is woman given as a loving
  Companion,—and when she obeys great Nature
  She serves most worthily the will of Heaven.
  And once you have performed sufficiently
  Your God's behest, who called you to the field,
  Then you will lay aside your weapons and   2210
  Return once more among the gentler sex
  That you have up to now denied and which
  Is not called to the bloody work of weapons.

JOAN: Reverend Sir, I cannot tell yet what
  The Spirit will command me to perform.
  But when the time arrives, its voice will not
  Be silent, and I shall obey it then.
  Right now it bids me finish up my task.   ·
  The forehead of my Lord is not yet crowned,
  The holy oil has not yet wet his head,   2220
  Nor does my Lord yet bear the name of King.

CHARLES: We are well on our way to Rheims, however.

JOAN: But let us not stand still, for enemies
  Are busy round about to block your path.
  Yet I shall lead you through the midst of them!

DUNOIS: But when once everything has been completed,
  When once we will have entered Rheims in triumph,
  Then will you, holy Maiden, grant to me—

JOAN: If Heaven wills that I emerge in triumph
  Out of this mortal battle, my work will   2230
  Be finished—and the shepherdess has no
  More business in the household of her King.

CHARLES (taking her hand):
  It is the Spirit's voice that stirs you now,
  And love is silent in your God-filled bosom.
  It will, believe me, not be silent always!
  Arms will be laid at rest, and Victory
  Will lead Peace by the hand, and Joy will then
  Come back to every bosom, and more gentle
  Emotions will awake in every heart—

They will awake in your heart equally,   2240
And you will weep sweet tears of longing then
Such as your eye has never shed. — This heart,
Which Heaven occupies entirely now,
Will turn in love unto an earthly lover —
Your rescue has brought happiness to thousands,
And you will end by making one man happy!

JOAN: Dauphin! Are you already weary of
Divine manifestation, that you would
Destroy its vessel and pull down to dust
The sinless Maiden whom God sent to you?   2250
You blinded hearts! You men of little faith!
The majesty of Heaven shines about you,
Before your eyes its miracles are wrought,
And you see nothing in me but a woman.
But should a woman case herself in steel,
Intrude amidst the battles fought by men?
Woe would betide me if I took my God's
Avenging sword in hand and in my vain
Heart bore affection for an earthly man!
It would be better I had not been born!   2260
Not one word more of this, I tell you, if
You do not wish to rouse the Spirit in me
To fury. A man's eye desiring me
Is horrible to me and sacrilegious.

CHARLES: Enough. It is in vain we seek to move her.

JOAN: Command the trumpets to be blown for war!
This truce oppresses me, this war unwon;
Up from this idle rest where I now wait
It drives me to complete my task begun,
Imperious in its summons toward my fate.   2270

(Enter a Knight in haste.)

CHARLES: What is it?

THE KNIGHT: The enemy has crossed the Marne
And taken battle stations.

JOAN *(inspired)*:   War and battle!
The soul is now delivered from its bonds.

Go fetch your weapons. I will form the ranks.
(She hurries out.)

CHARLES: La Hire, go with her.—At Rheims gate itself
They mean to make us battle for the crown.

DUNOIS: True courage does not drive them on. This is
The last attempt of futile desperation.

CHARLES: I do not spur you, Burgundy. Today
Could well atone for many evil days.   2280

BURGUNDY: You shall be satisfied with me.

CHARLES: I will
Advance before you on the path of fame,
And in sight of the coronation city
I'll fight and win myself a crown.—My Agnes,
Your loyal knight bids you farewell!

AGNES *(embraces him):*
I shall not weep, nor shall I tremble for you.
My confidence extends up to the clouds!
So many signs of grace could not have been
Vouchsafed by Heaven only for our sorrow.
I shall embrace my Lord with victory crowned 2290
Within the conquered walls of Rheims tomorrow.

(Trumpets resound with spirited tones, and while the scene-change is being effected, pass over into wild battle scrimmage. When the curtain rises on the new scene the orchestra strikes up and is accompanied by martial instruments offstage.)

SCENE 2

(The scene is transformed into an open country bordered by trees. During the music soldiers are seen withdrawing swiftly across the rear of the stage.

Enter Talbot, leaning on Fastolf and accompanied by soldiers.)

TALBOT: Now set me down here underneath these trees,

While you go back again into the battle.
I have no need of any help to die.

FASTOLF: O this deplorable, unhappy day!
          (Enter Lionel.)
  Alas! the sight you find here, Lionel!
  Here our Commander lies with mortal wounds.

LIONEL: Oh, God forbid! Stand up, my noble Lord.
  This is no time for sinking with exhaustion.
  Do not give way to death, but order Nature   2300
  By virtue of your mighty will, to live.

TALBOT: In vain! The day of destiny has come
  That is to overturn our throne in France.
  In futile and in desperate struggle I
  Had hazarded the utmost to avert it.
  Felled headlong by the lightning, here I lie,
  Not to arise again.—And Rheims is lost.
  Make haste to salvage Paris!

LIONEL: Paris has made a treaty with the Dauphin.
  That was the news a courier just brought us.   2310

TALBOT *(tears off his bandages)*:
  Then ebb away, you brooklets of my blood,
  For I have looked my fill upon this sun!

LIONEL: I cannot stay here.—Fastolf, you will take
  The General to a place of safety; we
  Can not hold out much longer in this place.
  Our troops are fleeing on all sides, the Maiden
  Is pressing forward irresistibly.

TALBOT: Inanity, you win, and I must perish!
  With stupidity the gods themselves contend
  In vain. Sublimest Reason, light-clear daughter   2320
  Sprung from the godhead's brow, wise founder of
  The universe, directress of the stars,
  Who are you, if, tied to the horse's tail
  Of Idiocy, that frenzied steed, and crying
  With helpless cries, you see yourself paired with
  The drunken and hurled down to the abyss!
  A curse on any man who turns his life

To great and worthy things and with wise spirit
Devises well-laid plans! The King of Fools
Is winner of the world.—

LIONEL: My Lord, you have   2330
But few more moments yet of life.—Think now
Of your Creator!

TALBOT: If we had been conquered
As brave men by brave men, then we could take
Some comfort from that universal Fate
That turns its globe with constant alternation.—
But to succumb to such gross trickery!
Was our industrious and earnest life
Not worthy of more dignified conclusion?

LIONEL (*gives him his hand*):
My Lord, farewell. Your rightful due of tears
I'll pay you when the battle has been fought,   2340
Provided I am still alive. But now
Fate summons me, which on the battlefield
Still sits in judgment and still shakes its lots.
Until we meet, then, in another world.
Brief is our parting for so long a friendship.
                    (*Exit.*)

TALBOT: Soon all will end, and I to earth give back,
And to the everlasting sun, the atoms
That were conjoined in me for joy and sorrow,—
And of the mighty Talbot who had filled
The world with warrior's fame, there will be nothing   2350
Left but a handful of light dust.—Such is
The end of man,—and as for profit, all
We gain out of the struggle of our lives
Is insight into nothingness, and cordial
Contempt for everything that once had seemed
Sublime to us or worth the wishing for.
            (*Enter Charles, Burgundy, Dunois, Du Chatel,
            and soldiers.*)

BURGUNDY: The redoubt has been stormed.
DUNOIS: The day is ours.

CHARLES *(noticing Talbot):*
  See who it is that yonder takes unwilling
  And hard farewell from the light of the sun.
  His armor signifies no common man.   2360
  Go lend him aid, if aid can still avail him.
        (Soldiers from the King's retinue
           step up.)
FASTOLF: Stand back, and have respect for this man dead
  Whom while he lived you did not want close by!
BURGUNDY: What's this! It's Talbot lying in his blood!
        (He walks toward him. Talbot stares
          at him fixedly, and dies.)
FASTOLF: Back, Burgundy! Sight of a traitor should
  Not poison the last gaze of this great hero!
DUNOIS: The dreaded Talbot! The invincible!
  Can you make do with this so little space
  When the wide earth of France could not suffice
  For the ambition of your giant spirit?   2370
  —Now for the first time, Sire, I hail you King.
  The crown was still unsteady on your head
  As long as life remained within this body.
CHARLES *(after he has viewed the dead man silently):*
  A Higher One than we has conquered him.
  Upon the soil of France he lies here like
  A hero on his shield which he would not
  Desert. Take him away.
       (Soldiers lift the corpse and
       carry it away.)
              Peace to his ashes!
  A monument of honor shall be his.
  Here in the midst of France his bones shall rest
  Where his course as a hero was concluded,   2380
  As far as his no foeman's sword advanced.
  His epitaph is the spot where he now lies.
FASTOLF *(surrenders his sword):*
  My Lord, I am your prisoner.
CHARLES *(gives the sword back to him):*   Not so!

Harsh warfare honors pious duty also,
Follow your master freely to his grave.
Now hurry, Du Chatel. — My Agnes trembles. —
Relieve her of anxiety for us. —
Tell her we live and are victorious,
Give her triumphant escort into Rheims.

(Exit Du Chatel.)
(Enter La Hire.)

DUNOIS: La Hire! Where is the Maiden?

LA HIRE: I ask that   2390
Of you. I left her fighting at your side.

DUNOIS: I thought she was protected by your arm
When I rushed off to lend the King assistance.

BURGUNDY: In the foe's thickest press I saw her white
Flag flying just a little while ago.

DUNOIS: Alas! where is she? I surmise misfortune!
Come on, come on, let's set her free. — I fear
Her daring spirit has led her too far.
By foes surrounded, fighting all alone,
She may be now succumbing to their numbers.   2400

CHARLES: O hurry, save her!

LA HIRE: Coming!

BURGUNDY: All of us!   [2401]

(They hurry away.)

SCENE 3

*Another desolate area of the battlefield. The towers of Rheims
are visible in the distance, gleaming with sunlight.*
*Enter a Knight all in black armor, with closed visor. Joan pursues
him to the front of the stage, where he stops and waits for her.*

JOAN: You thing of craft, I see your cunning now!
Deceitfully and by pretended flight
You lured me from the battlefield, averting
Death and destiny from British heads.

But your own ruin overtakes you now.
THE BLACK KNIGHT: Why do you thus pursue me, and why do
  You cling with burning fury to my heels?
  I am not destined to die by your hand.
JOAN: You are abhorrent to my deepest soul,   2410
  As is the night, whose color is your own.
  An overwhelming impulse drives me to
  Obliterate you from the light of day.
  Who are you? Open up your visor.—If
  I had not seen the warlike Talbot fall
  In battle, I would say that you were Talbot.
THE BLACK KNIGHT: Has your prophetic spirit voice gone silent?
JOAN: It loudly speaks out of my bosom's depths
  To tell me that Misfortune stands beside me.
THE BLACK KNIGHT: Joan of Arc! Up to the gates of Rheims 2420
  You have advanced on wings of victory.
  Let thus much fame achieved suffice you and
  Dismiss the Fortune that has served you like
  A slave, before it frees itself in anger;
  It hates faith and serves no one to the last.
JOAN: Why do you bid me stop in mid career
  And turn aside to leave my task unfinished?
  I shall complete it and fulfill my vow!
THE BLACK KNIGHT: Nothing can withstand you, mighty Maiden,
  In every battle you have been triumphant.—   2430
  But enter no more battles. Heed my warning!
JOAN: I shall not let this sword out of my hand
  Until proud England has been overcome.
THE BLACK KNIGHT: Look yonder! There Rheims rises with its
  Your journey's goal and end.—And there you see   [towers,
  The high cathedral's spires aglow with light.
  There you will enter in triumphal splendor,
  And crown your King, and see your vow fulfilled.
  —Turn back and do not enter! Heed my warning!
JOAN: Who are you, creature false and double-tongued,   2440
  Who seek to terrify me and confuse me?
  How dare you thus presume the treachery

Of giving me false oracles?
>   *(The Black Knight starts to go away.*
>   *She steps athwart his path.)*
>   No, you
Shall answer me or perish at my hands!
>   *(She starts to deliver a blow at him.)*

THE BLACK KNIGHT *(touches her with his hand; she stops
>   motionless):*
Kill something that is mortal!
>   *(Darkness, lightning, and a clap of thunder.*
>   *The Knight sinks into the earth.)*

JOAN *(stands in astonishment at first, but soon recovers her self-
>   control):*
It was no living thing.—A phantom shape
It was from Hell, or some rebellious spirit
Arisen out of the abyss of fire
To quell my noble heart within my bosom.
Whom do I fear with the sword of my God?   2450
I shall fulfill my course triumphantly
Though Hell itself comes riding to the lists,
My courage neither falters nor desists!
>   *(She starts to leave.)*
>   *(Enter Lionel.)*

LIONEL: Accursed girl, turn and prepare to fight.—
For we shall not both leave this place alive.
The best men of my nation you have slain.
The noble Talbot has breathed forth his soul
Upon my bosom.—I shall take revenge
For that brave man or else share in his fate.
And so that you know who confers your fame   2460
By his death or his triumph,—I am Lionel,
The last one of the Princes of our army,
And still unconquered is this arm of mine.
>   *(He attacks her. After a brief fight she
>   strikes his sword out of his hand.)*
Deceitful Fortune!
>   *(He wrestles with her.)*

JOAN (*seizes him from behind by the helmet crest and wrenches his helmet open by force so that his face is revealed; at the same instant she brandishes her sword with her right hand*):
                    Suffer what you sought,
Through me the Blessed Virgin slaughters you!
                    (*At this instant she looks into his face. The
                    sight of him transfixes her, she stops motionless,
                    then slowly allows her arm to sink down.*)
LIONEL: Why do you falter and withhold the death-blow?
Take my life, you have my reputation
Already. I am in your hands. I want
No mercy.
            (*With her hand she gives him
            a sign to escape.*)
                I am to escape? And owe
My life to *you?*—I would much rather die!   2470
JOAN (*with averted face*):
Make your escape! I do not want to know
That your life was within my power.
LIONEL: I hate you and I hate your gift.—I want
No mercy.—Kill your enemy who loathes
You and who would be glad to kill you.
JOAN: Kill me, then,
    —And flee!
LIONEL: Ha! What is this?
JOAN (*hides her face*):   Alas for me!
LIONEL (*steps closer to her*):
They say you kill all Englishmen that you
Have overcome in battle.—Why do you
Spare none but me?
JOAN (*raises her sword against him with a sudden movement, but
    lets it drop again as she looks into his face*):
                    O Holy Virgin!
LIONEL: Why
Call on the Holy One? She does not know you.   2480
Heaven has no part in you.
JOAN (*in the most intense anguish*):

What have I done? My vow is broken now!
>   *(She wrings her hands in despair.)*

LIONEL *(observes her with sympathy and steps nearer to her)*:
Unhappy Maiden, I am sorry for you.
You touch me. You show magnanimity
To me alone. I feel my hatred melting.
I cannot help but sympathize with you.
—Who are you?

JOAN: Flee! Away! Make your escape!
LIONEL: I am grieved by your beauty and your youth.
The sight of you strikes to my heart, and I
Would like to save you.—Tell me, how can I   2490
Accomplish that? Come, come! Renounce this monstrous
Alliance.—Cast them from you now, these weapons!
JOAN: I am unworthy now to bear them.
LIONEL: Cast
Them from you, quickly. Come with me.
JOAN *(with horror)*:   What! Come
With you!
LIONEL: You can be saved. Come, then, with me
And I will save you. But do not delay.
I am seized with tremendous sorrow for you
And with a nameless longing for your rescue.
>   *(He seizes her arm.)*

JOAN: Here comes the Bastard! They are looking for me!
And if they find you here—
LIONEL: I will protect you!   2500
JOAN: O I will die if you fall at their hands!
LIONEL: Then you feel fondness for me?
JOAN: Saints of Heaven!
LIONEL: Will I see you again? Or hear from you?
JOAN: No, never!
LIONEL: This sword is my guarantee
Of seeing you again.
>   *(He wrests her sword away from her.)*

JOAN: You dare to, madman?

LIONEL: I yield to force now, but we meet again!
                          (Exit.)
                (Enter Dunois and La Hire.)
LA HIRE: Yes, there she is! Alive!
DUNOIS: Fear nothing, Joan!
  Your friends are standing mighty at your side.
LA HIRE: That fleeing man, is that not Lionel?
DUNOIS: Well, let him flee! The just cause triumphs, Joan,   2510
  Rheims opens up its gates, and all the people
  Are pouring forth exultant toward their King.
LA HIRE: What ails the Maiden? She turns pale, she faints!
      (Joan reels and is on the point of collapse.)
DUNOIS: She has been wounded.—Open up her armor.
  It is her arm, the injury is slight.
LA HIRE: Her blood is flowing!
JOAN: Let it with my life
  Stream forth!   [2517]
      (She lies unconscious in the arms of La Hire.)

ACT IV

SCENE 1

*A festively adorned hall. The columns are festooned; flutes and
oboes off stage.*

JOAN: Our weapons rest, the storms of war have found
    Their peace, song follows after battles dire,
    Through all the streets the merry dances sound,   2520
    In splendid festival shine church and choir,
    And arches of green boughs rise from the ground,
    And columns wear bright garlands for attire;
    Broad Rheims will not contain the welling tide
    Of guests now surging in from every side.

    One sense of joy exultant fills this place,
    And one thought beats in every heart tonight;
    What hate had sundered lately in disgrace
    Now shares the common pleasure with delight.
    Whoever claims descent from Frankish race   2530
    Now claims the name more proudly as his right.
    The splendor of the old crown is new won,
    And France does homage to her own King's son.

    But I who have achieved these glorious things,
    I am not touched by all this happiness;
    My heart is changed with many alterings
    And flees this merriment with sad distress,
    Unto the British camp it plies its wings,
    My gaze roams toward the foe and languishes,
    And from the joyous circle I must steal   2540
    That I my grievous guilt may best conceal.

Who? I? I hold the image of
A man in this pure heart of mine?
This heart can pulse with earthly love,
That Heaven fills with light divine?
I, who am my country's savior,
Almighty God's own warrior,
I for my country's foe dare yearn?
Do I dare to the chaste sun turn,
And will not shame annihilate me?   2550
    (The off-stage music passes over into a
       soft and melting melody.)
  Grief, o grief to me! These tones!
O how they beguile my ear!
Each one calls me with his voice,
Charms his image to appear.
  O if battle's storm would seize me,
Spears were whizzing round my head.
In the fury of the strife
Then I would regain my life!
  But these voices now, these tones,
How they twine and snare my heart!   2560
All the strength within my bosom
Is dissolved in tender yearning
And in tears of sadness burning.
    (after a pause, with greater
      animation.)
What if I slew him? Could I, after looking
Into his eyes? What! Slay him? I would sooner
Have aimed the mortal stroke at my own breast!
And am I guilty just for being human?
Is pity sinful?—Pity! Did you hear
The voice of pity and humanity
With all those others whom your sword has slain?   2570
Why was it silent when that youngster of a Welshman
With all his tender years begged for his life?
Sly heart, you lie to the Eternal Light,
It was not pity whose voice claimed its right!

Why did I have to look into his eyes?
Or see the features of his noble face?
It was with your glance that your crime began,
You luckless creature! God requires an instrument
Unseeing. With blind eyes you acted well!
But once you *saw*, God's shield abandoned you   2580
And you were caught in nets of Hell.

> *(The flutes resume; she falls into*
> *silent melancholy.)*

Harmless staff; Would that I
Had never changed you for the sword!
Or in your branches, sacred oak,
There had been no rustling word.
Would that you had not come down,
Queen of Heaven, wondrously,
I can not deserve your crown,
Take, o take it back from me.

I have seen the skies unfurled,   2590
Seen the saints with blessed eyes,
But my hopes are of this world,
Not on high among the skies.
Did you have to lay upon me
This dread call without appeal?
Could this heart of mine be hardened
Which was formed by Heaven to feel?

Choose when you proclaim your might
Those in your eternal sight
Who free of sin about you stand;   2600
To spirits pure give your command,
Deathless spirits, who will keep
Their vows, who neither feel nor weep!
The shepherdess, the virgin tender,
Do not choose her, do not send her!

Fates of battles, quarrels of kings,
Are these things of my concern?

  Guiltless I had guarded lambs
  On the silent mountain top.
  But you wrenched me forth to live   2610
  In a Prince's haughty hall,
  My choice it was not to give
  Myself to sin and guilty fall.
    (Enter Agnes Sorel in great agitation. When
  she catches sight of the Maiden, she hurries up
  to her and falls upon her neck. Suddenly she
  recollects herself, releases her, and kneels down
  before her.)

SOREL: No! No! Here in the dust before you—
JOAN *(tries to raise her up):*   Rise!
  What is it? You forget yourself and me.
SOREL: O do not hinder me. It is an impulse
  Of joy that casts me at your feet.—I must
  Pour out my overflowing heart to God,
  I worship Him Invisible in you.
  You are the angel who has led my Lord   2620
  To Rheims and placed the crown upon his head.
  What I had never dreamed of seeing is
  Fulfilled! The coronation rite is ready,
  The King stands in his gorgeous festive robes,
  Assembled are the peers, the great ones of
  The crown, to carry the insignia,
  The people pour in streams toward the cathedral,
  The dances sound, and all the bells are ringing,
  The happiness is more than I can bear!
    (Joan lifts her gently up. Agnes Sorel pauses
    for a moment as she peers more closely into the
    Maiden's eyes.)

But you remain severe and solemn. You   2630
Can create happiness but do not share it.
Your heart is cold, you do not feel our joy,
You have looked on the splendor of the heavens,
No earthly happiness can stir your heart.
    (Joan seizes her hand with vehemence,
    then quickly releases it again.)

If you could be a woman, feel like one!
Put off this armor, there is no more war,
Profess yourself one of the gentler sex.
My loving heart draws back from you in fear
As long as you are so like the dread Pallas.

JOAN: What do you ask of me?

SOREL: Give up these weapons!   2640
Put off this armor. Love is fearful of
Approaching such a bosom cased in steel.
O be a woman, and you will feel love!

JOAN: I should give up my weapons now! Right now!
No, I shall bare my breast to death in battle!
Not now.—O may steel seven-fold protect
Me from your festivals and from myself!

SOREL: Count Dunois loves you, and his noble heart,
Which only knows heroic virtue and
High fame, burns with a holy feeling for you.   2650
O it is fine to see oneself beloved by
A hero—finer still to love him also!

            (Joan turns away in revulsion.)

You hate him!—No, no, merely you can not
Love him.—How could you possibly hate him!
We hate none but the one who robs us of
A loved one, but for you there is no loved one!
Your heart is calm.—If only it could feel—

JOAN: Have sympathy for me! Lament my fate!

SOREL: What could be lacking to your happiness?
You have fulfilled your promise, France is free,   2660
And you have led your King triumphantly
Into the coronation city and
Achieved high fame. A happy people does
You homage, and from all tongues flows acclaim,
You are the goddess of this festival.
The King himself does not shine with his crown
More splendidly than you.

JOAN: O if I only
Could hide down in the deepest womb of earth!

SOREL: What is the matter? What a strange emotion!
   Who has a right to raise his eyes today   2670
   If *you* must keep your gaze cast down? Let *me*
   Blush, me, who feel so small compared to you,
   Who cannot rise up to the level of
   Your loftiness and your heroic strength.
   Shall I confess to you my total weakness? —
   It is not glory of my fatherland,
   Nor the new splendor of the throne, nor people's
   High jubilation over victory
   That occupies my gentle heart. There is
   But one alone who occupies it wholly.   2680
   It has room only for this one emotion:
   He is the one adored, the people shout
   For *him*, bless *him,* strew flowers in *his* path,
   And he is mine, he is the man I love.

JOAN: O you are fortunate! Count yourself blessed!
   You love where all else loves. And you may open
   Your heart and speak aloud of your delight
   And openly display it in men's eyes.
   The country's feast is the feast of your love.
   And all the people in their endless numbers   2690
   Now pouring at full tide into these walls,
   They all will share your feeling, they will bless it,
   They shout for you, for you weave wreaths and dance,
   With universal rapture you are one,
   You love that which gives joy to all, the sun,
   And all you see is your love's radiance!

SOREL (*falling upon her neck*):
   O you delight me, you have understood
   Me fully. I misjudged you, you know love
   And put what I feel into mighty words.
   From fear and shyness my heart is relieved   2700
   And it pours forth to you in confidence —

JOAN (*wrenches herself loose from her arms*):
   Leave me! Turn away from me, and do
   Not stain yourself with my pest-laden presence!

Be happy, go! Let me conceal in depths
Of darkness my misfortune, shame, and horror.
SOREL: You frighten me, I do not understand you.
But I have never understood you.—Your
Profound, dark self was always veiled from me.
Who can grasp what it is that terrifies
Your holy heart, your pure soul's tender feeling?   2710
JOAN: *You* are the holy one, *you* are the pure one!
If you looked in my heart you would reject
Your enemy with horror, your betrayer!
                *(Enter Dunois, Du Chatel, and
                La Hire with Joan's flag.)*
DUNOIS: We were looking for you, Joan. All
Is ready, and the King sends us to say
You are to march before him with the sacred
Banner. You shall join the ranks of Princes
And walk the last and closest to himself.
For he does not deny it, and the whole
World shall bear witness, that to you alone   2720
This great day's honor is attributed.
LA HIRE: Here is the banner. Take it, noble Maiden.
The Princes and the people are all waiting.
JOAN: I walk ahead of him! I bear the banner!
DUNOIS: Whom else would it befit! What other hand
Is pure enough to bear the sacred object?
You wielded it in battle; carry it
In honor now upon this joyous path.
                *(La Hire starts to give her the flag;
                she shrinks back from it in horror.)*
JOAN: Away! Away!
LA HIRE: What is the matter? Are you
Afraid of your own banner?—Look at it!   2730
                (He unfurls the flag.)
It is the same one that you waved in triumph.
It bears the image of the Queen of Heaven
Hovering above the globe of earth,
For that was how the holy Mother taught you.

JOAN *(glancing over in horror)* :
    Yes, it is she. Just so she stood before me.
    See how she looks at me and knits her brows
    And from beneath dark lashes burns with anger!
SOREL: She is beside herself! Come to your senses!
    You are not looking at an actual thing.
    That is her earthly simulated image,   2740
    She walks herself amid the choirs of Heaven.
JOAN: Dread Queen, do you come to chastise your creature?
    Destroy me, punish me, take up your lightnings
    And let them fall upon my guilty head.
    My covenant is broken, desecrated,
    I have blasphemed against your holy name.
DUNOIS: Alas, what is this? What unhappy words!
LA HIRE *(in astonishment to Du Chatel)* :
    Do you know what this strange emotion means?
DU CHATEL: I see just what I see. I have been long
    Afraid of this.
DUNOIS: What do you say?
DU CHATEL: I may not   2750
    Say what I think. Would God that it were over
    And that the King already had his crown!
LA HIRE: What? Has the terror emanating from
    This flag reversed itself to turn on you?
    Let Britons fall to trembling at this symbol,
    To France's foes it is a thing of dread,
    But to its faithful subjects it is gracious.
JOAN: Yes, you are right. To friends it is benign
    And in our enemies it strikes a terror.
                (The coronation march is heard.)
DUNOIS: Then take the banner. Take it up. They have   2760
    Begun the march, no moment must be lost!   [2761]
            *(They force the flag upon her. She takes hold
            of it with intense reluctance and leaves. The
            others follow.)*

SCENE 2

The stage is transformed into an open square before the cathedral.
Spectators fill the background, and from their midst step forth
Bertrand, Claude Marie, and Etienne, with Margot and Louison
following. The coronation march is heard muffled in the distance.

BERTRAND: I hear the music. Here they come! They are
  Not far away. What would be best to do?
  Shall we stand on the terrace, or shall we
  Press through the crowd not to miss any of it?

ETIENNE: We never will get through it. All the streets are packed
  With people both on horseback and in wagons.
  Let us step over here next to these houses.
  We can see the procession comfortably
  From here when it comes by.

CLAUDE MARIE: It's just as if   2770
  Half France had congregated here. The flood
  Of them has poured so overwhelmingly
  That it has even caught us up in our
  Far province of Lorraine and washed us here.

BERTRAND: Who would
  Sit idly in his corner when the great
  Event is happening in the fatherland!
  It surely cost enough of blood and sweat
  To get the crown placed on the proper head.
  And *our* King, who is the one true King, and
  To whom the crown is given, shall not   2780
  Be worse escorted than the Paris one
  That they had crowned at Saint Denis. No man
  Of proper mind would stay away today
  Or fail to raise the cry: Long live the King!
        (Margot and Louison join them.)

LOUISON: My heart is pounding. Margot, we will see
  Our sister.

MARGOT: We will see her in her glory
  And her exalted state, and we will say:
  That is our sister, that is Joan!

LOUISON: I

  Cannot believe it till I see with my

  Own eyes that this great person whom they call   2790

  The Maid of Orleans is actually

  Our sister Joan who was lost from us.

              (The march keeps getting nearer.)

MARGOT: You still doubt? You will see with your own eyes.

BERTRAND: See, here they come!

> *(Flute players and oboe players open the proces-*
> *sion. They are followed by children dressed*
> *in white and with branches in their hands. After*
> *them come two heralds. Then a procession of*
> *halberdiers. Magistrates in their robes follow.*
> *Next come two Marshals with their staves, the*
> *Duke of Burgundy carrying the sword, Dunois*
> *with the scepter, and other nobles with the*
> *crown, the orb, and the staff of justice; still*
> *others with sacrificial offerings. After these walk*
> *knights in the regalia of their orders, acolytes*
> *with censers, then two Bishops with the sacred*
> *ampulla, the Archbishop with a crucifix, and*
> *then Joan with her flag. She walks with bowed*
> *head and uncertain step. Her sisters show signs*
> *of amazement and joy at the sight of her. Behind*
> *her walks the King beneath a canopy carried*
> *by four barons. Courtiers follow him, and*
> *soldiers bring up the rear. When the procession*
> *has entered the church the march is concluded.)*

MARGOT: You saw her then?

CLAUDE MARIE: The one in golden armor,

  The one that held the flag before the King!

MARGOT: That was the one. That was our sister Joan.

LOUISON: She did not recognize us, did not dream

  How close her sisters' bosoms were to her.

  But she looked at the ground and seemed so pale,   2800

  And walked so tremblingly beneath her flag. —

  As I looked at her I could not feel happy.

MARGOT: Now I have seen our sister in her glory
And her magnificence. — Who would have ever
So much as fancied in a dream or thought
When she was herding flocks upon our mountains
That we would see her in such lofty splendor?
LOUISON: Our father's dream has been fulfilled, that we
Would bow before our sister here at Rheims.
That is the church our father saw in that   2810
Same dream, and everything is now fulfilled.
But our father saw sad images as well,
And I am troubled seeing her so great.
BERTRAND: But why do we stand idly here? Come into
The church to watch the holy ceremony.
MARGOT: Yes, come! Perhaps we'll meet our sister there.
LOUISON: We have already seen her. Let us go
Back to our village.
MARGOT: What? Before we have
Met her and spoken with her?
LOUISON: She no longer
Belongs to us. She has her place with kings   2820
And Princes now. — And who are we to force
Ourselves with idle boast upon her glory?
She was alien even when among us.
MARGOT: Will she be ashamed of us, and scorn us?
BERTRAND: The King himself is not ashamed of us,
And he has friendly greetings for the humblest.
However high she may have risen, still
The King is greater.
                (Drums and trumpets are heard
                    within the church.)
CLAUDE MARIE: Come into the church!
                (They hurry toward the rear where they are
            lost in the crowd.)
                (Enter Thibaut dressed in black. Raimond is
            following him and trying to hold him back.)
RAIMOND: Stay, father Thibaut, stay behind out of
The crowd. You will see only happy people,   2830

And your grief will affront this festival.
Come, let us flee this city with quick steps!
THIBAUT: Did you see my ill-fortuned child? Did you
Observe her closely?
RAIMOND: O I beg you, flee!
THIBAUT: And did you notice her unsteady steps,
How pale she was of face, and how distressed?
The hapless creature senses her position;
This is the time to save my child, and I
Intend to use it.

    (He starts to go.)

RAIMOND: Stop! What are you going
To do?
THIBAUT: I will surprise her, bring her down   2840
From her vain happiness; yes, and by force
I mean to lead her back to her God whom
She has renounced.
RAIMOND: Consider what you do!
Do not plunge your own child into destruction!
THIBAUT: If only her soul is alive, her body
May perish.

    *(Joan comes rushing out of the church with-
    out her flag. The people crowd up, adore her
    and kiss her garments. She is detained at the
    rear of the stage by the throng.)*

        There she comes! She rushes pale
Out of the church. Her anguish drives her from
The holy place. It is God's judgment that
Proclaims itself in her.—
RAIMOND: Farewell!   2850
Do not ask me to bear you further company.
I came all hope, and I now go all sorrow.
But I have seen your daughter once again
And feel as though I had lost her anew.

    (Exit.)
    *(Thibaut withdraws to the
       opposite side.)*

JOAN *(has fended off the crowd and comes forward)*:
  I cannot stay here.—Spirits drive me onward,
  The organ tones resound like peals of thunder,
  The high cathedral vaults collapse upon me,
  I am compelled to seek the free sky's breadth!
  I left my flag there in the sanctuary,
  And never shall my hand touch it again.
  —I seemed to see my well beloved sisters,   2860
  Margot and Louison, go drifting past me
  As though they moved within a dream.—Alas,
  That was an apparition, mere illusion.
  They are far, far away, not to be reached,
  As is my childhood and my innocence.
MARGOT *(stepping forth)*:
  It is she, it is Joan!
LOUISON *(hurries up to her)*:   O my sister!
JOAN: Then it was not a dream.—It is you.—I
  Embrace you, Louison, and you, Margot.
  Here in the alien, thronging emptiness
  I clasp my cherished sisters to my heart.   2870
MARGOT: She still knows us, is our good sister still.
JOAN: Your love has brought you all this way to me,
  So far, so far! You are not angry with
  Your sister who left you without farewell!
LOUISON: God's own dark dispensation led you forth.
MARGOT: The fame of you, which has the world a-stir
  And bears your name afar upon all tongues,
  Awoke us also in our quiet village
  And guided us here to this festival.
  We journeyed to behold you in your glory,   2880
  And we are not alone.
JOAN *(quickly)*:   Our father is with you?
  Where, where is he? Why does he hide himself?
MARGOT: Our father is not with us.
JOAN: No? He does not want
  To see his child? You do not bring his blessing?
LOUISON: He does not know that we are here.

JOAN: He does
  Not know? Why not?—You are abashed and silent,
  You keep your eyes cast down? Where is our father?
MARGOT: Since you left us—
LOUISON (*motions to her*):   Margot!
MARGOT: Our father has
  Become quite melancholy.
JOAN: Melancholy?
LOUISON: Take comfort. You know his foreknowing soul.   2890
  He will regain composure, be content,
  Once we tell him that you are happy here.
MARGOT: But—you *are* happy? Yes, you must be happy
  Because you are so great and honored.
JOAN: I
  Am happy seeing you again, and hearing
  Your voices, that beloved sound, and taking
  My memory home and to our father's meadows.
  When I was herding flocks upon our mountains
  I was as happy as in Paradise.—
  Can I not be so once again,—become so?   2900
      (*She buries her face in Louison's bosom.*
      Claude Marie, Etienne, and Bertrand appear
      and remain standing shyly some distance away.)
MARGOT: Come, Etienne! Bertrand! Claude Marie!
  Our sister is not proud, she is more gentle
  And speaks more kindly than she ever did
  When she was living with us in our village.
      (*The others come closer and start to offer her*
      their hands. Joan looks at them with a fixed
      stare and is in profound astonishment.)
JOAN: Where have I been? Tell me: Was all that only
  A long dream, and have I awakened now?
  Am I away from Dom Remi? Is it
  Not true that I had gone to sleep beneath
  The magic tree, and have awakened now,
  And your familiar forms stand here around me?   2910
  These kings and battles and these feats of war

Existed only in my dream—They were
Mere shadows that have passed before me there;
For dreams are vivid underneath that tree.
How would you get to Rheims? Or how would I
Get there? I never have left Dom Remi!
Confess that frankly and make my heart glad.

LOUISON: We *are* in Rheims. You have not merely dreamed
About those feats; you actually performed
Them all.—O look around you, recognize   2920
Yourself. Feel of your gold and gleaming armor.

> *(Joan raises her hand to her bosom, recollects
> herself, and starts with fright.)*

BERTRAND: And from my hand you did receive this helmet.

CLAUDE MARIE: It is no wonder you think you are dreaming,
For what you have accomplished and performed
Could not occur more wondrously in dreams.

JOAN *(quickly)*:
Come, let us flee! I will go back with you
To our own village, to my father's bosom.

LOUISON: O come, come with us!

JOAN: All these people have
Exalted me far, far beyond my merits.
You saw me when I was a child and weak;   2930
You love me, but you do not worship me.

MARGOT: Could you think of abandoning this glory?

JOAN: I throw it all away, this hated pomp
That separates your hearts from mine, and I
Shall once again become a shepherdess.
And I will serve you like a lowly servant
And thus atone with the severest penance
For having vainly raised myself above you.

> *(Trumpets resound. The King in coronation
> regalia emerges from the church. Enter also
> Agnes Sorel, the Archbishop, Burgundy,
> Dunois, La Hire, Du Chatel, Knights, and
> Courtiers.)*

ALL VOICES *(shout over and over as the King comes forward)*:

Long live the King! Long live King Charles the Seventh!
> (*The trumpets strike up. At a sign from the
> King the Heralds command silence with their
> raised batons.*)

THE KING: My loyal people! Thank you for your love!   2940
  The crown that God has placed upon our head
  Was won and conquered by the sword, and it
  Is wet with noble blood of citizens;
  But may green sprays of olive twine in peace
  About it. Thanks to all who fought for us,
  And to all those that fought against us, let
  There be forgiveness. God has shown us mercy,
  Let our first royal word be also—Mercy!   [Good!
THE PEOPLE: Long live the King! Long live King Charles the
THE KING: From God alone, the highest Ruler of   2950
  All rulers, France's kings receive their crown.
  But we, however, have received it from
  His own hand *manifestly.*
> (*turning to the Maid*)

  Here stands the Maid whom God has sent, who gave
  You back your true, hereditary King
  And broke the yoke of foreign tyranny.
  Her name shall stand on equal plane with that
  Of Saint Denis, protector of this country,
  And to her fame an altar shall be raised.
THE PEOPLE: Hail to the Maid, hail to the rescuer!   2960
> (*Trumpets.*)

THE KING (*to Joan*):

  If you are born of human kind as we are,
  Then tell us what good fortune can delight you.
  But if your native region is up yonder,
  If in your virgin's body you contain
  The shining rays of a celestial nature,
  Then take away the blindfold from our senses,
  Reveal yourself in that same shape of light
  In which the heavens see you, so we may

Adore you from the dust.
> (*General silence. All eyes are directed toward
> the Maid.*)

JOAN (*with a sudden cry*):   My father! There!
> (*Thibaut steps forth from the crowd and
> stands just opposite her.*)

SEVERAL VOICES: Her father!

THIBAUT: Yes, her miserable father,   2970
Begetter of this wretched child, impelled
By God's decree now to denounce my very daughter.

BURGUNDY: Ha! What is this!

DU CHATEL: Now comes a dreadful dawning!

THIBAUT (*to the King*):
You think you have been rescued by God's might?
O Prince betrayed! O blinded Frankish people!
You have been rescued by the Devil's arts.
> (*Everyone falls back in horror.*)

DUNOIS: Is this man mad?

THIBAUT: Not I, but you are mad,
And all these people here, and this wise Bishop,
Who think the Lord of Heaven would reveal
Himself through a mere lowly serving girl.   2980
Now let us see if to her father's face
She still asserts her brazen, cheating lie
With which she has deceived her King and people.
Now by the Triune God tell me for sure:
Are you among the saintly and the pure?
> (*General silence. All eyes are fixed upon her.
> She stands motionless.*)

SOREL: She does not speak!

THIBAUT: Nor does she dare do so before
The dread name that is feared within
The depths of Hell itself! —What! She a saint
Sent forth by God! —In an accursed place
It was contrived, beneath the magic tree   2990
Where through the ages evil spirits have
Held Sabbath.—There to mankind's enemy

She bartered her immortal part so he
Would glorify her with brief earthly fame.
Let her roll back her sleeve and you will see
The markings with which Hell has stamped her there!

BURGUNDY: Monstrous! — But we must believe a father
Who testifies against his very daughter.

DUNOIS: No, we must not believe a madman who
Brings shame upon himself through his own child!   3000

SOREL *(to Joan)*:
O speak! Break this unhappy silence! We
Believe in you! We trust you utterly.
Just one word from your lips, a single word
Will be enough for us. — But speak! Destroy
This monstrous accusation. — Merely state
That you are innocent, we will believe you.

> *(Joan stands motionless. Agnes Sorel steps
> back from her in horror.)*

LA HIRE: She is frightened. Horror and amazement
Have closed her mouth. — Why, innocence itself
Must tremble at such ghastly accusation.

> *(He goes up to her.)*

Rouse from your terror, Joan. Innocence   3010
Has its own language, and a victor's glance
To blast a slander with its mighty lightnings.
Rise up in noble anger, lift your eyes,
Beshame and punish this unworthy doubt,
This outrage to your sacred virtue.

> *(Joan stands motionless. La Hire falls back in
> horror. The commotion increases.)*

DUNOIS: Why is the crowd dismayed? Why are the Princes
So agitated? She is innocent. —
I pledge my princely honor for her sake!
And here I cast my knightly gauntlet down:
Who here will dare to call her guilty now?   3020

> *(A violent clap of thunder. Everyone stands
> horrified.)*

THIBAUT: Now answer by the God that thunders yonder!

Say you are innocent. Deny the Foe
Is in your heart, and prove that I have lied!
>   (*A second, louder clap of thunder. The crowd
>   takes flight in all directions.*)

BURGUNDY: God save us now! What dreadful signs are these!

DU CHATEL: Come, come, my King, and let us flee this place.

THE ARCHBISHOP (*to Joan*):
In God's name now I ask you: Are you silent
Out of a sense of innocence or guilt?
If the voice of this thunder speaks *for* you
Then grasp this crucifix and give a sign.
>   (*Joan remains motionless. New, violent claps
>   of thunder.
>   Exeunt the King, Agnes Sorel, the Archbishop,
>   Burgundy, La Hire, and Du Chatel.*)

DUNOIS: You are my wife.—I have believed in you   3030
Since first our glances met, and think so still.
I have more faith in you than all these signs,
More than that very thunder speaking yonder.
From noble anger you maintain your silence;
Enveloped in your sacred innocence,
You scorn denial of such base suspicion.
—Disdain it, but confide in *me;* for I
Have never doubted of your innocence.
Do not pronounce a word, but merely give
Your hand to me as pledge and sign that you   3040
Serenely trust my arm and your good cause.
>   (*He extends his own hand to her but she turns
>   away from him with a convulsive movement.
>   He stands in blank horror.*)
>   (*Reenter Du Chatel.*)

DU CHATEL: Joan of Arc! The King deigns to permit
You to depart unharmed out of this city.
The gates stand open to you. Fear no harm.
The royal peace protects you.—Follow me,
Count Dunois.—You will gain no honor by
Remaining any longer.—What an outcome!

(Exit.)

*(Dunois rouses from his stupefaction, casts
one final glance at Joan, and leaves. The latter
stands for a moment completely alone.*

*Enter finally Raimond. For a while he re-
mains some distance away observing her with
silent sorrow. Then he steps up to her and takes
her by the hand.)*

RAIMOND: Seize the moment, come! The streets are empty.
Give me your hand, and I will guide your way.   [3049]

*(At sight of him she shows her first sign of
feeling, gazes fixedly at him, and looks toward
heaven. Then she seizes his hand with vehemence, and leaves.)*

ACT V

SCENE 1

A wild forest. Charcoal burners' huts in the distance. It is completely dark. Violent thunder and lightning, intermittent firing. Enter a charcoal burner and his wife.

THE CHARCOAL BURNER: This is a murderous and cruel storm, 3050
    The heavens threaten to disgorge themselves
    In streams of fire, and in the broad daylight
    It is so dark that one might see the stars.
    The storm is raging like a Hell unleashed,
    The earth is quivering, and with a crash
    The ancient ash trees bow their time-worn crowns.
    And this horrendous warfare up above,
    That teaches even wild beasts to be gentle
    So that they tamely cower in their dens,
    Cannot establish peace among mankind.— 3060
    Amid the howling of the wind and storm
    You still may hear the booming of the cannon.
    Both armies stand so close to one another
    That just the forest separates them, and
    Each hour the fearful crisis may be on us.

THE CHARCOAL BURNER'S WIFE:
    May God protect us! Why, I thought they had
    Completely crushed the foe and scattered them.
    How is it that they trouble us anew?

THE CHARCOAL BURNER:
    Because they have lost their fear of the King.
    For ever since the Maid became a witch 3070
    At Rheims the Evil One no longer helps us
    And everything goes wrong.

THE CHARCOAL BURNER'S WIFE: Hark! Who comes there?
    (Enter Raimond and Joan.)

RAIMOND: I see huts here. Come on, here we will find
  Some shelter from this raging storm. You cannot
  Stand this much longer. Three days now you have
  Been wandering, avoiding human eyes,
  And nothing but wild roots have been your food.
        (*The storm subsides; it becomes
                clear and fair.*)
  Come, these are kindly charcoal burners. Come.
THE CHARCOAL BURNER: You seem to be in need of rest. Come in!
  Whatever our poor roof may have to offer   3080
  Is yours.
THE CHARCOAL BURNER'S WIFE:
  Why does this tender girl wear weapons?
  But, to be sure, this is a troubled time
  When even women have to put on armor.
  The Queen herself, Dame Isabeau, they say
  Appears with weapons in the foeman's camp,
  And they say too, a maid, a shepherd's lass,
  Has fought in battle for the King, our master.
THE CHARCOAL BURNER: What kind of talk is this? Go in the hut
  And fetch this girl a cup for her refreshment.
        (*The charcoal burner's wife goes
                into the hut.*)
RAIMOND (*to Joan*):
  You see, all people are not cruel. Even   3090
  Here in the wilderness dwell gentle hearts.
  Be of good cheer! The storm has raged its fill,
  And, shedding peaceful rays, the sun goes down.
THE CHARCOAL BURNER: Since you are journeying with weapons, I
  Suppose you want to get to our King's army.—
  Beware! The English have their camp near by
  And their patrols are roaming through the forest.
RAIMOND: How can we get away from them?
THE CHARCOAL BURNER: Stay here
  Until my boy comes back from town. Then he
  Will lead you by some hidden paths where you   3100
  Will not have anything to fear. We know

The trails.

RAIMOND (*to Joan*):   Take off your helmet and your armor.
They make you known and give you no protection.
                    (*Joan shakes her head.*)

THE CHARCOAL BURNER:
    The girl is very sad.—Hark! Who comes here?
                    (*The charcoal burner's wife comes out of the
                    hut with a goblet.
                    Enter the charcoal burner's son.*)

THE CHARCOAL BURNER'S WIFE:
    It is our boy that we expected back.
                    (*to Joan*)
    Drink, noble maiden. May it do you good!

THE CHARCOAL BURNER: You're here, Anet? What news?

THE CHARCOAL BURNER'S SON (*has fixed his eyes on the Maid
    just as she is lifting the cup to her lips. He recognizes her,
    steps up to her, and snatches the cup from her mouth.*)
                                        What are you doing?
    Whom have you taken in? This is the witch
    Of Orleans.

THE CHARCOAL BURNER AND HIS WIFE TOGETHER:
    Now God have mercy!
                    (*They cross themselves and flee.*)

JOAN (*calmly and softly*):
    You see, the curse pursues me, everyone   3110
    Takes flight. Look to yourself and leave me too.

RAIMOND: I leave you! Now! And who will be your guide
    And go with you?

JOAN: I do not go alone.
    You heard the thunder over me. I am
    Led by my destiny. Have no fear, I
    Will reach my goal without my seeking it.

RAIMOND: Where will you go? Here stand the Englishmen,
    Who have sworn fierce and dire revenge against you—
    There stand our people, who have cast you out.—

JOAN: Nothing will befall me, save what must be.   3120

RAIMOND: But who will find you food? Who will protect

You from wild beasts and from still wilder men?
Take care of you when you are sick and wretched?
JOAN: I know all the herbs and all the roots,
　　And from my sheep I learned to tell the good
　　Ones from the poisonous.—I understand
　　The courses of the stars and of the clouds,
　　And I can hear the hidden springs that murmur.
　　A human being needs few things, and Nature
　　Is rich in life.
RAIMOND (*takes her by the hand*):
　　　　　　　　Will you not search your heart?   3130
　　And reconcile yourself with God—return
　　Repentant to the arms of Holy Church?
JOAN: You too believe me guilty of that sin?
RAIMOND: How can I help it? You acknowledged by
　　Your silence—
JOAN:　　　　You, who followed me to exile,
　　The only one who has been loyal to me,
　　Who bound himself to me when all the rest
　　Rejected me, you take me for an outcast
　　Who has renounced her God.—
　　　　　　(*Raimond is silent.*)
　　　　　　　　　　O that is hard!
RAIMOND (*astonished*):
　　Then you are really not a sorceress?   3140
JOAN: A sorceress!
RAIMOND:　　　And all those miracles,
　　You did perform them by the power of God
　　And of His saints?
JOAN:　　　　　　How else should I perform them?
RAIMOND: And you kept silence at that horrible
　　Denunciation?—You speak now, and yet before
　　The King, when speech was vital, you kept silence!
JOAN: I bowed in silence to the destiny
　　Which God, my master, then enjoined upon me.
RAIMOND: You could withhold an answer from your father!
JOAN: Because it had come from my father, it   3150

Had come from God. Correction too will come
From him.
RAIMOND: But Heaven too vouched for your guilt.
JOAN: The Heavens spoke and therefore I was silent.
RAIMOND: What? With one word you could have cleared yourself
   And yet you left the world in dismal error?
JOAN: It was an act of Providence, no error.
RAIMOND: You suffered all this shame in innocence
   With not a word of protest from your lips!
   —I marvel at you and I stand aghast,
   My heart is stirred down to its deepest depths!   3160
   O I will gladly take your word for truth,
   For it was hard for me to think you guilty.
   But could I dream a human heart would bear
   Those monstrous things and still maintain its silence!
JOAN: Did I deserve to be God's messenger
   Without acceding blindly to His will?
   And I am not so wretched as you think.
   I suffer want, but that is no misfortune
   For one of my rank; I am banished, outlawed,
   But in the wilderness I found myself.   3170
   When honor's radiance surrounded me
   Then there was conflict in my heart. I was
   The most unhappy of all creatures when
   I seemed most envied in the world.—But now
   I have been healed, and this great storm in Nature
   That threatened to destroy her, was my friend
   And it has purified the world and me.
   Now there is peace within me.—Come what may,
   I am aware now of no further weakness.
RAIMOND: O come, come, let us hurry to proclaim   3180
   Your innocence aloud to all the world!
JOAN: The One who sent confusion will resolve it.
   The fruit of Destiny will only fall
   When it is ripe. A day will come to clear me,
   And those who now have cast me out and damned me
   Will then become aware of their delusion

And tears will flow then for my destiny.

RAIMOND: I should endure in silence until Chance—

JOAN *(taking him by the hand)*:

You see the natural phase of things alone,
The earthly bond is still upon your sight.   3190
With my eyes I have seen immortal things.—
No hair may fall from any human head
Without the gods.—Do you see yonder where
The sun is setting in the sky?—As surely
As it returns tomorrow in its brightness,
The day of truth inevitably will come.

> *(Queen Isabeau with soldiers appears in the distance.)*

ISABEAU *(still off stage)*:

This is the way into the English camp!

RAIMOND: The enemy!

> *(Soldiers enter, notice Joan, and reel back in fright.)*

ISABEAU: Why is the column stopping?

SOLDIERS: God save us!

ISABEAU: Are you frightened by a ghost!

What! Are you soldiers? Cowards, you are cowards!   3200

> *(She pushes her way through the others, steps out, then falls back as she catches sight of the Maid.)*

What do I see!

> *(She quickly gets control of herself and advances toward her.)*

                    Surrender! I claim you

My prisoner!

JOAN: I am.

> *(Raimond flees with signs of despair.)*

ISABEAU *(to the soldiers)*:

                    Put her in chains.

> *(The soldiers advance gingerly upon the Maid. She holds out her arms and is chained.)*

Is this the mighty creature so much dreaded

That frightened all your hosts away like lambs,
Who now cannot protect herself at all?
Does she do feats for her believers only,
And turn to woman when she meets a man?
                    (to the Maid)
Why have you left your army? And where is
Count Dunois, your protector and your knight?

JOAN: I have been banished.

ISABEAU *(falling back in astonishment)*:
                              What! You have been banished? 3210
Banished by the Dauphin?

JOAN: Do not ask.
I am in your hands now. Decide my fate.

ISABEAU: You have been banished for delivering him
From the abyss, and crowning him at Rheims,
And making him the King of all of France?
Banished! Ah, there I recognize my son!
— Lead her inside the camp and show the army
The dreadful phantom at which it so trembled.
This girl a sorceress! Why, all her magic
Is your delusion and your coward hearts!   3220
She is a *fool* who sacrificed herself
For her King's sake and now receives his royal
Reward for that. — Take her to Lionel. —
I send him the Luck of the French in chains.
I'll be there soon myself.

JOAN: Kill me at once
But do not give me up to Lionel!

ISABEAU *(to the soldiers)*:
Obey the order! Off with her at once!
                    (Exit.)

JOAN *(to the soldiers)*:
Do not allow me to escape alive
From your hands, Englishmen! Take your revenge!
Out with your swords, plunge them into my heart,   3230
And drag me dead to your Commander's feet!
Remember that I was the one who killed

Your finest, who felt no compassion for you,
Who shed whole rivers of good English blood,
And robbed your brave and your heroic sons
Of the day of their joyous coming home.
Exact revenge in blood by killing me!
You have me now. You may not always see me
As weak as this.—

LEADER OF THE SOLDIERS: Do as the Queen has ordered you.

JOAN: Must I   3240
Become more wretched than I was before!
O fearful Holy One, your hand is hard.
Have you expelled me wholly from your grace?
No God appears, no angel shows its face,
The marvels rest, and Heaven's gates are barred.
                (She follows the soldiers.)

SCENE 2

The French Camp.
Dunois between the Archbishop and Du Chatel.

THE ARCHBISHOP: Control your sombre indignation, Prince.
Come with us. Come back to your Lord and King.
Do not desert the common cause right now
At just the moment when we are again
Hard pressed and in need of your hero's arm.   3250

DUNOIS: Why are we pressed? Why is the enemy
Up on his feet again? All had been done,
France was triumphant and the war concluded.
You banished her who rescued us, now rescue
Yourselves! I do not want to see
The camp in which she is no longer present.

DU CHATEL: Accept our better counsel, Prince. Do not
Dismiss us with this answer.

DUNOIS: Du Chatel,
I hate you and I will not listen to
A word from you. You were the first to doubt her.   3260

THE ARCHBISHOP: But who was not in doubt about her, who

Would not have wavered that unlucky day
When all the portents testified against her!
We were surprised, bewildered, and the shock
Drove deep dismay into our hearts. — Who could
Weigh and examine in that hour of terror?
But now our self-possession has returned.
We see her as she used to walk among us
And we can not discover any blame in her.
We are confused. — We fear that we have done   3270
A grievous wrong. — The King repents his action,
The Duke upbraids himself, La Hire is wretched,
And every heart has veiled itself in grief.

DUNOIS: What! She a liar! If the truth is ever
Incarnate in a form that can be seen,
Then it will bear her features! And if faith
And innocence and purity of heart
Dwell anywhere on earth — then they must dwell
Upon her lips and in her shining eyes.

THE ARCHBISHOP: May Heaven intervene with miracle   3280
To clarify this mystery which cannot
Be penetrated by our mortal eyes. —
But let it be untangled as it may,
We have incurred guilt one way or the other:
By having used infernal magic weapons
For our defense, or else by banishing a saint.
And both things call down Heaven's anger and
Chastisement on this poor, ill-fortuned country.

        (Enter a Nobleman.)   [Highness.

THE NOBLEMAN: There's a young shepherd asking for your
He urgently requests to speak with you.   3290
He claims he has come from the Maid. —

DUNOIS: O hurry
And bring him in. He comes from her.

        (The Nobleman opens the door for Raimond.
        Dunois hurries to met him.)

                      Where is she?

Where is the Maid?

RAIMOND: Hail, noble Prince! And I
  Am blessed too to find this pious Bishop
  With you, this holy man, the shield of all
  Who are oppressed and father of the lost.
DUNOIS: Where is the Maid?
THE ARCHBISHOP: Yes, tell us that, my son.
RAIMOND: My Lord, she is no wicked sorceress!
  By God and all His saints I swear to that.
  The people are mistaken. You have banished   3300
  The innocent and cast God's own away.
DUNOIS: Where is she? Tell us!
RAIMOND: I was her companion
  During her flight through the Ardennes forest,
  There she confessed her inmost heart to me.
  May I die under torture, may my soul
  Have no share in salvation everlasting
  If she is not pure, Lord, of any guilt!
DUNOIS: The sun itself in heaven is not purer!
  Where is she? Tell us!
RAIMOND: O if God has changed
  Your hearts—then hurry! Go and rescue her!   3310
  She is a prisoner among the English.
DUNOIS: A prisoner!
THE ARCHBISHOP: O the unhappy creature!
RAIMOND: In the Ardennes where we were seeking shelter
  She was surprised and captured by the Queen
  And put into the hands of Englishmen.
  O save her now, as once she was your savior,
  From a hard and an awful death!
DUNOIS: To your weapons! Up! Sound the alarm! Beat drums!
  Lead all the troops to battle! Let all France
  Take arms! Our honor is at stake, I say!   3320
  Crown and Palladium are snatched away.
  Risk all the blood in France, risk life itself!
  Free she must be before the close of day!   [3323]
(Exeunt.)

SCENE 3

A watchtower with an opening above.
Joan and Lionel. Enter Fastolf in haste.

FASTOLF: The people can no longer be restrained.
  They shout in fury for the Maid to die.
  You will resist in vain. Kill her and throw
  Her head down from this tower's parapets.
  Her blood alone will pacify the army.

                    (Enter Isabeau.)

ISABEAU: They're putting ladders up to mount attack.
  Appease the people. Do you want to wait   3330
  Until in their blind rage they have surrounded
  The entire tower and destroy us all?
  You cannot shield her now. Surrender her.

LIONEL: Let them attack, and let them rage in fury!
  This fort is strong, and I will lie beneath
  Its ruins rather than be forced by their
  Will.—Answer me, now, Joan. Be my wife,
  And I will shield you from an entire world.

ISABEAU: Are you a man?

LIONEL: Your people cast you out.
  You are free from all obligation now   3340
  Toward your unworthy fatherland. The cowards
  That wooed you have abandoned you. They did
  Not venture into battle for your honor.
  But I will fight your cause against *my* people
  And *yours.*—You did once lead me to believe
  My life was precious to you. I stood then
  In battle as an enemy against you.
  And now you have no friend but me.

JOAN: You are
  Mine and my people's hated enemy.
  Between us there can be nothing in common.   3350
  Love you, I never can. But if your heart
  Inclines toward me, then let it be a blessing
  For both our peoples.—Take your armies from

The territory of my fatherland,
Surrender up the keys of all the cities
That you have conquered, make good all the thefts,
Set free the prisoners, send hostages
By compact of a sacred treaty, then
I offer peace to you in my King's name.

ISABEAU: Do you in fetters claim to give us terms?   3360

JOAN: Do this in time, for you will have to do it.
France never will endure the bonds of England.
No, that will never, never happen. Sooner
It will become a wide grave for your armies.
Your finest men already have been slain.
Think of your safe return. Your reputation
Is lost in any case, your might is ended.

ISABEAU: Can you endure this raving girl's defiance?

(Enter a Captain in haste.)

THE CAPTAIN: Commander, hurry to draw up the army
For battle. On with flying banners come   3370
The Franks. The valley glitters with their weapons.

JOAN *(inspired)*:
The Franks are coming on! Now, haughty England,
Out to the field! Now is the time to fight!

FASTOLF: You frenzied creature, moderate your joy!
You will not live to see this day's conclusion.

JOAN: My people will have victory, and I
Will die. Those brave ones need my arm no more.

LIONEL: I scorn those weaklings! We have driven them
In terror on before us in a score
Of battles until this heroic Maid   3380
Fought for them. I despise the entire nation
Except for one, and her they banished. — Fastolf,
Come on, and we'll give them another day
Like those at Crécy and at Poitiers.
You, Queen, will stay inside this tower and guard
The Maid until the battle is decided.
I leave you fifty knights for your protection.

FASTOLF: Are we to go to meet the enemy

And leave this crazy girl behind our backs?

JOAN: You fear a woman chained with fetters?

LIONEL: Joan,   3390
Give me your word not to make your escape.

JOAN: My only wish is to make my escape.

ISABEAU: Put threefold fetters on her. I will pledge
My life that she shall not make her escape.

> (*She is fettered with heavy chains around her
> body and around her arms.*)

LIONEL (*to Joan*):
You want it thus! You force us! You still have
Free choice. Renounce France! Carry England's flag,
And you are free, and those wild lunatics
Who now call for your blood will be your servants!

FASTOLF (*urgently*):
Come on, come on, Commander!

JOAN: Spare your words.
The Franks are coming on. Defend yourself.   3400

> (*Trumpets sound. Lionel hurries off.*)

FASTOLF: You understand, Queen, what you have to do.
If Fortune turns against us, if you see
That our troops are in flight—

ISABEAU (*drawing a dagger*):   Have no fear there!
She shall not live to look upon our fall.

FASTOLF (*to Joan*):
You know what to expect. Now pray for Fortune
Upon your people's weapons!

> (*Exit.*)

JOAN: That I shall!
On that score no one shall prevent me.—Hark!
That is my people's war march.—O it rings
With victory and valor in my heart.
Ruin to England! Triumph to the Franks!   3410
Up, up, my brave ones, up! The Maid is near you.
She cannot bear the flag ahead of you
As formerly—now heavy fetters bind her—
But from her prison her soul swings up free

Upon the pinions of your martial song.

ISABEAU *(to a soldier)*:
Go to the lookout there that faces toward
The field, and tell us how the battle turns.
                    (The soldier goes up.)

JOAN: Be brave, my people! This is the last fight.
One victory more and then the foe is finished!

ISABEAU: What do you see?

THE SOLDIER: The fighting has begun.   3420
A wild man on a barbary steed and in
A tiger skin rides out with cavalry.

JOAN: That is Count Dunois. Boldly now, brave fighter!
Yours is the triumph!

THE SOLDIER: The Burgundian
Attacks the drawbridge.

ISABEAU: O would that ten lances
Had run his false heart through, the sorry traitor!

THE SOLDIER: Lord Fastolf gives him manly opposition.
They're off their horses, fighting man to man,
The Duke's retainers and our men.

ISABEAU: But don't
You see the Dauphin? Don't you recognize   3430
The royal emblems?

THE SOLDIER: Everything is lost
In dust. I cannot make out anything.

JOAN: If he had *my* eye, or if I stood there,
The slightest thing would not escape my glance.
I can count wild fowl in their flight, I can
Discern the falcon on the heights of air.

THE SOLDIER: There is a fearful press beside the moat,
The foremost nobles are in combat there.

ISABEAU: But does our flag still fly?

THE SOLDIER: It streams aloft.

JOAN: If only I could peer through these walls' rifts   3440
I would control the battle with my glance.

THE SOLDIER: What do I see? O our Commander is
Surrounded!

ISABEAU *(draws the dagger on Joan):*
          Die, you wretch!
THE SOLDIER *(quickly):*   They set him free.
  Now from the rear the brave Fastolf attacks
  The enemy—he breaks their densest ranks.
ISABEAU *(withdraws the dagger):*
  There spoke your angel!
THE SOLDIER: Triumph! They are fleeing!
ISABEAU: Who is?
THE SOLDIER: The Franks and the Burgundians.
  The field is covered with the fugitives.
JOAN: My God! My God! You will not thus desert me!
THE SOLDIER: A badly wounded man is being led,   3450
  And many troops are riding to his aid.
  It is a Prince.
ISABEAU: Of ours or of the Frankish?
THE SOLDIER: They take his helmet off. It is Count Dunois.
JOAN *(grasps her chains with a convulsive exertion):*
  And I am nothing but a girl in chains!
THE SOLDIER: Look! Who is that one in the sky-blue mantle
  With hem of gold?
JOAN *(eagerly):*   That is my Lord the King!
THE SOLDIER: His steed is shy—it rears—it plunges, now
  He winds his way with heavy effort forward—
          *(Joan accompanies these words with vehement
          exertions.)*
  Our men are moving forward at full gallop—
  They have caught up with him—surrounded him—   3460
JOAN: O does Heaven have no angels left!
ISABEAU *(with mocking laughter):*
  Now is the time! Now rescue, rescuer!
JOAN *(falls to her knees, praying with a voice of intense emotion):*
  Hear me, my God, in my supreme distress!
  Up unto You in ardent imploration
  I send my soul aloft into Your Heaven.
  You can make the threads of a spiderweb
  As strong as cables of a ship; and to

Change bonds of iron to thin spiderwebs
Is a slight thing to Your omnipotence. —
If You but will it, these chains will fall off   3470
And the walls of this tower split. — You once
Helped Samson when he was in chains and blind,
Enduring bitter mockery from his
Proud enemies. — Relying then on You,
He seized the pillars of his prison with
His might, and leaned, and brought the building crashing. —

THE SOLDIER: Triumph! Triumph!

ISABEAU: What now?

THE SOLDIER: The King is captured!

JOAN (*jumps up*):
May God be merciful to me!

> (*She had seized her chains with both hands
> mightily and wrenched them asunder. At the
> same instant she throws herself upon the nearest
> soldier, tears his sword away from him, and
> rushes out. Everyone stares after her in blank
> astonishment.*)

ISABEAU (*after a long pause*):
What was that? Was I dreaming? Where can she
Have gone? How did she break those heavy bonds?   3480
I would not have believed it from a world
Had I not seen it with my very eyes.

THE SOLDIER (*at the lookout*):
Does she have wings? Or was she swept away
By storm-winds?

ISABEAU: Tell me, is she down below?

THE SOLDIER: She stalks amid the battle. — Her pace is
More swift than sight. — Now she is here — now there —
I see her all at once in many places.
— She parts the ranks. — They all give way before her,
The Franks stand firm, they form their ranks anew!
— Alas, what do I see? Our troops throw down   3490
Their weapons and our flag begins to sink. —

ISABEAU: Will she wrest this sure victory from us?

THE SOLDIER: Right toward the King she presses.—She has
   She snatches him by force out of the fighting.   [reached him.—
   —Lord Fastolf falls! —Our General is captured!
ISABEAU: I want to hear no more. Come down from there.
THE SOLDIER: Flee, Queen! You are about to be attacked.
   Armed men are pressing forward to this tower.
                    (He comes down.)
ISABEAU *(drawing a sword):*
   Then fight, you cowards!
              *(Enter La Hire with soldiers. At his entrance
              the Queen's troops lay down their arms.)*
LA HIRE *(approaching her respectfully):*
                         Queen, surrender to
   Our total power.—Your knights have all surrendered   3500
   And further opposition is quite futile.
   —Accept my services. Command me where
   You wish to be accompanied.
ISABEAU: Any place
   Will do where I do not confront the Dauphin.
              *(She surrenders her sword and follows
                 him with the soldiers.)*

                    SCENE 4

The stage is shifted to the battlefield.
Soldiers with flying banners fill up the rear. In front of them are
the King and the Duke of Burgundy. In the arms of both princes
lies Joan, mortally wounded and without any sign of life. They
come slowly forward.
Agnes Sorel rushes in and throws herself on the King's bosom.
SOREL: You are alive—and free! —And you are mine
   Again!
THE KING: Yes, I am free—and at this price.
                    (Points to Joan.)
SOREL: It's Joan! She is dying!
BURGUNDY: She is dead.
   Behold an angel parting. See how she

Lies still and painless like a child asleep.
The peace of Heaven plays about her features.   3510
No breath stirs in her bosom, but there is
Still some life to be felt in her warm hand.

THE KING: She has departed—no more to awake.
Her eyes will not see earthly things again.
She floats above us, a transfigured spirit,
Who sees our grief no more, nor our repentance.

SOREL: Her eyes are opening, she lives!

BURGUNDY (astonished):   Has she
Returned to us out of the grave? Has she
Defeated Death? She rises, stands!

JOAN (stands completely up and looks about):
                    Where am I?

BURGUNDY: Among your people, Joan. With your loved ones. 3520

THE KING: In the arms of your friends and of your King.

JOAN (after gazing fixedly at him for a long while):
No, I am not a sorceress. Indeed
I am not.

THE KING: You are holy as an angel.
But darkness of the night had veiled our eyes.

JOAN (looking about with a cheerful smile):
And am I really back among my people,
Despised and scorned no more, no more cast out?
No longer cursed, but looked upon with kindness?
—Now I see everything again distinctly.
Here is my King. And those are flags of France.
And yet I do not see my flag.—Where is it?   3530
I must not come without my flag. It was
Entrusted to me by my Master. I
Must lay it down before His throne. I can
Show it because I bore it faithfully.

THE KING (with face averted):
Give her her flag.
            (It is given to her. She stands erect and un-
            supported, the flag in her hand.—The sky is
            suffused with a rosy glow.)

JOAN: O do you see the rainbow in the air?
  The skies are opening their gates of gold,
  She stands in glory in the choir of angels
  With the eternal Son upon her bosom
  And stretches out her arms to me and smiles.   3540
  But what has happened! —Light clouds bear me up.—
  My heavy armor has become winged raiment.
  Upwards—upwards.—Earth is rushing back.—
  Brief is the pain, and joy is everlasting.   [3544]

      (The flag drops from her hand, she sinks dead
     upon it.—Everyone stands for a long time in
     mute emotion.—At a slight gesture from the
     King all the flags are laid down over her so that
     she is completely covered by them.)